Snobbery

Snobbery

THE AMERICAN VERSION

Joseph Epstein

Houghton Mifflin Company

BOSTON · NEW YORK

2002

For information about permission to reproduce selections from
this book, write to Permissions, Houghton Mifflin Company,
215 Park Avenue South, New York, New York 10003.

Visit our Web site: www.houghtonmifflinbooks.com.

Library of Congress Cataloging-in-Publication Data
Epstein, Joseph, date.
Snobbery : the American version / Joseph Epstein.
p.   cm.
Includes bibliographical references and index.
ISBN 0-395-94417-1
1. Social status — United States. 2. Snobs and
snobbishness — United States. I. Title.
HN90.S6 E67 2002
305.5'0973—dc21   2001051623

For Kathleen and Lily

MY CALIFORNIA GIRLS

ACKNOWLEDGMENTS

Whatever gaiety this book has is largely owing to the charm and verve of the magical music of Fats Waller, which I listened to almost constantly over the past two years. Whatever melancholy and errors the book contains have been supplied by the author.

Contents

Preface

This is a book about snobbery, its perplexities and its perils, its complications and not least its comedy. Behind its composition lies the perpetual question — never, I hope, pressed too insistently but always looming in the background — of whether snobbery is a constituent part of human nature or instead an aberration brought about by particular social conditions. The book has been written for those who, after having looked into themselves and into the life around them, have acquired sufficient detachment to exclaim, rather unoriginally perhaps, but nonetheless with ever-fresh astonishment: "What a piece of work is man!"

Whenever I happened to mention that I was attempting to write a book on snobbery, someone was sure to respond by saying that he or she hoped I was going to cover this or that aspect of the subject — the snobbery of PBS television, of shades of skin color among African Americans, of health food, of contemporary art — that was, almost invariably, not included in my book. But snobbery, like bacteria, is found everywhere; this is part of its fascination and part of the difficulty it presents to its chronicler.

Snobbery also seems to have existed, in however attenuated a form, from the Tuesday of the week following that in which God created the universe. A brief illustration will reinforce my point. For more than a century after the Emperor Constantine moved the seat of the Roman Empire from

Rome to Constantinople, some people would say, with pride but more with snobbery, that their family had "come over with Constantine." Sound familiar?

Because snobbery is of such long standing and so very widespread, I early made a decision to concentrate my coverage of the subject to its role in America. In these pages, then, I have tried to make out the larger patterns of snobbery within the broad canvas of American life since the decline of what, later in the book, I call the Waspocracy. If your own favorite snobbery is missing, please accept my apology and take some (possibly snobbish) comfort that your awareness of snobbery exceeds that of the author of an entire book on the subject.

Part One

We will drink a little
and philosophize a little
and perhaps we both
who are made of blood and illusion
will finally free ourselves
from the oppressive levity of appearance.

— Zbigniew Herbert, "A Parable of King Midas"

1

It Takes One to Know One

RATHER THAN imply his superiority to his subject, the author of a book about snobbery ought to set out, fairly briefly, his own experience of snobbery. He ought to let his readers know if he has been a victim of snobbery, and of the sorts of snobbery to which he is susceptible, to allow them to judge his own relationship to the subject.

Perhaps the best way for me to begin, then, is to explain my social origins. These are a bit complicated. They seem to have been culturally lower middle class but with middle- and, later, upper-middle-class financial backing. Neither of my parents went to college. My father, growing up in Canada, in fact never finished high school; my mother took what was then known as "the commercial course" at John Marshall (public) High School in Chicago. They were both Jewish, but, against the positive stereotype of Jews loving culture and things of the mind, my parents had almost no cultural interests apart from occasionally going to musical comedies or, in later years, watching the Boston Pops on television. Magazines — *Life, Look,* later *Time* — and local newspapers came into our apartment, but no books. I don't recall our owning an English dictionary, though both my parents were well spoken, always grammatical and jargon-free.

Politics was not a great subject of family conversation. The

behavior of our extended family and neighbors, money, my father's relations with customers at his business, these made up
the main conversational fare — unspeculative, nonhypotheti-
cal, all very specific. Education was another subject of little
interest; no time was spent, say, discussing the differences between Amherst and Williams colleges, for the good reason
that neither of my parents had ever heard of such places.

My father, I believe, hadn't a speck of snobbery. It would
not have occurred to him to want to rise socially in the world,
and the only people he looked down upon — apart from
crooks of one kind or another — were people who seemed to
be without the ambition to take measured risks in business.
We had a distant cousin who was a lieutenant colonel in
the U.S. Army, and my father was baffled by the notion of a
Jewish man settling for a career in the regular army. It pleased
my father to give ample sums to charities (many of them
Jewish charities) and, in later years, to travel to foreign
countries — once, with my mother, to Paris on the *Concorde*
and back from London on the *QE2*. Above all, it pleased him
to have made enough money to help out his family and be
able to establish his financial independence, which he did at
the age of seventeen. But he barely acknowledged the social
realm in which snobbery takes place. For him the world of
status, where style, rank, and social climbing were central,
was a mystery he felt no need to fathom.

My mother, though no snob either, had a greater awareness
of snobbery. She was on the alert for snobberies used against
her, and could be vulnerable to them. In her friendships she
sought out women who were goodhearted, for she was good-
hearted and generous herself. She also had an unashamed
taste for what, by her standard, passed for *luxe*, which meant
driving big cars (Cadillacs), owning lavish furniture, dressing
well (furs, expensive dresses, Italian shoes, jewelry). She was
made a bit nervous by people who had more money than
she, and tended to arrange her social life among people who
were her financial equals or inferiors. But I never saw my
mother — or my father — commit a single socially mean act:
I never saw them fawn over anyone better off than they, or put

down anyone beneath them for reasons one would think to call snobbish.

Why, then, did the eldest of their two sons, the author of this book, have so keen a sense, almost from the outset of his consciousness, of the various arrangements that make for snobbery: social class, money, taste, religion, admired attainments, status of all kinds. As a small boy, I sensed who was richer than whom, noted people who lived more grandly and more poorly than we, immediately grasped what excited the envy of others, felt stirrings of incipient envy of my own. Where this came from I cannot even now say, but it was, beyond argument, in place. Nor, to this day, has it ever left me.

When men gathered in my parents' apartment to talk about world affairs, I could not help noticing that the wealthier ones generally did most of the talking, or at least talked most authoritatively and were listened to most closely. A pleasant man named Sam Cowling, living in the apartment building next to ours, was a comedian on a popular radio show called *The Breakfast Club*, and this, clearly, lent him a certain allure. Money and celebrity, I early recognized, counted for quite a bit in the world. Some work in life carried greater prestige than other work — as in baseball, shortstop was a more admired position than second base, and in football, quarterback was more admired than interior lineman.

In grammar school I was able to arrange to play both shortstop and quarterback. I also became a fair tennis player, a sport with all sorts of interesting connections to snobbery, from its then country-club settings to its emphasis on stylishness, which tends to vaunt appearance over reality — a phenomenon at the heart of much snobbery.

I went to a high school where status was spelled out with a brute clarity I have not since encountered elsewhere. At Nicholas Senn High School on the North Side of Chicago, status was at least as carefully calibrated as at the court of the Sun King at Versailles, though the food was less good and the clothing nowhere near so elegant. The school had roughly fifty clubs, fraternities, and sororities for boys and for girls, each with its own colorful jackets. Some had Greek-letter names — Alpha, Beta, Delta; some had the names of animals, real and mythological — Ravens, Condors, Gargoyles; some had names with aristocratic shadings — Dukes, Majestics, Imperials, Gentry; some had neologisms for names — Raynors, Chiquitas, Fidels, Iaetas. But each club, each fraternity and sorority had a social character that was distinct and apparent to the student body: this club represented the best athletes, this sorority the cutest girls, this fraternity the most fearsome thugs, this the dreariest nerds ("science bores," we called them).

It didn't take me long — perhaps a couple of months at the outside — to decode all these groups with their various social gradations. Because I had in those days a superficial charm that allowed me to make friends easily, I was soon invited to join the best of the clubs and fraternities, which meant those whose members were among the best athletes and most socially fluent of the school's male students. The ease with which I was able to do this may have left me a touch jaded. Sufficiently so, at any rate, so that during my senior year in high school I was invited to join a boys' honor society called Green & White and turned it down, perhaps the first boy in the history of the school to do so. I didn't want it, I didn't need it, and, besides, I understood that turning it down would confer greater status upon me than accepting it. From a fairly early age, then, I was a fairly cunning statustician.

Because I was not an uninterested student, and because my family had no knowledge of the social and financial implications of attending the better American colleges and universities — which for snobbish reasons remain, I believe, considerable — I went to the University of Illinois in Champaign-Urbana, which in those days had, for residents of the state, an open-enrollment policy and low fees. Illinois turned out to be one of the most Greek — that is, most fraternity- and sorority-ridden — campuses in the United States. With my small talent for making myself acceptable, I arranged to be invited to join the best *Jewish* fraternity on campus. (And let me add that — with a feeling of slight shame

I cannot shake off even now, more than forty years later — I left behind my two best friends, who were not invited to join the same fraternity.) I italicize the word *Jewish* not only because the fraternity's membership was exclusively made up of Jews, but because fraternities and sororities during the middle 1950s were strictly segregated by religion, with almost all Gentile fraternities and sororities not accepting Jews and some not permitting Catholics to become members.

Here I ought to underscore that my being Jewish may well have increased my sensitivity to the realm of snobbery. Although an agnostic in religion, my father was keen on sniffing out anti-Semitism, having lived with a great deal of it among the Quebecois in Montreal when he was a boy and then through the nightmare that Hitler created during World War Two. One of his few repeated and heavily emphasized lessons to me was to be on the qui vive for anti-Semitism, which could crop up anywhere. "People might hate you," he said, "for no better reason than your name. Be careful. Stay on the alert." Anti-Semitism may itself be the first and perhaps the longest lasting and most virulent form of snobbery, though when stepped up to the level of pogroms, not to say genocide, it becomes, like racism, something much greater than mere snobbery.

Given all this, I never found myself much upset by the religious segregation practiced in the Middle West in the years I grew up there. That Jews were not wanted in Gentile fraternities at the University of Illinois was not in the least troubling to me. Jewish snobbishness of its own, reinforced by Jewish chauvinism, doubtless kicked in (who needs them!), but I never felt it a serious social deprivation not to be able to join any fraternity or country club, or even live in certain then *Judenrein,* or restricted, neighborhoods or suburbs in and around Chicago, of which there were quite a few.

I soon became bored by this fraternity and what seemed to me its rather pathetic social aspirations. Chief among these was the hope of joining forces with a high-status Gentile sorority in a musical-comedy sketch called Stunt Show. I was, in fact, about to change radically the status system under which

I operated, then and forever. After a year at the University of Illinois, I applied to and was accepted at the University of Chicago, which turned out to be an entirely different kettle of caviar.

Mike Nichols, the movie director and former comedian, who was at the University of Chicago roughly four years before I went there — pity he didn't attend later, so that I might have known him and thus dropped his name, a good one, at this point — Mike Nichols has said, "Everyone at the University of Chicago was neurotic, weird, strange — it was paradise." I'm not so sure about the paradise part, but about the neurotic, weird, and strange no argument is possible. One of the most astonishing things of all was that life at Chicago was not founded on status — which is also to say, on snobbery — at least not as I had been hitherto accustomed to it. People were not ranked by physical beauty, or athletic skill, or wealth, or family connections. None of these things seemed to matter. All that did was intelligence — or, more precisely, intellectuality, which I would define as the ability to deal in a sophisticated way with the issues, questions, and problems presented by art, science, politics, and things of the mind generally. Since my own intellectual quality was then of a low order, my status as a student at the University of Chicago was commensurately low. Hiding my ignorance as best I could, I looked on, fascinated. Here was a new game, and one I felt, if then still somewhat inchoately, I wanted to play.

The University of Chicago, I was to discover, had its own built-in status system. No one announced what it was, but anyone at all attentive couldn't fail to note that in this system only four kinds of work in life had any standing. These were: to be an artist; to be a scientist (and not some dopey physician, treating people for flu or urological problems — only a research physician qualified); to be a statesman (of which there were none then extant); or — and here was the loophole — to be a teacher of potential artists, scientists, and statesmen. To be anything else, no matter how great one's financial or professional success, was to be rabble, just another commoner, a natural slave (in Aristotle's term), out there struggling under the blazing sun with the only shade available that provided by Plato's cave for the uninitiated ignorant.

Henceforth the snobbish system under which I would operate would be artistic, intellectual, cultural. Had I gone to Harvard, Princeton, or Yale (unlikely, since the latter two schools in those days had strict quotas against Jews, and, besides, my mediocre grades would not have qualified me for entrance), I might have adopted snobbery of a social kind, though, so barren of social distinction was the family I grew up in, this would not have been easy to bring off without extraordinarily thin pretensions. Meanwhile, artistic, intellectual, and cultural snobbery gave me quite enough to do. I began to think of myself as an intellectual and a highbrow, interested in art only in its exalted forms. As a would-be intellectual, I found myself comfortably contemptuous of the middle class (even though it was the class from which I happily derived), its values and general style of living. As someone with declared cultural interests, I tended to look down on businessmen, on philistinism, on anyone, really, who thought there were more important things in life than art and ideas. Other people might achieve success in life — I would seek *significance*.

Of course, for the most part I kept these snobbish notions to myself. I believe — at least I hope — I never came across as preposterous as I assuredly was in the inner drama I was then living. Still, deep down (deep down, that is, for a shallow young person) I tended to forgo the more innocent affectations by which people hope to establish superiority — through possessions, through memberships in clubs and groups, through socially favorable marriages — in favor of a heavy freight of artiness and intellectuality.

This lasted for several years, certainly till my thirties. I feel touches of it invade my thinking even today, when I sense my superiority click in as some friend or relative expresses admiration for a book or movie or play I think beneath seriousness. What is operating here is the snobbery of opinion, or, more precisely, of correct opinion. Someone tells me that he

thinks, say, *Death of a Salesman* is a great play, and my mind
goes — click — foolish opinion, betraying a want of intellectual subtlety, a crudity of sensibility. (My view of that
play has come to be close to that of the salesman who, leaving
the theater after the play, is supposed to have said to his
friend, "That New England territory was never any goddamn
good.") A person who is not a snob is content merely to think
a wrong opinion mistaken and let it go at that; it surely
doesn't speak to the character or anything else essential about
the person who has expressed it. For the snob, a wrong opinion is usually more than stupid; it's an utter disqualification.

The tricky part of judging snobbery, in oneself or others, is
in determining the intrinsic value of a thing, or act, or person and the value that society assigns that thing, or act, or
person. Behind all acts of snobbery is, somehow or other, a
false or irrelevant valuation. I drive a Jaguar S-type; it is a
fairly expensive car — costing roughly $45,000 — and has, I
recognize, some snobbish cachet. But it is also a very reliable
and comfortable and handsomely designed car, a pleasure to
drive. I bought it, I like to believe, for its inherent quality and
not for what other people think of it. Yet sometimes I feel
myself unduly pleased with this car. It is not as vulgar as a
Mercedes, I have concluded; it has none of the gaudiness
of a Cadillac or the parvenu feeling of a Lexus. These are, of
course, purely snobbish notions. The only questions that
probably need to be asked of a car are: Does it do well what I
want it to do and is it worth its price? But cars have long since
passed the stage of being merely vehicles of utility and entered the murky realm of status.

Because I wanted to divest myself of the silly realm of cars
and status, I used to make it a point to drive dull cars: Chevys
and mid-sized Oldsmobiles. A case, this, clearly, of reverse
snobbery: the chief mechanism in reverse snobbery is to find
out which way that snobs are headed and then turn oneself
in the opposite direction. Reverse snobbery — about which
more later in this book — may be more difficult to shuck off
than actual snobbery, for it proceeds in part from a distaste for
snobs and snobbishness, but also in part from a wish to assert

one's superiority to snobbery generally, which itself can seem suspiciously like a snobbish act.

I have, for example, a little thing about San Francisco, which, despite all the virtues of its climate and topography, is one of the great centers of snobbery in America. The boosters of the city, who seem to include everyone who lives there, imply by their manner that they above all their countrymen have found the secret of good living, and, with their insistence on their good taste in daily life, San Franciscans can be richly, profoundly off-putting. I find myself sufficiently put off by them to have come to think of their extolling of their own city as unbearable Bayarrea.

I have found that certain fads in dining, clothes, travel, hotels, neighborhoods, artworks, and other items and subjects that bring out the snob in people bring out the reverse snob in me. Sometimes all it takes for me to drop an enthusiasm is the knowledge that someone I think commonplace has picked it up. Twenty-five or so years ago I thought Humphrey Bogart a swell actor; the Bogart cult killed it for me. I mock — though never to their faces — people I know who buy what I think crappy modern art, pretending to enjoy it and hoping it will increase in value. If lots of what I take to be indiscriminate, and therefore nondiscriminating, people take something up, I can almost always be relied upon to put it down, at least in my mind.

Yet I continue to feel that snobbish sense of false superiority when, say, I stay in an expensive hotel, as I did recently in a suite at the Plaza in New York (at someone else's expense, let me quickly add), though a small superior hotel will set my snob glands flowing even more profusely. Wearing good clothes can also elevate my spirits. I've not any food snobbery, I believe, and I have also managed to evade wine snobbery altogether, and think that spending more than thirty dollars for a bottle of wine an almost immoral act. But I am a sucker for the small fine things that a not really wealthy person can acquire: fine stationery, a splendid fountain pen, an elegant raincoat. I don't own an expensive watch, chiefly because I'm not much for jewelry, and spending a thousand dollars or more for a wristwatch is not my notion of a good time, but I am not opposed to buying a knockoff of a Cartier tank watch or of a Bvlgari watch on the streets of New York or Washington, D.C., for fifteen or twenty-five dollars. ("An André Knokovsky," I say, if anyone asks what kind of watch I'm wearing.) Snobbery, I know, still courses through my bloodstream.

It's time it be flushed out. My eldest son not long ago reminded me that, when he was applying for admission to college, I gave him the following advice: "I want you to go to one of the country's best schools, at any rate as the world reckons these things. What you will discover when you get there is that it's not all that good, which is fair enough. But having gone there, you will at least not have to spend any further portion of your life in a condition of yearning, thinking to yourself, Ah, if only I had gone to one of the better schools, how much grander my fate would have been." My son, a good student, went to Stanford, and he says that things have worked out just as I had prophesied.

But, pathetic truth to confess, I am also a little pleased that my son went to Stanford, for nothing better, I fear, than snobbish reasons. I am too often a little pleased with myself on other snobbish fronts. Allow me to present a few candid snapshots. Here I am giving a lecture at an English university — how nice! Here I am being praised in print by a writer I have long admired in a magazine of high status — splendido! Here I am being paid obeisance by the wealthy — and, lo, the world seems a just and good place!

Time to grow out of such thoughts. Time to extrude all such snobbish feelings. Time to see the world, as the philosophers put it, as in itself it really is, which snobbery, even in small doses, makes it all but impossible to do.

2

What Is a Snob?

IN THE BEGINNING was *not* the Word. The Thompson gazelle, that elegant beast, existed well before either Thompson or the word *gazelle.* So it has been with snobs and snobbery: the phenomena existed long before the words arose to describe them. When the word *snob* was first used and what its true origins might be are both in the flux of controversy. "The etymology of the word snob," Margaret Moore Goodell wrote in a 1939 study of Thackeray, Meredith, and Proust, "has not found a universally accepted explanation, although a great deal of ingenuity has been expended in searching for one." At a minimum, one can say that to call someone a snob, as the philosopher George Santayana once put it, "is a very vague description but a very clear insult."

Four notions of origin predominate. In the first, the word *snob* is thought to be Scandinavian and carries the meaning of "a dolt, idiot, with the notion of impostor or charlatan, a boaster." In the second, the word is thought to derive from an abbreviation of the Latin *sine-nobilate,* or "s.nob," which, as Professor Goodell remarked, "is supposed to have been appended to the names of commoners as opposed to noblemen in certain official lists, especially at the universities." A third notion has it that *snob* derives from its antonymic relation to the word *nob:* nobs were people with genuine position and power; snobs, having neither, were people who urgently sought both. A fourth speculation is that the word derives from the elision of French peasants in pronouncing the phrase *c'est noble,* referring to that which is of the upper class. *Snob* could also possibly derive from *snub,* though it might just as easily have been the other way around. Etymology, though complicated enough, isn't crucial.

Nor is an absolutely lucid definition easily established. The word *snob* has taken on slightly different connotations in France, Germany, Spain, Italy, and the United States. The French, for example, had a fairly extensive vocabulary for describing the epiphenomena of snobbery — including the words *parvenu, arriviste, nouveau riche* — well before they took up *snob* and formed *snobisme* from it. A writer named Emile Faguet, in 1907, speculated that his countrymen liked the word's *"impertinence monosyllabique,"* or single-syllable sauciness, which it certainly has. The 1907 *Petit Larousse* defined *snobisme* as "an artificial and foolish admiration for all that is in fashion," which suggests that in France snobbery seems to have had more to do with absorption in fashion than the yearning for rank, with the chic rather than the socially enviable.

In the United States the word *snob* has taken on its own special twist. In a country still in the making, it had been a bit tricky, especially at first, to imitate the higher social ranks when it was not always clear which these might be. After all, almost all *riches* had to be *nouveaux,* everyone was an *arriviste,* and everybody could count himself *parvenu.* In its early decades, nearly the entire United States was engaged in one vast social climb. To be in on the climb, though, was never the social crime here that it was deemed in Europe. The crime in America was less in wanting social rank than in claiming it. The snobs in America have more often than not been those who have chosen to look down their noses at their countrymen. In the United States, contempt for social inferiors more than anything else marked the snob.

By way of preliminary definition: a snob is someone who

practices, lives by, exults in the system of distinctions, discriminations, and social distractions that make up the field of play for snobbery. "The essence of snobbery is that you wish to impress other people." So wrote Virginia Woolf, who allowed that she was herself a snob. But that definition is not only too slack but much too generous. (The world does contain, after all, a small number of people whom it is worthwhile to impress.) The essence of snobbery, I should say, is arranging to make yourself feel superior *at the expense* of other people. Which is a different, really a much more wicked, little proposition.

And while we're at it, be warned against people who too readily admit to being snobs, as Virginia Woolf does in her essay "Am I a Snob?" They probably are snobs, but often in ways rather uglier than they are willing to admit, because much more shameful than they are likely to confess. While owning up to her weakness for people with titles, Woolf neglects to mention her nagging anti-Semitism — more than nagging, certainly, if one is a Jewish reader — even though she was married to Leonard Woolf, who was himself Jewish. Thus of her meeting with Isaiah Berlin, the Oxford political philosopher, she wrote to a friend, describing a dinner at Oxford: "There was Isaiah Berlin, a Portuguese Jew by the look of him [he was, in fact, from Riga], Oxford's leading light; a communist, I think, a fire-eater." She could also use snobbery as a weapon in literary rivalry, snobbishly referring to James Joyce, a writer greatly superior to her, as "underbred."

Snobbery often entails taking a petty, superficial, or irrelevant distinction and, so to say, running with it. It is sitting in your BMW 740i and feeling quietly, assuredly better than the poor vulgarian (as you cannot help judging him) who pulls up next to you at the stoplight in his garish Cadillac. It is the calm pleasure with which you greet the news that the son of the woman you have just been introduced to is majoring in photojournalism at Arizona State University while your own daughter is studying art history at Harvard. It is the delight you feel when an associate at your law firm walks into your

office wearing an ill-tailored Italian suit that costs three times
your own better-fitting traditional clothes. In such comforts,
and many more minuscule and subtler ones, does the snob
find paradise.

Paradise, however, figures always to be temporary, because
the snob resides in a world of relentless one-upmanship, even
though, unbeknownst to him, he may be the only one playing
the game. He can almost be certain that one day, at another
stoplight, a Bentley will pull up next to his pathetic BMW;
that he will be introduced to a woman whose son is studying
classics at Oxford; and another colleague will enter his office
wearing a bespoke English suit, a wafer-thin Patek Philippe
watch, and Italian shoes made from, let us say, the foreskins of
Norwegian rams. In such minor discomforts does the snob
find his or her hell.

So little does it take to lift a snob's spirits, and so little, too,
to send him or her plunging, that the life of a snob is likely to
be fairly jumpy. The snob can have only one standard, that of
comparison. And comparison inevitably implies competition,
rivalry, almost full-time invidiousness. The snob is always po-
sitioning himself. He needs to know that he is in a better position than the next person. The true snob can know no lengthy
contentment. If he doesn't feel his own superiority, he is likely
to feel an aching sense of inferiority, or of at least not being in
the position he wants to be in.

Snobs divide into those whose snobbery consists of looking down on others and those whose snobbery consists of
looking up to, and being ready to abase themselves before,
their supposed betters. The upward-looking snob feels envy
more acutely than ordinary people. One can of course be
both kinds of snob simultaneously: an all-round snob looks
both up and down, also over his shoulder and to both sides of
him, as befits a person making a steep climb or even someone
standing at the top of a precipice. He, the snob, is happiest
when he feels himself gaining ground on his superiors and
putting more ground between himself and those whom he
takes for his inferiors, with whom he never wants to be con-

fused. No easy job, that of the snob; the pay is entirely psychic and the hours are endless.

"Life," wrote William Hazlitt, "is a struggle to be what we are not and to do what we cannot." If Hazlitt is to be believed, we are, as he goes on to say, "very much what others *think of us.*" At the heart of snobbery is the snob's hope that others will take him at his own (doubtless) extravagant self-valuation. It is his high if shaky opinion of himself that he needs to have confirmed, and at frequent intervals. Since the world often does not concur in this valuation, the snob is usually left feeling raw, resentful, agitated.

There is something deeply antisocial about the snob. He is, in a profound sense, in business for himself. Hugh Kingsmill, in a book on D. H. Lawrence, wrote: "Snobbishness is the assertion of the will in social relations as lust is in the sexual. [Snobbishness] is the desire for what divides men and the inability to value what unites them." Like the poor guy without rhythm in the old Louis Armstrong song, the snob can be the loneliest man in town.

The *Concise Oxford English Dictionary* defines *snob* as a "person with exaggerated respect for social position or wealth and a disposition to be ashamed of socially inferior connections; behaves with servility to social superiors, and judges of merit by externals; person despising those whose attainments or tastes he considers inferior to his own." Marcel Proust, in his early life a great snob and later a great — the very greatest — connoisseur and critic of snobs, asserted that snobbery "is admiration of something in other people unconnected with their personality" — by which he meant things extrinsic to them. (Proust also called snobbery, in his essay "On Reading Ruskin," "the greatest sterilizer of inspiration, the greatest deadener of originality, the greatest destroyer of talent." When he said this, he was still unable to begin his great novel, and so the remark is probably best read as a wholly autobiographical, self-accusatory utterance. The shedding of his own snobbery made it possible for Proust to write *The Remembrance of Things Past.*) The snob measures himself and others by extraneous things: ancestry, wealth, power, social connections, possession of glittering or elegant objects — with everything that is connected with status in the world, or with that portion of it that vibrates alluringly for him.

I have chiefly been using masculine pronouns in this chapter, but it is far from clear which of the sexes provides the greater number of snobs. Only a guess is possible here, and my own would be that snobbery, like bad judgment, is evenly divided between men and women, although the world's most famous snobs — the Duc de Saint-Simon, Lord Chesterfield, the Comte Robert de Montesquiou — have been men. Nothing exclusively feminine about snobbery, but it does sometimes suggest, in the full pejorative sense, the effeminate. The emotions, the values, the gambits of snobbery seem, in their indirectness, less than virile. Generally the most infuriating snobs I have encountered happen to have been men, though the single most tiresome snob I know is a woman. So there we are. Best perhaps to conclude that in snobbery at least, men and women have reached something like perfect equality.

"I have never met a snob who was not also a liar," writes Paul Theroux, "and that was what was wrong with snobbery." This quotation becomes all the more interesting when one considers that Theroux, especially in his travel writings, has often been thought a considerable snob. (Can it be that Theroux is himself lying in saying he has never met a truthful snob? This is a bit like the paradox presented by the Cretan who announced that all Cretans are liars.) Perhaps a greater sin inherent in snobbery is that it purports always to be above vulgarity, while it is in fact a central branch of vulgarity. The novelist Anthony Burgess once referred to another writer's "ill-bred snobbery," but that may well be a tautology, for all snobbery is, in some sense, ill bred — in the sense that everything is ill bred that does not seem to have behind it kindness, generosity, and a good heart.

For a beginning or working definition, then, I take the snob to be someone out to impress his betters or depress those he takes to be his inferiors, and sometimes both; someone with an exaggerated respect for social position, wealth, and all the accouterments of status; someone who accepts what he reckons to be the world's valuation on people and things, and acts — sometimes cruelly, sometimes ridiculously — on that reckoning; someone, finally, whose pride and accomplishment never come from within but always await the approving judgment of others. People not content with their place in the world, not reconciled with themselves, are especially susceptible to snobbery. The problem here is that at one time or another, and in varying degrees, this may well include us all.

3

How Snobbery Works

S<small>NOBBERY</small>, like religion, works through hope and fear. The snob hopes to position himself securely among those whom he takes to be the best, most elegant, virtuous, fashionable, or exciting people. He also fears contamination from those he deems beneath him. Snobs who have arrived do what they can to encourage hopelessness among those who haven't. Snobs who haven't arrived fear rejection the way other people fear cancer — it represents death, of a social kind.

Some snobs take special pleasure in looking down on others; some snobs dream of rising higher than they now are; and yet other snobs — reverse snobs — derive their comfort (and cold comfort it usually is) from feeling themselves outside the snobbery game altogether. The way you can tell a snob is by the energy he puts into these various operations: climbing, stopping others in mid-climb, rather too strenuously disassociating himself from the climb. The snob cares a little — and often a lot — more about these things than he or she ought.

What the snob wants is deference, inevitably quite a bit more than he deserves. He believes that deference comes through rank, which is not an altogether false belief. The grounds for deference differ in various societies at different times, and the determinants of rank can be inconstant, shifting, changing. High birth, by which is meant distinguished ancestry, can earn one deference. So can merit or extraordinary accomplishment. ("Better to be an ancestor," said Freud, neatly covering this point, "than to have them.") Considerable wealth, accompanied by an admired style of living, can also ring the gong for deference. Power in its differing forms almost always commands deference. High educational or cultural attainment may sometimes receive deference. Sometimes mere closeness, or even suggested closeness, to people who receive deference is sufficient to garner deference. Hence the snobbish tic of name-dropping, which implies that, through knowing the great or powerful or wealthy or famous, one is also owed deference. All these items will be taken up in the chapters that follow.

To have other people recognize your quality is no small pleasure. The lack of deference can seem no less displeasing. I occasionally go to lunch, at his club, with a friend who is a federal judge, who is greeted by the maitre d' and by waiters as Your Honor. This is fair enough — in fact, his job apart, he is an honorable man — but I always undergo a slight letdown at being unaddressed, feeling a bit like that bereft figure in newspapers, "man at left unidentified."

Deference, to be sure, can be lovely. Even unearned deference isn't bad. I had a taste of the latter in my late twenties at an excellent Chicago steak house called The Black Angus, where I believe I was taken, mistakenly, as "connected" by the owner, who also served as maitre d'. Connected, in the Chicago of those days, meant connected to the Syndicate, or Mob, or The Boys, as the Chicago mafia was then known. Perhaps I was taken for the son or nephew of someone important. Whatever the case, when I came into the restaurant, which was fairly often (this was in the BC, or Before Cholesterol, era), I was given precedence over already waiting customers — "Right this way, Mr. Epstein" — and escorted to one of the better tables. Shocking to report, I never corrected the owner, taking him aside, straightening him out, explaining to him that I was actually nobody.

All societies are at least partially organized along lines of deference. These lines can alter, often subtly. But deference always implies hierarchy or an ordering — sometimes implicit, sometimes explicit — by respect, which itself can bring automatic privilege. Sometimes these privileges seem just — those accorded the United States Supreme Court justices, the seeding accorded tennis players based on their previous performances — but sometimes they will seem unearned, excessive, stupid in the extreme.

Whatever the reality of his or her social position, everyone feels entitled to respect, which can be another, softer, slightly more euphemistic word for deference. "I don't get no respect," the old refrain of the comedian Rodney Dangerfield, spoken in a juddering voice while pulling nervously at his necktie, is one we have all, at one time or another, uttered — or more likely muttered — to ourselves. Nearly every human being deserves respect, but the question is, how much? And who does the calculations? By one's own reckoning, it is safe to say that a great deal of respect is owed. By the world's reckoning, the estimate is, somehow, almost inevitably likely to be lower. Journals kept by the young tend to give off a strong whiff of depression, chiefly because the world doesn't yet recognize the youthful journal keeper's genius, however unproven it may be. Sometimes one feels one isn't getting the consideration (another euphemism for deference) one deserves as a veteran, senior man or woman, someone whose mettle has been established. Awaiting a decision from an editor that takes longer than I think it ought, I find myself mumbling about the ignorance of people who don't understand that I am much too important to be kept waiting so long. Comic stuff, true, but also, I suspect, endemic.

Gauging one's significance not as you but as the world reckons it is no small problem. "Whenever I think I'm famous," the composer and critic Virgil Thomson once remarked, "I have only to go out into the world." By which he meant that he would find plenty of evidence that the world didn't concur. I recall, in this connection, the meeting of two distinguished intellectual figures — one a scholar of high international reputation, the other a Nobel novelist — who were joined by an administrative vice president at the university where both men then taught. After ten or fifteen minutes, the vice president departed, and the scholar said to the novelist, "Ah, me, I see that X is suffering from delusions of equality."

Is this a tale of snobbery or merely a devastatingly witty remark? I think the latter. First, because the remark wasn't made in front of the person at whom it was aimed. And second, because (as I happen to know) that person is himself a considerable snob, a double snob actually, one who sucks up to his betters and looks down on those he takes to be beneath him. The context gives its own special, happy twist to the story.

The true downward-looking snob not only feels too good about his own position in the world but is most genuinely pleased when encouraging a deep feeling of hopelessness in the upward-looking snob, who wishes to establish equality with him. The former, by making plain the disqualifying deficiency of the latter — wrong family, wrong schools, wrong connections, wrong clothes, wrong taste, wrong manners, wrong almost anything, really, will qualify — puts up a clear stop sign: swine do not pass here, and that, pal, means you.

Most people are readier to admit to being a downward-looking than an upward-looking snob. A man who wasn't was Chips Channon, a transplanted Chicagoan who became a minor English politician; socially well connected, he regularly gave parties for royalty from various countries during the 1930s. He made no bones about his idea of a good time being one in which he spent an evening with a king and a princess or two, or an afternoon on which a queen comes to call. At the end of one such night, he noted in his diary: "Our party then went on for some time, everyone agreeing, I think and hope, that it had been sensationally successful. They all left about 1:30, exalted and impressed, and exhausted, I crept up to bed. The atmosphere had been terrific; so many royalties, so many jewels." Hard to be angry at a man so open about his own light-hearted (and -headed) superficiality.

But the reason most people aren't ready to admit to

upward-looking snobbery is that it suggests envy. And envy, as Melville, in *Billy Budd,* writes, is "universally felt to be more shameful than even felonious crime." The upward-looking snob is happiest when he is mingling — better, perhaps, commingling — with the people he envies, which allows him to believe, however momentarily, that he is one of them. The upward-looking snob usually also turns out to be a downward-looking snob, for the pleasure that he takes being among his betters is not fully enjoyed unless he is also able to make plain to his former circle that he has now, thank you very much, risen well above it. Both parts — acceptance from those above, rejection of those below — must be in place for the upward-looking snob to feel the full elation of his victory. To be one up, someone else must be pushed one down, and so there has always been the element of one-upmanship about snobbery. But it is not one-upmanship of the kind put into play on the golf course or tennis court, where it is meant to throw an opponent off his game. It is one-upmanship played for higher emotional stakes.

The snob—be he upward or downward looking — needs above all to feel superior. "Nothing fortifies friendship," wrote Balzac in *Cousin Pons,* "more than one of two friends thinking himself superior to the other." Snobbery inheres in those things (wine connoisseurship, the acquisition of art) the knowledge or possession of which confers upon us — sometimes in spite of our best efforts to fight it off — a feeling of superiority. Yet, whatever one's specialty in this line, sustaining the feeling of superiority is no easy task, for, terrible truth to tell, human beings are not naturally superior. Hence the jumpy mental state of the snob, who almost perpetually requires confirmation of a superiority that doesn't truly exist.

Yet the real snobbery question is whether one is taking pleasure in a thing or activity for itself or because the pleasure is that other people — most people, in fact — are for one reason or another excluded from it. The two points are not so easily separated. One is driving along the Pacific Coast Highway in a two-seater Mercedes convertible, top down, an automobile of extravagant expense and on which great craftsmanship has been expended. Is the pleasure in the car itself, or is it partly in the knowledge that few people can afford such luxury? A bit of both, my guess is, and the pleasure is likely to be heightened by the mixture.

Neither will it do to call everything that is extravagant, elitist, highbrow, or a minority taste snobbish. Something can have all the earmarks of snobbery and turn out to be — of all things! — absolutely worth it. Some while ago I took myself to an expensive three-star restaurant in Chicago called Le Francais, which has long had a strong press, and discovered that — bad news here — it seemed worth the expense. I say bad news because if the restaurant were mediocre, I could write it off as a piece of snobbish obtuseness and never have to think about it again. Now, from time to time, I do.

The test for snobbery is finally a quality-control test. Is the thing desired worthy on its own and not for extrinsic (usually social) reasons? Is the car — the restaurant, the school — genuinely excellent? Or is it only that the world, in its characterless ignorance, has agreed that it is excellent. If the latter, then the standard in use is a snobbish one. Nothing wrong with wanting the best; the problem — the snobbery problem — enters in making sure it really is the best one wants, and not merely something whose prestige comes from its being *known* as the best, a very different thing.

A further problem is that snobbery often works. Sometimes things that had true quality — certain once elite American universities, for example — have long lost it in substance, but the world conspires to keep this from being known, for the good reason that people who have gone to them do not want to knock the pins out from under themselves. Having gone to these schools still works to gain entrée into all sorts of places that might otherwise be closed to one: jobs and clubs and other social connections. Even after a radical hysterectomy, some golden geese continue for decades to lay their eggs.

Putting one's own pleasures to the snobbery check can be a tiresome business. Snobs aren't, after all, always wrong. An elegant bit of design, a particular food or drink, a line of cloth-

ing needn't be disqualified just because it is taken up by
snobs, though this is certain to deter the reverse snob. On the
other hand, does enjoying one's own exclusivity make one a
snob? I recall, in the late 1970s, a friend telling me that for
years she had had an interest in serious cookery and in house-
plants, and now she was disappointed to see that nearly everyone had taken up these interests. She maintained the former
and deserted the latter.

Not wanting to run with the general herd, nor wanting to
run with that higher herd — the herd of independent
minds — does not qualify one as a snob. It makes one, I
would say, a person struggling to be an individual. Being discriminating isn't necessarily being snobbish, either. "All
artists are snobs," Diana Trilling wrote, "whatever the social
group with which they make common cause, if only to the extent that they live by discriminations." The trick is to be independent of fads, trends, passing phases, to make one's choices
and take one's actions, think one's thoughts as free as possible
from social pressures, yet at the same time try to get the best
that one's time has to offer. Never, this, easily brought off.

I have to inject here another form of snobbery, which I have
come to think of as infuriating snobbery — infuriating, that
is, if aimed at you. This is the snobbery that one is sometimes subjected to by people who don't understand what
matters to you. Beer connoisseurs — and there are such —
who are amused by your ordering a Budweiser; designer-
clothes idiots who make plain they find your clothes crude
because they carry no logos; visual-art fools who buy expensive though dubious art yet look down on you for not knowing the name of a painter from Carmel, California. Vulgarity is
the hubris of the snobbish. It can be excruciating to be the
victim of snobbishness in a realm where one is not even
mildly interested but in fact, insofar as one can get up any interest at all, rather looks down on oneself. One wants to explain to the people looking down on you that they really must
get it clear that your own standards are well out of the range of
their pathetic snobberies.

Nor does having high standards make one a snob. I, for example, have long scoffed at the habit — now practically a full-blown tradition — of universities conferring honorary degrees on movie actors and television journalists. In doing so, I believe, they degrade themselves, showing that they are quite as gone on celebrity as the average reader of *People* or viewer of *Entertainment Tonight.* In giving an honorary degree to Robert Redford or Oprah Winfrey or Ted Koppel they pander to their students, turning them into another audience and turning themselves into low-grade impresarios.

High standards generally — about workmanship in the creation of objects, about what is owed in friendship, about the quality of art, and much else — far from being snobbish, are required to maintain decency in life. When the people who value these things are called snobs, the word is usually being used in a purely sour-grapes way. "Elitist," a politically supercharged word, is almost invariably another sour-grapes word, at least when used to denigrate people who insist on a high standard. The distinction, I believe, is that the elitist desires the best; the snob wants other people to think he has, or is associated with, the best. Delight in excellence is easily confused with snobbery by the ignorant.

4

The Democratic Snob

WILLIAM MAKEPEACE THACKERAY, in his *Book of Snobs,* reports that "first, the World was made, then, as a matter of course, Snobs." Yet it is not altogether certain that this is true. One hears little about snobbery before the eighteenth century, and scarcely anything at all about it then. The Snob, one would think, would be a staple figure in Restoration comedy, but not so. Neither are there any snobs in Shakespeare, Dante, Aristophanes, or the Bible. Not that there isn't plenty of truckling to superiors, parasitism, heavy-handed flattery, back-scratching and bottom-kissing, all calculated to bring special advantages to its purveyors. Pretension, too, has never been in short supply. We see much pretension that veers on the snobbish in the plays of Molière. The painter Benjamin Robert Haydon, friend to Wordsworth, Keats, Lamb, and Hazlitt, practically swooned when in the company of the highborn. But snobbery as we know it today, snobbery meant to shore up one's own sense of importance and to make others sorely feel their insignificance, was not yet up and running in a serious way. It took the spread of democracy to make that possible.

The reason is that, until the nineteenth century, there was a ready acceptance of rank and social position and, accompanying this, an understanding that most people were everlastingly locked in their place. Where social rank is clearly demarcated, as it is when a nobility and a gentry are present, jockeying for position of the kind that is at the heart of snobbery tends to play a less than strong part in daily life; nor is it quite so central in the interior dramas of men and women whose hearts are set on rising in the world.

Snobbery thrives where society is most open. It does particularly well under democracy, even though, theoretically, it is anathema to the democratic spirit. Snobbery is, wrote the political philosopher Judith N. Shklar in *Ordinary Vices,* "a repudiation of every democratic value." The social fluidity that democracy makes possible, allowing people to climb from the bottom to the top of the ladder of social class in a generation or two, provides a fine breeding ground for snobbery and gives much room to exercise condescension, haughtiness, affectation, false deference, and other egregious behavior so congenial to the snob.

The unavoidable Alexis de Tocqueville, in *Democracy in America,* reminds his readers that "democratic institutions most successfully develop sentiments of envy in the human heart." He also remarks that in America he "found the democratic sentiment of envy was expressed in a thousand different ways." In a democracy there are so many ways of rising in society: through the acquisition of money, through marriage, even through, *mirabile dictu!,* merit. But such is the spirit behind democracy that no one really believes that, apart from innate talent, anyone is intrinsically better than anyone else, and especially is no one better than oneself; therefore any difference in social status between one person and another is taken to constitute an injustice of a kind — and one that can be remedied and rectified by careful plans. From the early Henry James ("Daisy Miller") to Edith Wharton (*The Custom of the Country*) to Theodore Dreiser (*An American Tragedy*) to F. Scott Fitzgerald (*The Great Gatsby*), some of the best nineteenth- and early-twentieth-century American novels are about the attempts to carry such plans to fruition. The attempt to rise in American democracy may be the primary, the central, the essential American story.

One finds touches of snobbery in our nation's early history. John Adams must have felt he was scoring heavily when he called Alexander Hamilton "the bastard brat of a Scotch pedlar," and the tragic rivalry between Hamilton and Aaron Burr has always seemed to have about it a social-class tinge. But for the most part the Founding Fathers felt that honor was more important than social position. If one wished to sink a man, the best way to do it was not to attack his birth or manners but his reputation. "Probably nothing separates the traditional world of the Founding Fathers from today," the historian Gordon S. Wood has written, "than its concern with honor. Honor was the value genteel society placed on a gentleman and the value a gentleman placed on himself. . . . Honor subsumed self-esteem, pride, and dignity, and was akin to glory and fame."

Little snobberies existed even in this rarefied atmosphere. Some American families considered themselves aristocratic; some states felt their place was higher than that of other states — the gentry of Virginia and Maryland early took on aristocratic pretensions. The phenomenon of *Mayflower* passengers — that is, that of claiming status through precedence — was part of the mythos of the American founding. As late as the last half of the past century, this was continued by such organizations as the Daughters of the American Revolution. But whereas the DAR, as it was then known, once carried some punch in its disapproval, its current-day existence seems largely a joke.

Snobbishness, Proust noted, implies that there are people to whom one feels oneself inferior. In democratic America, where everyone was thought to be created equal, this became a dubious proposition — at least officially, if not realistically, so. In a country with so brief a history, no one could say, as Aimery de La Rochefoucauld is supposed to have said, when refusing to invite a family to his home, that "they had no position in the year 1000." Snobbery therefore became identified with pretension — the snobs were those who pretended to be above the ruck. Yet in the new America this didn't mean that great numbers of people did not wish to rise as high as possible. Thank goodness the law of contradiction has never been enforced in social life, for the jails would overflow.

Elsewhere in the world the social system was fixed because of the stability of a class system, with aristocracy at its top, a substantial peasantry below, a thinnish middle class between. Samuel Johnson felt "subordination is very necessary for society, and contentions for superiority very dangerous." A firmly locked-in social system, with little mobility either upward or downward, can be the best stifler of snobbery.

By the time the United States was founded, the first tremors of the forthcoming collapse of aristocracy were being felt. The French Revolution, in 1789, provided more than mere tremors. Tocqueville, himself of an aristocratic family, knew the game was up well before his visit to our shores in 1831. Behind the writing of *Democracy in America* was the fear that then rising equality would destroy liberty. He never mentions snobbery in his book, but he is unlikely to have been surprised by the fact that the spirit of equality could only excite the behavior that goes into the making of the snob. Let us add to this the underbelly emotions the snob suffers of uncertainty, uneasiness, and a worrisome self-consciousness about his true status.

In public life, a political candidate could be attacked on what were essentially snobbish grounds. Even so cultivated a gent (as he now seems) as Thomas Jefferson took a number of hits about his wardrobe, his grooming, his too easy manners. Andrew Jackson was called by his opponents "the Tennessee barbarian," and his poor spelling was mocked. Abraham Lincoln, progenitor of the main American myth — that in the United States one can go from a log cabin to the White House — was put down in his day by the *New York Herald* as "a fourth-class lecturer who can't speak good grammar." Henry Adams, the consummate American snob, devoted an entire novel, *Democracy*, to excoriating the coarseness of American senators, and in that novel, after setting out their low principles, called political corruption "the dance of democracy." Adams's friend Henry James wrote a story, "Pandora," with characters modeled on Adams and his wife, who

are planning a party and in which the Adams character remarks, "Hang it, there's only a month left; let us be vulgar and
have some fun — let us invite the President."

Perhaps there is something fraudulent about democracy,
not as a method of conducting politics but as a social arrange-
ment. In America this was highlighted by the predominantly
middle-class makeup of the country. Vague and wide-ranging
though the term *middle class* may be, it does render anyone
who is part of this class capable of, if not intrinsically susceptible to, snobbery in both directions. To be middle class positions one nicely to be both an upward- and a downward-
looking snob, full, simultaneously, of aspiration to rise to the
position of those above and of disdain for those below.

H. L. Mencken makes this same point, possibly with more
glee than is absolutely required, but then his prose glands
were always stimulated by the contemplation of what he liked
to refer to as *Boobus Americanus.* In an essay he titled "The
Pushful American," Mencken, along with George Jean Na-
than (though the voice of the essay is dominantly Mencken's),
claimed that Americans are distinguished above all by their
desire to climb socially. But this appetite for the climb was
strongly hedged by a fear of slipping and losing one's original
place.

Mencken's larger point is that socially the American is on a
perpetually icy slope, wanting to climb "a notch or two" but
"with no wall of caste . . . to protect him if he slips." He wrote:
"Such a thing as a secure position is practically unknown to
us." Without a true aristocracy, with full titles and the rest of
it, he argued, no American is ever securely lodged. (Tocqueville wrote that "in no country of the world are private
fortunes more unstable than in the United States.") With a
title — especially a title handed down to one and handed on
in turn to one's children — one can act the utter rascal or
rogue without worry about losing one's place; one can be
drunk, stupid, immoral, with insane politics, but one is still an
earl, marquis, count, grandee, which cannot be taken away.
Lacking a true aristocracy, what we have had, Mencken contends, are cities "full of brummagem aristocrats," who have

turned out to be little more than plutocrats coarsely aping aristocratic behavior. Instead of a settled society, Americans have a regular rhythm of rise and fall. "The grandfather of the Vanderbilts," Mencken writes, "was a bounder; the last of the Washingtons is a petty employee in the Library of Congress."

Americans attempting the social climb Mencken found pitiful, and the group at the top contemptible, with its "shameless self-assertion, its almost obscene display of its importance and of the shadowy privileges and acceptance on which that importance is based." These arrangements gave way to an almost inevitable snobbery — though Mencken, too, doesn't use the word — with those who may be said to have arrived anxious to keep down the newcomer, and the newcomer ready to abase himself, to "sacrifice his self-respect today in order to gain the hope of destroying the self-respect of other aspirants tomorrow."

Mencken's description of American life, with every city having its own upper-caste groups, with various undergroups plotting to slip past the gates to enter a social Valhalla of sorts, is now so badly dated as to be quite without reality. But where Mencken wasn't wrong was in noting that democracy "is always inventing class distinctions, despite its theoretical abhorrence of them." The Ins and Outs, especially in recent years, change with considerable rapidity. Capital-S Society, which once stood for *le gratin,* the upper crust, in every modest-sized town and above all in New York City — where such groups existed as Ward McAllister's Four Hundred, the number of people who could fit into Mrs. Astor's private ballroom — and which once dominated American social snobbery, is all but finished. This was Society of the Society page, where the cotillions, debutante balls, marriages, and other doings of the putative upper class were reported on regularly, generally in a tone of gushing admiration. No one knows who killed Society, or even the date of its death, but one can fix the demise around the time that the Society pages were banished from the newspapers, to be replaced by the Style sections, which began to happen in the 1960s.

The disappearance of a formal, structured Society didn't

mean the end of snobbery, for social envy continued un-
abated, only becoming more amorphous and turning on
things other than birth or wealth alone. "A degree of proximity is required between two classes to make possible envy of
the upper by the lower," the sociologist Robert Nisbet wrote,
adding: "This is why envy proliferates during periods or in
societies where equality has come to dominate other values."
Nisbet felt that the American competition for "status becomes in its own way as tyrannical as anything before it."
Making roughly the same point, the English journalist Malcolm Muggeridge reported that, at lunch with the editor of
Burke's Peerage, he was told of the great interest in titled
Englishmen among Americans. "I said that, inevitably, the
more egalitarian a society became, the more snobbish."

While Society was still running strong in America, there
was much copying of the English aristocracy, in the naming of
suburbs, schools, housing developments, even children. In
no other country than in America was the ennobling suffix,
usually awarded only to kings and popes, sometimes added to
names, resulting in J. Bryan III, or Daniel Thomas V. Americans, for all their official allegiance to the notion of democracy, seemed to long for an aristocracy.

If a full-blown aristocracy could not be brought off, then
something resembling a patriciate was thought acceptable.
The ultimate effort in this direction, which is not over yet, is
the attempt on the part of many Americans to render the
Kennedy family our patriciate. The assassination of John F.
Kennedy aided this effort immensely. Panegyrists there have
been in plenty to stoke and keep the sacred flame. But too
much scandal elsewhere in the family — including the near
fascism and anti-Semitism of the Founding Father, as Joseph
Kennedy, Sr., came to be known — and the serious want of
talent among Kennedy descendants has made it difficult to
sustain. Even now the desire refuses to be quite extinguished,
as witness the good-night-sweet-prince press treatment of the
sad accidental death of the son of Jack Kennedy. Not even
Ted Kennedy, a bloated Falstaffian figure without any of the
winning humor, can put it to sleep.

Perhaps the most striking evidence of this is the mythical aura that arose around Jacqueline Bouvier Kennedy Onassis, or Jackie O., in the grocery-press and fashion-magazine styling of her name. Here was a woman of modest attainments, who put up with a frightful amount from her philandering husband, supplied a veneer of culture over his presidency, but whose personal motto, finally, might have been — what the hell, let's Frenchify it — *Montrez-moi l'argent:* Show me the money. One cannot say that she longed for the role, yet she became our older, longer-suffering Princess Diana. And not through any intrinsic merits but chiefly because of her connection to the Kennedys, she became, in that thinnest of over- and misused words, an icon. (In the one joke I have ever heard attributed to Mao Zedong, the Chinese leader is supposed to have said, "If Aristotle Onassis was interested in power, I wonder why he didn't propose to the widow of Nikita Khrushchev.")

At the same time that Americans may long for a patriciate, a royal family even, we hate what seem to us distinctions of rank not based on merit. The only time I ever encountered such arrangements was in the peacetime U.S. Army, where the officer class did not seem to me to earn its privileges. (Only a handful of sergeants, most of them black, impressed me as truly able men.) Many of the officers I had to do with were ROTC-trained, seemed dullish, undeserving of the deference that was theirs by right of rank. Not that I rebelled. In my dealings with them, I merely fell back on what I took to be my intrinsic superiority, reminding myself that they may be majors or colonels in a military setting, but outside this setting, in the larger world in which I planned to act, they were corporals at best. If this was the snob in me reacting to what I took to be an undeserving hierarchy, it was, I now think, even more an almost purely American reaction.

Perhaps Americans in their democracy were especially prone to snobbery because they felt themselves so snobbishly judged by Europeans. Right out of the gate, it was old world versus new, with the new having little going for it besides a certain raw energy. When Mrs. Frances Trollope, the mother of the novelist, arrived here in 1827, to report on *Domestic Manners of the Americans* — eventually the title of her once famous book on America — she had almost nothing good and plenty dreary to say about her subject. Of Americans generally, and American soldiers in particular, she wrote: "I do not like them. I do not like their principles, I do not like their manners, I do not like their opinions." Here she is on Americans at table:

> The total want of all the usual courtesies of the table, the voracious rapidity with which the viands were seized and devoured, the strange uncouth phrases and pronunciation; the loathsome spitting, from the contamination of which it was absolutely impossible to protect our dresses; the frightful manner of feeding with their knives, till the whole blade seemed to enter into the mouth; and the still more frightful manner of cleaning the teeth afterwards with a pocket knife, soon forced us to feel that we were not surrounded by the generals, colonels, and majors of the old world; and that the dinner hour was to be anything rather than the hour of enjoyment.

Lots more of the same issued from Europeans during the nineteenth and well into the twentieth century. Charles Dickens, in *Martin Chuzzlewit*, devoted the better part of a thickish novel to attacking American manners and mores. The main charge of Europe against America was coarseness and vulgarity. With the exception of Tocqueville, whose criticisms were not so superficial and whose admirations were genuine, scarcely any Frenchman missed taking a shot at American life when the opportunity was presented. The Germans were not more charitable. But the English were the most relentless in this line, allowing no one, but no one, to get off. Here is Virginia Woolf, in her diary for September 12, 1921, while complaining about Henry James's *The Wings of the Dove:* "Not a flabby or slack sentence, but much emasculated by this timidity or consciousness or whatever it is. Very highly American, I conjecture, in the determination to be highly bred, and the slight obtuseness as to what high breeding is."

This of Henry James, the man who T. S. Eliot said achieved the status of being a complete European but of no known country. James himself reminded Americans not to be cowed by Europe. But many Americans, especially those with high social and cultural aspirations, chose, rather than to fight it, to join it by deciding to view themselves outside European social condemnation and turning essentially the same criticisms on their countrymen, thus beginning a chain of snobbery that, from the top down, would never quite end, even in our own day.

5

Snob-Jobbery

IN EUROPE, it used to be said, people want to know *who* you are. In the United States they want to know *what you do*. A useful distinction, this, for it implies that in Europe whom you derive from, your family line, is the crucial datum, whereas in America what you do defines you. In America one's work marks one socially — and, often, snobbishly.

Once upon a time, and not so long ago as all that, the best answer to the question of what one did was to say that one was a professional man or (more and more nowadays) woman. To be a professional man or woman meant that one had had more higher education than others, albeit of a vocational kind, was earning a serious sum of money, was held in respect in one's community. Some professions were of course thought better, were ranked higher, than others. Within each of the professions — medicine, law, clergy, engineering — there was a hierarchy, and even a hierarchy within each element of the hierarchy. In medicine an M.D. was above an osteopath, an osteopath above a dentist, a dentist perhaps above a veterinarian, a veterinarian above a chiropractor, a chiropractor tied in a panting dead heat with a podiatrist. One can cut things further and finer by setting up a hierarchy among M.D.s, beginning perhaps with the neurological surgeon and ending with the general practitioner.

Yet in America today all the professions have lost a good deal of their social prestige. Consider medicine, in which most parents would probably still be pleased to find their grown children working, if only because it meant they were doing something worthwhile (healing the sick) and almost always for an excellent wage. We all rely on the services of medicine, but we no longer revere physicians, at least not in the way we once did. This is owing in part to the attainment of physicians of what we might revere in others but find off-putting in them: their interest in moneymaking. The loss of prestige in physicians can be traced in significant part to their gain in earning power, though this is now said to be much reduced.

Beginning in the middle 1960s, with the advent of Medicare in the United States, doctors suddenly found ways to become multimillionaires, or at least they had the potential to do so. Around the same time they ceased to make house calls, increasingly specialized, and more and more became businessmen whose products were health and the promise of longevity. Their former separation from general society, once thought to be elevated by an assumed idealism that automatically put them on a high moral plane, was now all but eradicated. Empty babble about the special doctor-patient relationship would continue, but doctors had come to seem like everyone else — in business for themselves, out to make a buck, with the added mark against them that their money-mongering could result in their actually doing harm by refusing poorer patients or making decisions based on profit rather than health. The HMOs, with their many strictures and qualifications on what they will allow in the way of treatment, demonstrate in heightened form the idea of medicine as merely another business. One index of the slip in prestige of physicians is the absence within the last forty years of any towering national figure — of the stature, say, of William Osler — in medicine.

That lawyers have slipped in social prestige is almost too obvious to require mention. Evidence for this is everywhere, from lawyer jokes (Why don't sharks attack lawyers? Answer:

Professional courtesy) to the representation of lawyers in popular culture. Two recent novels by young writers evidence a cool disdain for the legal profession: "Law school was a word I kept lodged at the back of my mouth," notes the young protagonist of Jonathan Rosen's novel *Eve's Apple,* "like a cyanide tablet, *just in case.*" In Valerie Block's *Was It Something I Said?,* a character dating a woman lawyer notes that law was an "unimaginative choice" as a career for a man but still acceptable in a woman.

Lawyers were once thought erudite, honorable, trained for leadership. They are now thought, at best, a dreary necessity to negotiate an astonishingly intricate web of laws that, the suspicion is, these spiderish creatures have themselves erected to add to their profits; at worst, and perhaps more often, they are viewed as corrupt, without integrity, pigs at the trough, the enemies of decency. Famous lawyers there are in America — Johnnie Cochrane, Alan Dershowitz, Vernon Jordan — but none seems in any way admirable, another index of the drained prestige of the law as a profession. Some of the most interesting careers in America today seem to be those led by men and women who went to the Harvard or Yale Law School but chose not to practice.

Although there is much talk about increased church attendance in America, and religious revivals are announced almost monthly, the clergy, too, has lost its standing in American life. As recently as fifty years ago, clergymen of all faiths were figures of prominence: the Reverend Norman Vincent Peale, Rabbi Stephen Wise, and Bishop Fulton Sheen are only a few of the names that had national resonance. Billy Graham may be the last clergyman to have had fame of this kind, but somehow he has lost it, perhaps because of his too close connection with Republican politicians. Today the only names associated with religion are also bathed in the greenish light of the deeply dubious: the Reverends Jerry Falwell and Jesse Jackson, or the scandalous Jim Bakker and what seemed for a while the endless parade of priests accused of child molesting, or the vaguely comic Reform rabbis vying with one another to see who could depart further from Jewish tradition and do the first nude bar mitzvah. The Catholic Church in America, as is well known, cannot marshal a sufficient number of priests to staff all its institutions, which is one reason why Catholic higher education, no longer taught by an impressive priesthood, has seemed so sadly diminished in recent decades.

Part of the loss of prestige, social and intellectual, of the American clergy is to be found in the loss of authority of religion itself, despite all the talk about religious revival. Religion has had to become flexible, to unbend, to meet its audience more than halfway, and in doing so has begun to seem as if it is selling itself. Retaining dignity — not to speak of assuming grandeur — while selling is not an easy trick, and contemporary religion has not come anywhere close to mastering it. One result of this is that its cadre of clergy for the most part no longer retains the admired position among the professions or in the greater society that it once held.

The loss of prestige among engineers and inventors — whose founding figure in American life is Benjamin Franklin — is more complicated. Toward the close of the nineteenth century, engineers and inventors were the nation's great heroes. Such was the popularity of Alexander Graham Bell that he was photographed more than any man in the United States except the president. Thomas Edison, who did not bother to go to high school, was a source of endless stories, most having to do with his natural genius. Henry Ford was another such figure: the self-made man who improves his society — building cars, inventing the assembly line, raising wages — while also immensely enriching himself. The man with mechanical skills and inventive capacity was everywhere admired. Charles Lindbergh, the Lone Eagle, along with being the first pilot to cross the Atlantic on a solo flight, was also an inventor of some seriousness, having a number of patents to his credit. Until he besmirched his reputation by naively allowing his name to be connected with some of the leading Nazi figures, he was easily the greatest American hero of the first third of the twentieth century.

Engineers and inventors, with their pragmatic spirit, were

doing the work of building the country: laying down roads, setting up bridges, building the vast and complex infrastructure of immense cities. Hoover Dam, the world's greatest single piece of practical sculpture, was the work of American engineers. Competence was the trademark of engineers. The least mistake on their part and many lives would be forfeit. Astonishingly few such mistakes were made. Engineers brought water, spread light, helped crops to grow, extracted fuel and minerals and wealth from the earth — they did the work that men once invoked the gods to do.

Yet engineers, too, have now lost their standing. Not through earning too much money, nor through a reputation for lubricity, nor even through a loss of belief in the aims behind their work. The twentieth century is likely to be remembered for its blessed advances in labor-saving and health-restoring technology. "We are now in the midst of a technological revolution that is full of surprises," the philosopher John Searle not long ago wrote. "No one thirty years ago was aware that one day household computers would become as common as dishwashers." Yet at the close of the century engineers seemed figures of little or no interest, greatly limited, dull, déclassé. Why?

Even though a high level of technology is absolutely required and everywhere enjoyed, the people who produce it seem a good deal less than elegant, as elegance is currently construed. Nerds we call some among them. Dullards we tend to think most of the rest of them. (Even Bill Gates, said to be the world's richest man, can't quite excite the American imagination.) Whether designing bridges or computer software, they lack panache, a sense of participation in the wider and subtler and more stylish life of the country. Poor clods, most of them don't seem to recognize that there is a world out there in which what one wears, eats, drinks, holds opinions about can count for a great deal — for almost everything, really. All they seem to worry about is the job at hand — and then, when that is done, the next job. No longer good enough.

Teaching, particularly university teaching, once held prestige, at least in some quarters, but today this is less and less so.

The old criticism of university teachers is that they were "academic," a word that stood in nicely for "theoretical" and therefore "out of it"; Shaw did teaching grave damage with his famous aphorism: "He who can, does. He who cannot, teaches." The title "professor" always conveyed a slight comic tinge, and was also conferred on the man who played the piano in the bordello.

Still, a kind of idealism attached to the job: professors were after all working with the young, entrancing, inspiring, instilling passion for things of the mind. The element of sacrifice also entered in: professors worked for low wages because of their love for the work. But professors are now often quite decently paid, with many full professorships bringing in well over $100,000 a year, and in certain subjects (chiefly in the sciences and social sciences) a great deal more money is available through consulting. Then, too, professors as a general group have shown so little courage in times of university crises that it was difficult to think of them standing for much of anything but going with the flow, in whatever direction it happens to lead. Perhaps I am biased against the professoriat, having taught in a university for too long, but my own sense is that the serious teaching nowadays is done in grammar and high schools — important, necessary work that is less recognized and vastly under-appreciated.

For a brief spurt, jobs with a large payload of idealism in them were much admired. Young people thought to become investigative journalists, after the pattern of Bob Woodward and Carl Bernstein, who helped bring down the Richard Nixon administration. Marine biology was big for a time, with its promise of saving the whales and talking to the dolphins. Becoming a forest ranger, or anything to do with the environment — which really meant anything to do with helping save the environment — also put many points on the board. But today all these do-gooding jobs seem peripheral, nowhere any longer quite center ring.

Somehow the emphasis in American life is on a different order of work, and hence of worker. The agent, the broker, the trader, the marketer, the investment banker, the all-purpose executive, the operator, the entrepreneur, the man or woman who does not provide the service or the product but helps bring it to market, usually acquiring a solid profit for him- or herself along the way — these are the figures who seem most admired in American life just now. (One of the most sought-after jobs by recent graduates at the better universities is that of junior-grade consultant, working for Andersen Consulting, McKinsey & Company, or other such firms.) "Just now" is a time when the country has shifted from a strong manufac-turing, mining, farming, logging country to one where the main emphasis is on service and information and entertain-ment. Such people aren't everywhere openly admired — they may even be despised a little — but they are nonetheless thought to be the insiders, the people with the lowdown on how things work, the folks at the controls, the smart money.

Less and less in the middle and upper middle classes in America does one encounter anyone who actually makes something; instead most people work at shuffling paper, play-ing with numbers, making deals, disseminating knowledge, conveying news. People who make things have been given the title "content providers" — helluva phrase, that — but for the most part they are not the powerful players. The action has gone elsewhere, to the purveyors, conveyors, middlemen. (Al-though the children of the upper middle class are allowed a slightly fashionable dip in downward mobility: one's daugh-ter may become a chef, or one's son do restoration carpentry, without social disgrace resulting.)

The one major exception is that of artists: painters, per-forming musicians, even not very successful writers have been able to retain a purchase on prestige. "Artists," Saul Bellow has said, "are more envied than millionaires." Oddly, those lit-erary artists in our era who have been most handsomely rewarded — Arthur Miller, E. L. Doctorow, Toni Morrison, Edward Albee, Cindy Sherman — seem to be those who have been most critical of what they think the corruption of the country in which they have flourished. The gods of capital-ism, we must assume, love a joke. Because of the cachet that culture has in contemporary America, to be even a not very good poet or a hopeless painter is still to be thought "creative," to have a higher calling. Besides, if one isn't good at one's art, one can always teach it in universities, turning out hundreds of young people quite as mediocre as oneself.

Allied with the prestige of art, even bad art, the great gong of fashionable success is perhaps most resoundingly rung by young men or women who work in the movies or television. Some years ago I was hired by Warner Brothers to write a screenplay based on a short story I had written, and nothing I had done until then had attracted anything like the same excited interest on the part of family, friends, acquaintances, even strangers. During this time, too, I learned that a good number of young people working in the movies or television had earlier gone to Harvard, Yale, Princeton, and other of the country's tonier schools. They work in movies and television, I believe, not for the money alone — many of them come from wealthy parents, or could themselves make big money by going to superior law schools or doing an M.B.A. and subsequently getting a well-paid job in a corporation. They choose to do so because they sense that in the business of mass entertainment lies the greatest *gloire* — that combination of fame, riches, power, and leisure — now available in America, even if it entails heartbreaking compromise, turning out meretricious work, and sucking up to some clearly loathsome characters. Although most Americans cannot name three screenwriters or two television producers, although it does not say much for the United States at the beginning of a new century, mass entertainment appears to be where the real action is, at any rate as measured by the admiration of the young.

Still, something has changed in the very nature of ambition that has altered snobbery in regard to occupations, or what I think of as snob-jobbery. The traditional pattern of ambition posited a success built on solid foundations, coming to fruition after long and careful work, with the ease of more than sufficient money nicely in place to massage the worn muscles used in accruing genuine achievement. No longer. Ours is an age that needs to retire the word *millionaire,* since it has made a million dollars seem rather a piddling sum. It's an age when one hopes to score early, not to have to wait long past forty to retire to some artificial community such as Santa Fe, New Mexico, there to live in a vastly expensive house on an unpaved road. (Houses on well-paved roads — such are among the twists of snobbery in our time — are less expensive in Santa Fe.) It's an age when loyalty even to one's own creations — the product one has designed, the company one has developed, the pride of ownership — is made to seem a little, make that a lot, beside the point. The new ideal of ambition is to get in, score early and big, and get out.

For a brief period, a new hero began to appear on the scene, the young entrepreneur, who started up a dot-com on Monday morning and by Friday was worth $60 million (a dream that seems now to have crashed). But the dot-coms, and these young men and women — jeans-wearing, scooter-riding, fruit-juice-drinking — seem to have succumbed to the stodgy laws of economics: a useful product with a real demand for it is required for any lasting success. In time all but the solidest of such enterprises began to go under.

Ambition and snobbery tend to be linked, except where ambition — in science, in serious art — is pure, which means that it does not entangle itself with worldly success. Snobbery, which rarely questions the world's valuations, goes with the flow, sometimes wishing to swim just a bit upstream ahead of most other people. The jobs the world values the snob values. In the snobbery sweepstakes, being a physician, though not what it once was, still counts for something; a successful lawyer, if making great sums, need not wince in perpetual shame; a clergyman, having become a variant of salesman, has a hellaciously hard row to hoe; and an engineer, if he is any good, probably won't notice or care how little he is regarded. But it's the day of the middleman: the fellow who creates little, builds less, changes lots, but develops nothing enduring — just takes the cash and makes certain he or she gets the vice presidency, the best table, the fine wine, the excellent opera tickets. Prestige, at this moment, lies with them.

6

O WASP, Where Is Thy Sting-a-Ling

THE HISTORY of the world, in one interpretation, is the history of fallen aristocracies. If true, no century was more intensely crowded with history than the twentieth. With all the talk of changes in the world around the time of the new millennium, quite overlooked was the all but complete closing down of the European aristocracy. Henry James once called aristocracy "bad manners organized," which may or may not have been so, but aristocracy stood for deference — and privilege and prestige — also organized.

The deference and privilege were genuine and extensive. In his elegant book *The Secrets of the Gotha,* Ghislain de Diesbach recounts how, in Europe, the upper aristocracy could stop trains when the mood to do so took them. "The Empress Elizabeth of Austria frequently did this to visit a chateau she had seen from the window of her compartment, or simply in order to relax a little by walking on foot in the country-side. The slightest journey involved a considerable display of forces, red carpets at the station, authorities clad in frock-coats to make speeches of welcome, platoons of cavalry, bouquets of flowers and above all fanfares to drown the

seditious shouts of the anarchists." Yes, it was good to be
empress.

The history of the past century — *poof!* — wiped all this
away. With the exception of the monarchy in England, the
principality of Monaco, the honorific monarchies in Sweden,
Spain, and a few other places, and the occasional pretender
wandering, dazed, around European spas, aristocracy today
is all but done, gone, kaput. The name of a European aristocratic family is sometimes licensed to a clothing or perfume
manufacturer, or an Italian or French aristocrat, usually hus-
tling wine, pops up in the pages of *Vanity Fair* or *Town &
Country* magazines, but that's about it. From the 1917 revolution in Russia through two world wars with a major economic
depression in between and through the smash-up of empire
everywhere in the world, aristocracy emerged as one of the
permanent casualties of the twentieth century.

An argument could be made that it was on its way out
long before the Russian Revolution sounded its first death
knell. In the middle of the nineteenth century, what became
known as the title search — that of American heiresses seeking down-on-their-uppers aristocrats for husbands — was
well under way. This provided Henry James and Edith Wharton with a swell literary subject. When in 1895 the Comte
Boni de Castellane married Anna Gould, the daughter of Jay
Gould, the American financier, he threw a fete for three thousand in the Bois de Boulogne, on you'll never guess whose
money; and it took the shameless Comte eleven years to go
through $5.5 million of Gould money before a divorce — and
nine years later an annulment — was arranged. This didn't
stop Miss Gould from next marrying the Prince de Sagan, of
the house of Talleyrand-Périgord.

If these and other such marriages speak to the impoverish-
ment of European aristocracy, ready to barter pedigree for
purse, they speak quite as vociferously to the American yearning for aristocracy. This yearning, though it could never be
openly declared, seems always to have been present. ("Only
stupid people," wrote Horace, "assess people by their geneal-
ogy," but stupid people have never been in short supply, and

they continued to be so long after the fall of the Roman Empire.) A group of Americans after the successful revolution from England wanted to declare George Washington our king. Aaron Burr always carried himself as an aristocrat; Alexander Hamilton, the more talented man, was thought vulnerable because of his illegitimate birth. Members of the Adams family, itself immensely talented, never had qualms about asserting their social primacy by way of their intellectual distinction. Henry Adams, the best writer among them, was entirely comfortable in his hauteur.

To this day the longing for aristocracy on the part of Americans crops up in odd places. Royalty in close proximity seems to make Americans lose their balance, if not get positively goofy. Princess Diana, not long before she died, visited Northwestern University, where I teach. The spectacle of the university president, a smallish man in glasses, following the Princess about the campus, yapping away, reminded one of nothing so much as that of a chihuahua attempting to mount an Afghan hound. A plaque has been placed on a rock on the campus commemorating in perpetuity the sad, rather airheaded princess's completely perfunctory visit.

As for an actual American aristocracy, regional patriciates burgeoned in nineteenth-century America and long before in New England, in New York and Philadelphia, in the South. Where they weren't bogged down in mossy fantasy, as in the postbellum South, they could be impressive. Not all of them were philistine — the Boston Brahmin class was intellectually extraordinary — but they could also be impressive even in their philistinism. In *A Backward Glance,* Edith Wharton records one such family, her own, the Joneses of New York (not, one suspects, those very Joneses with whom others felt they had always to keep up). Although Edith Wharton was in her seventies and acknowledged as a great American writer, in her memoir she still felt it necessary to inform readers that ancestors on both sides of her family had been in America for nearly three hundred years. Her own lineage was composed of bankers, lawyers, and merchant traders. Dullish though she allows her own parents and their social set to have been, their value lay "in upholding two standards of importance in any community, that of education and good manners, and of scrupulous probity in business and private affairs."

Good manners and reverence for education (of a certain kind) ran deep through the established American upper class. Edith Wharton reports bringing her first effort at story writing to her mother. The eleven-year-old author's opening sentences were " 'Oh, how do you do, Mrs. Brown?' said Mrs. Tompkins. 'If only I had known you were going to call I should have tidied up the drawing-room.' " To which her mother's icy reply was: "Drawing-rooms are always tidy." Neither of Wharton's parents could be said to be serious readers, but their reverence for careful English was genuine; it "was more than reverence," their daughter reports, "it was love," for they had "sensitive ears for pure English." In their set, careful language and careful manners went together. "It would have been 'bad manners' to speak 'bad' English, and 'bad manners' were the supreme offense."

The weakness of her class, Edith Wharton felt, lay in their "blind dread of innovation" — of any sort. Her father kept an impressive library in which the young Edith read freely and capaciously. The only writers held to be respectable were dead writers. Actually to become a writer was itself unthinkable, quite beyond the pale. In the case of her own parents, "they were genuinely modest and shy in the presence of any one who wrote or painted." The world of art — excluding singing, still a drawing room accomplishment — suggested the possibility of political or moral contamination. New ideas generally were not welcome. Standards were set high, but they existed, in good part, to induce conformity.

Edith Wharton was born into an American *rentier* class, that class of people who lived mainly off their real estate and land. If the men of this class worked, it usually wasn't under great strain. "The group to which we belonged was composed of families to whom a middling prosperity [I'm not sure Wharton's notion of "middling" is to be trusted, for her own tastes in later life, from limousines to mansions, were very grand] had come, usually by the rapid rise in value of inherited real estate, and none of whom, apparently, aspired to be more than moderately well-off [compared, say, to the Astors and Goelets]."

Money, though ample quantities of it were assumed, was not yet taken to be the point of the game. "I never in my early life," Wharton writes, "came in contact with gold fever in any form, and when I hear that nowadays business life in New York is so strenuous that men and women never meet socially before the dinner hour, I remember the delightful week-day luncheons of my early married years, where the men were as numerous as the women, and where one of the first rules of conversation was the one early instilled in me by my mother: 'Never talk about money, and think about it as little as possible.' " Of course it is much easier not to think about money when one has gobs of it.

Edith Wharton was highly ambiguous about the quality of her social class. In *The House of Mirth*, she put on display the heartlessness that was at the center of it. In *The Custom of the Country*, she showed the eagerness with which *parvenus* longed to become part of it and took pleasure in describing their coarseness. In *The End of Innocence*, the best of the novels of her maturity, she showed what an extraordinary mixture of admirable strength and yet crushing narrow-mindedness propelled her class. She wrote the emotional history of the American upper class from the inside, and it has had no subtler chronicler than she.

Edith Wharton's family was unusual chiefly because in its daughter it raised a considerable literary artist. So, too, did the family of Henry James, Sr., which threw in a great philosopher for good measure, though it was not so well placed socially as the Joneses, for Henry and William James's grandfather, an Irish immigrant, made his killing in real estate in Albany, New York; and Albany was not New York City, as Irish most assuredly wasn't English or Dutch. Yet in Boston and New York the Jameses gained entry to the best Society through a combination of talent and money. In America, entrée into Society, itself a euphemism for the upper class, was not utterly sealed off by birth.

Talent might be admitted a place. So, more often, might money, even hideously new money, if allowed a generation or so to dry off and clean itself up by carefully chosen good works. Think of a figure such as John D. Rockefeller, Sr., a Baptist, whose father was accused of horse stealing and was once indicted for rape. Rockefeller himself wasn't eligible for Society, but his children and grandchildren qualified easily. With enough money, a single generation could do it. "In America," said the Russian-born painter Pavel Tchelitchew, "there are two social classes, those who are rich and those who aren't." In Chicago the children of Swifts and Armours, butchers and meatpackers, came to play central roles in local Society.

In American cities small or large, money could bring one into the inner circle, where, it was assumed, life was lived on a more elevated, more pleasurable, generally happier plane. With money, if one moved gingerly, one could not so much crash as slide through the gates, where entrée to the best neighborhoods and clubs and among the best families awaited. Not that this was everyone's idea of a good time. Oscar Wilde, in the words of one of his biographers, said that he enjoyed Society because he "found in it both the satisfaction of his vanity and an inexhaustible source of fatuity." But most people, when offered the chance to become part of what passed for Society, did not turn it down.

If one looks at the occupations of the members of Ward McAllister's Four Hundred in New York City, one finds a preponderance of bankers, brokers, lawyers, and manufacturers, with only the occasional "clubman" or "sportsman," the latter two living, clearly, either on investments or on Father. Yet in New York and elsewhere the people who constituted Society were of great municipal earnestness — movers, you might say, who weren't usually noisy shakers. They were almost always the people who underwrote public institutions: the libraries, the art and natural history museums, many of the private universities, the symphony orchestras. At least three ways of viewing such people are possible: that they were astonishingly selfish and privileged, which they certainly were;

that they were immensely generous and civic-minded, which they also were; and that, most convincingly, they were both. (A kind word needs to be inserted here for the too crudely named Robber Barons — Rockefeller, Carnegie, Morgan, Frick, Huntington, Stanford, and company — without whom American cultural and educational life would look very different than it does today. Worth recalling also that these men gave away vast sums without the inducement of tax write-offs, since the income tax had not yet come into being during the period of their greatest benefactions. The view that they did so out of guilt doesn't persuade; if they were the monsters that the name Robber Baron suggests, they should scarcely have been hampered in any way by guilt.)

From the Gilded Age (roughly the 1880s until World War One) such people dominated in the larger American cities. They were able, moreover, to hand on their position of dominance to their children, and these children to their children. Some families fell out, room was made for energetic and socially ambitious newcomers, but by and large the club—for tight-knit clubs this clustering of important families tended to be — remained intact. They commanded the presidencies and a considerable majority of the students at Ivy League universities; they comprised the exclusive membership of the most admired city and country clubs; their voice in politics wasn't always supreme, true, but they were always a force that had to be taken into serious consideration.

Moving now into the third decade of the twentieth century, in a purely New York deviation, they became known, at least in the press, as Café Society, so called by one its chroniclers, Lucius Beebe, himself a great snob who nonetheless earned his living writing about the goings-on of these people for the old *New York Herald Tribune.* "A general definition of Café Society might be," Beebe wrote, "an unorganized but generally recognized group of persons who participate in the professional and social life of New York available to those possessed of a certain degree of affluence and manners." Beebe thought the number of such people never rose above five hundred.

One can see how smoothly all this worked — the interlocking of genealogies, social relationships, institutional affiliations, and financial arrangements — in the career of Joseph Alsop (1910–1989), the political columnist of impeccable upper-class connections. Alsop came out of Harvard — where he was an enthusiastic member of the Porcellian Club and an indifferent scholar — with an incipient drinking problem, little ambition, and no known aptitude. His mother, through her connection with "that nice Helen Reid," wife of Ogden Reid, then the owner of the *New York Herald Tribune,* got him a job on that paper. He moved to New York, worked as a reporter, but kept a valet and cook. In 1935, toward the close of Franklin Delano Roosevelt's first term as president, he was transferred to the paper's Washington bureau; Eleanor Roosevelt and Alice Roosevelt Longworth, both first cousins to his mother, resided in the capital, the former as wife to the president, the latter as the reigning social hostess. He had connections with many of Roosevelt's Ivy League Brain Trusters and also in the State Department.

Alsop was good at what he did, but his social connections put him on the inside of things — made him, in fact, an insider's insider. Journalists were second-class citizens in Washington in those days — hired help, really — but not Joe Alsop, who was part of Dining-Out Washington and in time himself became a major host in social-political Washington. Throughout a long career, he traveled first class in every way. To his credit, he never doubted that, despite such considerable journalistic talents as he came to possess, he was "very lucky," as he put it, "by way of being a very minor member of that ever diminishing group of survivors of the Wasp-ascendancy." In his memoirs, he claimed that his idea of heaven was to be well dressed at an outdoor New England wedding.

A club, as I say, and one that, if it sometimes allowed new members in, also drew the line, or lines, firmly and indelibly: the minimal but unrelenting qualification was to be white, Anglo-Saxon in heritage, and Protestant in religion. If one was Catholic, or surely Irish Catholic, or Jewish, forget about

it; if one was black, don't even think about it. E. Digby
Baltzell, the sociologist and historian of the club, was the
first man, in *The Protestant Establishment,* to use the acro-
nym WASP — for White Anglo-Saxon Protestant — and it has
since gone on to be misused to cover anyone who was white,
Anglo-Saxon, and Protestant: Presidents Jimmy Carter and
Bill Clinton are two notably mistaken examples. By WASP
Baltzell meant something much more specific; he intended
the term to cover a select group of people who passed
through a congeries of elite American institutions: certain
eastern prep schools, the Ivy League colleges, and the Episcopal Church notable among them. (As for the importance of
being Episcopalian, the journalist Nicholas Lemann refers to
the old Wasp leadership as "the Episcopacy.")

Bred-in-the-bone Wasps also tended to live in exclusive,
and often exclusionary, neighborhoods and suburbs: the
Main Line near Philadelphia, Back Bay in Boston, upper Park
and Fifth Avenues in New York, Lake Forest and Winnetka
outside Chicago. They worked for, or availed themselves of,
white-shoe law firms or blue-chip Wall Street houses. They
lived among their own kind, belonged to the same clubs, went
through the same social rituals, acquired affluence, assumed
power and authority and privilege as a matter of birthright.
The most impressive among them had a fine civic spirit, disinterested and generous, perhaps finer than our country will
ever see again. For decades they ran the State Department
as if it were a family business; occasionally they were to supply a United States president. Many among them considered
Franklin Delano Roosevelt, very much a member of the club
by birth, a traitor to his class. The last Wasp president
brought up under the old Wasp regimen was George H. W.
Bush (1988–1992). His son, George W. Bush, our current
president, has done everything he can to expunge the notion of his Waspishness — which has the bad odor of elit-
ism — and comes on as a Texan purely. He has even turned
the brilliant trick of pretending to be of the privileged under-
class, separating himself from the meritocrats who get into
good schools on the basis of educational achievement and

aligning himself with those who were poor students at such schools.

In a less than riotous but sociologically telling joke, two Jewish bees are flying about when one of them places a yarmulke on his head. "Why are you doing that?" the other bee asks. "I'm doing it," says the first bee, "so that no one will take me for a Wasp." The point of this joke, which was going the rounds in the early 1990s, is that it was not good to be taken for a Wasp. But things had begun to unravel long before. Some — E. Digby Baltzell prominent among them — claim things had begun to go sour as early as before 1964, when he published *The Protestant Establishment*. At that time Baltzell remarked that the Wasp "still remains an affluent class, [but] no longer possesses the qualities of an authoritative aristocracy." The reason it no longer possessed those qualities, Baltzell believed, was that "its standards of admission have gradually come to demand the dishonorable treatment of far too many distinguished Americans for it to continue, as a class, to fill the traditional function of moral leadership." Proust said that "each social class has its own pathology," and that of the Wasps included a serious want of imagination and sympathy.

When the shakeup of the 1960s was under way, one of the great public enemies was something called, with more vagueness than acuity, "the Establishment." The Establishment was a not-so-obscure code word, in good part, for the Waspocracy, which was thought to have tied the country up in a disastrous foreign policy (for which read: Vietnam and anti-Communism generally), a lingering anti-Semitism, a passive acceptance of racism, and a deep stagnation of spirit. In literature during these years, Jewish and black writers easily attracted the most attention. This same period saw the rise of ethnic pride. Everyone featured and vaunted his own ethnic ancestry, which hitherto tended to be played down, if not hidden. Ethnic food was everywhere the rage. The ethnic story was almost always a story of pride at overcoming, or pride in still attempting to overcome, one or another form of hardship or oppression. Such was the rush to claim ethnicity that feminists and homosexuals, when their political movements got started, assumed something like ethnic status. The oppressors, presumably, were the only people with no oppression story, and that would be the Wasps. Much better, it turned out, to be among the unwashed than to be overwashed.

If one's heritage was Wasp, one tended to play it down. Thus George Bush, Sr., when running for president in 1988, reinvented himself (in the cant phrase) as a good ole boy from Texas, even though he qualified as a Wasp among Wasps: his father (and uncles and cousins) had been tapped for Skull and Bones at Yale, and was a member of the investment firm of Brown Brothers Harriman; and George, in marrying Barbara Pierce of Rye, New York, had actually married up. But when Bush campaigned against Michael Dukakis he claimed the Oak Ridge Boys as his favorite singing group, campaigned with a female country-western singer in tow, and chomped on pork rinds. He sensed — correctly, judging by the results — that running as the patrician he was would have been a serious error.

Not that the American rejection of the Waspocracy was complete. For there remained a strong current, not quite dead even now, of what I should call Wasp longing on the part of people outside the club. I have felt it myself. About a quarter century ago, I took my son to Brooks Brothers, then the principal supplier of Waspish clothes, for a suit for his bar mitzvah, and the kindly woman who fitted him remarked, as my little son walked off into the dressing room, "He's a real Brooks boy, Mr. Epstein." I recall feeling a slight flutter, as if our family had, in its third generation, now at last arrived in America.

How could it be otherwise, for Wasp culture during its long reign set the tone, the criteria for excellence, and (not least) the standard for snobbery. Attesting to the endurance of this Wasp longing is the continued success of the designer Ralph Lauren, who began with a line of men's clothes that soon became what in the trade is known as lifestyle design, one that takes its imprimatur from his logo of a polo player. Lauren's career was built on the fantasies of a short Bronx-

born Jewish boy (né Lifshitz) of how Wasps live, or at least
ought to live. The way they ought to live, in Lauren's clothing
designs, is the way he imagines English patricians lived; and
he has taken those who can afford his expensive duds to a
Newport or a Kenya of his own commercial imagining.

Other outsiders have put deeper imaginations to the subject. The American novelists F. Scott Fitzgerald and John
O'Hara, both Irishmen, offer the perspective of the boy at
the candy store window who longs to get inside. Fitzgerald's yearning to live the good Wasp life was mediated by
his knowledge of the likes of Tom and Daisy Buchanan,
those Wasps to the highest power and the villains of *The
Great Gatsby:* she whose laugh had the ring of money, he
who was used to breaking things up. This knowledge didn't
prevent Fitzgerald, more than a bit of a snob himself, from trying to live as Waspily as possible. In his habits, John O'Hara
also lived his life on the Wasp model, and it was said of him
that the towering sadness of his life, never quite surmounted,
was not going to Yale.

Richard Brookhiser, in *The Way of the Wasp,* a book that
contends that "Wasp character is the American character,"
lists among the chief Wasp qualities "success depending on
industry; use giving industry its task; civic-mindedness placing obligations on success, and anti-sensuality setting limits
to the enjoyment of it; conscience watching over everything."
Not a bad statement of the case, really, but Brookhiser, in this
book written in 1991, wanted what we now know for certain
could never be: something like a return, if not to Wasp hege-
mony, then to the best of Wasp qualities, for the good and bad
Wasp social qualities were somehow hopelessly intertwined.

One can now begin to see that, for better *and* worse, at
least three things helped bring Wasp culture down. The first
was that the generation of Wasp descendants who went to
university in the 1960s and '70s began to feel an uneasiness
about their wealth and privileged position. One read stories
about Rockefeller and other great-grandchildren of the upper
class feeling guilty about their money, about not deserving
it. Elite culture, which was the culture that the Wasp aimed

for, was in bad odor, especially in universities, where the word *elite* itself became a buzz — that is, a bad — word. The Wasps, in short, began to lose their will and with it the authority necessary for leadership.

Then there were the incursions on those essential Wasp institutions, the elite prep schools and Ivy League colleges. As Nicholas Lemann reports in *The Big Test,* his study of the background and effects of the SAT in American life, allowing more children to enter the elite schools on the basis of testing rather than ancestry turned these schools more and more meritocratic in their admission policies. Not completely meritocratic, to be sure, for places in these schools were now reserved for minority group members, which cut down further on former Wasp dominance. At the same time, the meritocratic standard made the mating of the Wasp with non-Wasp fellow students more frequent, and this, too, served to dilute even more the mainstream of Wasp culture.

Recently, on the campus of Northwestern University, I was stopped by an acquaintance, a fellow teacher, a contemporary, himself a Wasp who goes about ill dressed, in ungroomed beard and jeans, and in conversation he mentioned a well-known journalist, saying that "he was my roommate at prep school." The reference — "my roommate at prep school" — sounded suddenly quaint, foreign, oddly marginal. Coming from the bearded mouth of this man, it might almost have sounded more American, I thought at the time, if he had said, "I knew him at yeshiva."

Everyone interested in this changing of the guard will have his own favorite anecdote or bits of evidence to show how complete it has become. Mine is about a philosophy professor of some academic eminence named Martha Nussbaum. Professor Nussbaum, I learned only a few years ago, was not born with the name Nussbaum, but is in fact a Wasp from the Philadelphia Main Line. Nussbaum is her long-departed first husband's name. In an age of feminism, she, a feminist, went against the grain and kept the name Nussbaum, which allows her to sidestep her Wasp antecedents while picking up a few Jewish victimhood points. The very name Nussbaum makes

the story all the more piquant to those of us old enough to recall, from the old *Fred Allen Show* on radio, Mrs. Nussbaum,
the character from that portion of the show known as Allen's
Alley, who was the matron of all Jewish matrons, greenhorn
accent and all, a stage Jew — rather, one might say, though in
a radically different way, like Martha Nussbaum.

Finally, the changes in the nature of the economy, with the
large mergers among banks, stockbrokerages, and department
stores, and the unsettling effect of the new technologi-
cally based but not geographically centered business world,
took the control of local businesses out of the hands of
long-established Wasp dynasties. Philadelphia banks were
no longer necessarily run by powerful figures who had grown
up in Philadelphia; hundred-year-old department stores in
Chicago were now run by national corporations in Houston
or Minneapolis or who knew where else; top New York law
firms were now staffed by young men and women (women —
this in itself was an astonishment) who may have been from
the best schools but who had no Wasp connections or antecedents whatsoever. After more than a century, the Wasp
domination of major institutions had drained and was fast
disappearing.

What amazes is that they, the Wasps, seem to have surren-
dered with so little struggle. In *Nineteen Eighty-four,* George
Orwell sets out four ways in which a ruling class can be dis-
lodged: "Either it is conquered from without, or it governs so
inefficiently that the masses are stirred to revolt, or it allows a
strong and discontented Middle Group to come into being,
or it loses its own self-confidence and willingness to govern."
Orwell adds that these ways usually act in combination, but in
the case of the Wasps, the fourth way, the mental attitude,
seems to have been dominant. The determination, the confidence, the energy to go on had somehow dissipated.

Perhaps the best analogy to the Wasp divestment of power
is that of the British giving up their empire. Both may have
felt the need to do so inevitable — and quite possibly it was
inevitable — but each came away disliked, diminished, maybe
even a little despised for having done so.

What the demise of the Waspocracy did for snobbery was to unanchor it, setting it afloat if not aloft, to alight on objects other than those connected exclusively with social class. A solid upper class, which is what the Waspocracy always provided, gave direction and something like a form to snobbery. With an upper class securely in place, the snob could locate his own position in the world; without it, things seemed much shakier, not by any means eliminating snobbery as a human habit, but altering its applications in dramatic ways.

The direction and shape that snobbery has taken in America since the close of the Wasp dominance is largely what this book is about.

7

....

Class (all but) Dismissed

WITH THE near-total displacement of the Wasps from their position as the unequivocal American upper class, a fairly sensitive status radar is required to determine the country's new hierarchical arrangements. It's difficult to have an actual class system without a clearly demarcated and convincing upper class, which seems to be the condition of American social life at the moment. Hierarchical arrangements there are always, of that one may be sure; even egalitarians have a strong sense of hierarchy, with some egalitarians naturally more egalitarian than others. The pressing question for the snob, as for the snobographer, is to find out who just now is on top and how social gradations are worked out from there down. Inquiring snobs want — make that *need* — to know.

Under the current disposition, *le nouveau régime,* what group or combination of groups constitutes the American upper class? Wealth, power, and culture have often vied for top place; and in socially static times, what is everywhere conceded to be the upper class will have a near monopoly on all three, as for so many years the Wasps did. All this is now less than clear. To illustrate how unclear, consider wealth. Now that the word *millionaire* has lost its luster, with really serious money apparently beginning around half a billion dollars, wealth alone is no longer sufficient to qualify one for the upper class. What's more, many of the country's wealthiest men — Ted Turner, George Steinbrenner, Donald Trump, Michael Milken, Bill Gates and other of the computer-made entrepreneurs — seem uninterested in qualifying: social class, (capital-S) Society, and social prestige in any form thus far known holds, insofar as one can discern, little magic for them.

Not only social class but the way people think about it is in a state of flux. The class struggle, that lumpish Marxist idea, seems to be long over, though every once in a while it rears up again. In *The New Yorker,* of all places, a man from Helena, Montana, in response to an article about servant problems, wrote that the article "filled me with paroxysms of class rage. As a forty-one-year-old working-class man who grew up poor . . . I've grown sick of watching people with money wring their hands and worry about the morality of hiring servants, and whether their servants love them, and how much working people deserve to be paid. Just understand that we don't love you, and that your money is always gained by our poverty and hard work, and that there is nothing noble about hiring somebody for pennies to do what you as an able-bodied person should be doing yourself." One doesn't often see that kind of cold class hatred so openly expressed anymore. At the same time, our man from Montana can, I think, relax his hatred, for nothing like a servant class any longer exists in America. Instead newly arrived immigrants do such work until they gain a foothold in the economy, at which point they are replaced by the next round of immigrants.

Karl Marx posited three social classes: landowners, capitalists, laborers. Remarking on this, the British historian David Cannadine writes that "on closer inspection, the best that could be said of Marx's three class-conscious classes was that they were ideal types, historical abstractions that grossly oversimplified." Landowners, after all, were large holders in capitalist concerns, and capitalists, at the first opportunity, like to set up as large-scale landowners. Social-class unity of the kind Marx needed for his model of the class struggle

never really existed; all social classes contained vast intramural disagreements. "Since Marx's time," Cannadine writes,
"old occupational groups have expanded, and new occupational groups have come into being that do not easily fit into
his three-level model: rentiers, managers, professionals, domestic servants, and the whole of the lower middle classes."

From nobility to peasantry, there have through modern
times been subtle gradations within every social class. Such
items as ancestry, income, education, taste, style of living, and
much else went to form one's social class. There has always
been the additional complication that your own view of your
social-class standing is often quite different from the next person's view of your social-class standing. Complicating things
further, people tend to describe social class from the perspective of their own social-class standing, or what they perceive
that standing to be.

One might hate all distinctions based on social class, but
even the largest-hearted of people find themselves playing the
class game. John Keats, who was surely a member of that best
of all minority classes, the genuinely goodhearted, could not
help but worry that his brother George, when he went off to
America to seek his fortune, not descend to working at
"trade," which is to say waiting on other people. For a long
while in Europe the idea of working at trade was the great
social curse. "The daughters of the iron monger refuse to
mix with the daughters of the woman who owns the pastry
shop," wrote Jules Renard in his *Journal,* apropos of the
early-twentieth-century French village in which he lived.
"Iron is more noble than pastry; and besides, *they* are never
seen working in the store!"

So class saturated is our equipment for social observation
that it is difficult not to put people into social classes. Something is "classy," people say, or they describe an object or an
act as having "class," or they refer admiringly to "a class act."
And yet R. H. Tawney, the English historian, was right when
he said that "the word 'class' is fraught with unpleasing associations, so that to linger upon it is apt to be interpreted as the
symptom of a perverted mind and a jaundiced spirit."

Social class, like bumps in phrenology, was once associated with characterological qualities. "At one time," Proust has his great character the Baron de Charlus say, "the word aristocrat meant the best people, in intellect and in heart." It also implied a certain stylish effrontery: Winston Churchill, having neglected to pay his tab at Wilton's, a famously excellent London restaurant, for fully eighteen months, was politely confronted by the manager, who suggested that perhaps his secretary had overlooked the bill. "Good heavens, Marks," replied Churchill, "didn't know you were hard up." Flaubert's distaste — fury is perhaps closer to it — was reserved chiefly for the middle classes, the petite bourgeoisie especially, judging them always guilty until proven innocent. In America, Sinclair Lewis heaped many choice coals on this particular fire. The working class, the so-called lower orders, received a boost from Dickens, for in any Dickens novel, someone from the working class is likely to be the repository of all loyalty, kindness, goodheartedness, and no-frills wisdom. All this is very close to nonsense, of course, for creeps and saints are to be found in every social class and exist across all class lines. Louis Kronenberg reports that W. H. Auden surmounted all this by seldom wasting time dissecting or passing judgment on people: "someone, to him, was either a gent or not a gent — this a judgment in terms of character, not class." The finest word of all on the subject, I believe, is that given to Madame Grandoni, in Henry James's *The Princess Casamassima*, who, after saying she has no use for the People in the abstract, adds, "An honorable nature, of any class, I always respect."

The novelists, as usual, are our keenest sociologists. And in the twentieth century through today the best novelists on questions of class have doubtless been the English. Anthony Powell's novels featured the English in their immense variety, which included higher civil servants, Oxbridge academics, minor aristocrats, people who drift into journalism, bohemians living on who knows what income. Kingsley Amis was excellent on the English social classes at their lower range, and in *Stanley and the Women* has a character remark that he is

"lower middle class, not working class. Very important distinction. My old dad got really wild if you said he was working
class. Worse than calling him a Jew." In John Lanchester's
novel *Mr. Phillips*, Lanchester says of the English that they
have in their brains "a top-of-the-range on-board computer
calculating the exact geographical and social locations of the
speaker every time someone opens their mouth."

When he was alive, George Orwell was much taken
up with social class; he used regularly to refer to the "class
racket," and once declared Britain "the most class-ridden
country under the sun." Although no Marxist, his was generally the class-struggle view of society, with sentimental so-
cialist overtones. In *Nineteen Eighty-four,* he set out three
groups, the High, the Middle, and the Low. "The aim of the
High is to remain where they are," he wrote. "The aim of
the Middle is to change places with the High. The aim of the
Low, when they have an aim . . . is to abolish all distinctions
and create a society in which all men shall be equal." He also
set out "a new aristocracy," which included "professors, pub-
licists, and journalists."

Things are now, and probably always have been, much
more complicated than that, in England and in America.
Peregrine Worsthorne, an English journalist with upper-class
pretensions, has said that "the class system has changed out
of all recognition in my lifetime." The decades of the 1960s
and '70s had a good deal to do with this. "The working
class," Jilly Cooper, another English journalist, wrote, "became beautiful and everyone from Princess Anne downwards
spat the plums out of their mouths, embraced the flat 'a' and
talked with a working class accent." The Beatles may have
contributed a lot to this. And then along came the Rolling
Stones, whom Tom Wolfe once described as like the Beatles,
"only more lower-class deformed."

In England, there is even controversy about the importance of class distinctions. "What is peculiar in Britain is not
the reality of the class system," Stein Ringen, the Oxford professor of sociology and social policy, writes, "but class psy-

chology: the preoccupation with class, the belief in class, and the symbols of class in manners, dress, and language." Is social class, as Professor Ringen's comment would seem to suggest, like sex for some people, mostly in the head?

Class distinctions exist, no one argues otherwise, but what seems to have changed is the widening of class opportunities. In a prosperous economy such as America has enjoyed for the past quarter century, nearly all possibilities are open to the talented, the industrious, those who possess desire, ability, and will power in the right combination. As early as the days of the founding of the country, Abigail Adams, wife of John Adams, referred to her fellow citizens as "the mobility," a prescient phrase, for social mobility has been one of the preponderant themes in American life.

Confronted with the fact of social class, and once one has sufficient social consciousness to determine one's own, some people struggle to rise into the next higher social class (and then the next and the next); some are content where they are; some remain where they are yet complain about all the obstacles set in their way. "The essence of a class system is not that the privileged are conscious of their privileges," Clive James writes, "but that the deprived are conscious of their deprivation." I'm far from certain either end of that sentence is true. One has to be a great ninny not to be aware of one's privileges; and deprivation, stinging though it surely is, does not — need not — seem so permanent as once it did, and thus is not so convincingly channeled into class resentment as once it might have been.

In America, with the demise of Wasp upper-class culture, it becomes less and less easy, as I have said, to describe the class system. One could, I suppose, begin with something called the superclass, which would include the vastly wealthy — people worth $500 million or more — but the number of such people, though it has grown in recent years, is nowhere large enough to constitute anything resembling a social class. At the bottom, one might posit a *lumpen* lower class, composed of habitual criminals, drug addicts, and people

who for one reason or another have taken themselves out of
the game. But all that lies in between — the vast majority of
the population — becomes fairly tricky social terrain.

In an old joke, a plumber presents a man with a bill for
$486. Staggered by the bill, the man says, "You weren't even
here an hour! I'm a neurosurgeon and I don't charge that
much." "I know," says the plumber, "that's why I left medical
school." Money, the point is, no longer defines social class.
Donald Trump is worth I don't know how many millions,
but his confident vulgarity will always keep him from being
viewed as other than monstrously rich (perhaps more mon-
ster than rich), and if he were to be certified as upper class,
many others put in that category would doubtless do what
they could to find a new social class to fit into. The huge sums
earned by athletes and entertainers has further confused notions of an orderly class structure. Nor can anyone easily define the middle, implied in the term *middle class*. Poverty lines
are set, based on annual incomes, but some years movie actors, choosing not to work and to collect unemployment insurance, may technically fall below the poverty line. It's all a
great mess.

George Orwell once described himself as lower-upper-
middle class, and in doing so brought what seems to me an
impressive precision to his social standing. His father had
been a civil servant; Orwell had gone to Eton, though not afterward to university; he had served as a young man in the im-
perial police in Burma; he was a writer and lived in a combined working-class and bohemian manner, and not yet a
landowner (as he would become in a minor way in Scotland
during his last years) nor wealthy, though at the close of his
life he would be well-off from the royalties of *Animal Farm*
and *Nineteen Eighty-four*. Lower-upper-middle class sounds
dead-on right.

I cannot place myself anywhere near so precisely. I write; I
have taught at a university of fairly high reputation (Northwestern); I went to one of the country's better universities
(the University of Chicago); I have arrived at a stage — partly

a function of my own and the prosperous age — where I do not worry overmuch about money; I have some friends who are very wealthy, others who scrape by; I know some distinguished people, and a few in high places. I know my social origins (Jewish and lower middle to middle class), but they seem to have less bearing on things today than they did thirty or forty years ago. I always think myself Jewish, but I have a far less clear conception of my class. Sometimes I refer to myself as among the so-called educated class, which I also say with a light salting of irony and an insistence upon that *so-called.*

Tom Wolfe, a man for whose status radar I have the highest respect, recently wrote: "Any fool sociologist could tell you there are only two objectively detectable social classes in America: people above the bachelor's degree line — i.e., people who have graduated from four-year colleges — and people below it, who haven't." This, though accurate enough, takes in only part of what I mean by the so-called educated class. What I mean is that I and my (social) classmates live lives bounded by ideas — *notions* is perhaps the better word — of elegance, by concern for our health, by interest in culture and entertainment, and by much else that derives not only from our having gone to college, but because our having done so has been one of the central experiences of our lives. Most members of the so-called educated class haven't had all that much firsthand experience of the sort of elegant lives they wish to live, and so many of the notions upon which they base their lives derive from books, journalism, movies, and other secondary experiences.

Members of the so-called educated class really think of themselves as the enlightened class. Taste ranks high in the scheme of what we value — higher perhaps than anything else — and gives our lives a nervous quality. This class, writes Jilly Cooper, calling them the upper middle classes, "are the silliest and most sensitive to every new trend." To accuse a member of the so-called educated classes of a want of taste is an insult of a profundity worthy of an invitation to a duel.

Always changing, being subject to the greatest disputation, taste is above all things susceptible to snobbery. This is perhaps why snobbery runs high among the educated class.

A new conception of this class has been suggested by David Brooks, who, in his book *Bobos in Paradise,* contends that there is a new upper class in America. This new upper class, Brooks finds, is marked by the old bourgeois ethos of moneymaking and acquisitiveness but is radically different from former American upper classes in its bohemian spirit. Brooks's Bobos go in for egalitarianism, environmentalism, health-mindedness. Their habits of consumption, though by no means inexpensive, tend to be inconspicuous. Brooks believes that this new spirit of the bourgeois combined with the bohemian, from which derive the term *Bobos,* is sweeping the boards. He nicely illustrates his point through the examples of current-day retailing, politics, and status arrangements, arguing that "even the scions of the old Wasp families have adapted to the new mode." Brooks's central idea, that the bourgeois and the bohemian spirit have now combined, is both an amusing and a useful one, but Boboism sometimes seems too thinly spread — just about anyone who has been in a Starbucks or has a penchant for Ben & Jerry's ice cream would seem to qualify — to constitute anything like a real social class.

Next to the novelists, the best sociologists — the sociologists themselves, I'm afraid, are almost never the best sociologists — are the marketing experts. And the marketing experts, in attempting to sell their goods, no longer think primarily of social class in doing so. Too many unpredictable things have happened in recent years to make social class any longer a reliable guide to marketing. Consider only the phenomenon of kids from wealthy white suburban families taking their cue on what's in style in footwear, jeans, and other apparel from inner-city black kids. In former days, fads tended to percolate from the wealthiest end of the social scale downward; now they seem quite as often to boil upward.

Instead of social class, marketers now talk about something

called "clusters," which have given them, the marketers, a new cartography of American life. Mobility, social fluidity, and new immigration are only a few of the social factors that have made the earlier division of upper, middle, and lower classes seem crude, if not altogether obsolete. One such marketer, Michael J. Weiss, in *A Clustered World,* sets out no fewer than 64 clusters, an increase of 55 percent, he tells us, over a few decades before. Thus people are divided by the settings in which they live (from Elite Suburbs to Rustic Living) and within these divisions into smaller groups defined by income or age or ethnic status (including "ethnically mixed urban singles," "mid-level white-collar couples," "middle-income empty nesters," "Hispanic middle-class families," and so on and on). Beyond the selling of goods, clustering seems rough-hewn, based as it largely is on that imprecise, blatant term *lifestyle.* But it does show up the greater crudity of a three- or even a nine-category class system as an adequate way of describing American life.

My own aspiration in connection with social class, which I suspect may be shared by a great many Americans, is to live, or at least think, altogether outside it. The ample middle class, whence I derive, has been derided, but I happen to think that there is much to be said on its behalf: it imbued one with, among other things, concern about the future, caring for one's family, bringing order to one's life — none of these insignificant things. Yet somehow measuring other people — above, below — from a middle-class perspective seems an irrelevance to the world we now live in, and therefore without much point.

At the close of his book *The Rise and Fall of Class in Britain,* David Cannadine invokes America as a model of a classless society. By classless he does not mean without inequalities of wealth and power, such as all societies have had, but one in which these do not translate into "corresponding inequalities of social prestige or social perceptions"; one whose members don't think of an unbridgeable divide between "us" and "them"; one in which the middle class swal-

lows up all else; one in which the chief difference between the
rich and the poor, as Lord Beaverbrook once remarked, is
that the rich have more money.

Is this a true picture of American social life? I'm not sure
that it is, but it does seem accurate as a description of the way
American society is tending. The word *class* came into being
in the middle of the eighteenth century to describe social differences; it may well be that by the end of the twenty-first it
will be retired for want of usefulness. But its gradual disappearance, as we shall see, scarcely means the disappearance of
snobbery. The absence of strict social-class boundaries may
even, in odd ways, work to increase it.

8

Such Good Taste

Taste has been one of the major ways of defining social class. For some, such as the French sociologist Pierre Bourdieu, it still is. The upper classes, in this reckoning, do not bowl, nor do the workers listen to J. S. Bach. But this, too, has long been shifting. Many years ago, for example, it was bruited about that the most affluent television audience was that which watched the rather brutish game of professional football — hence all those commercials for Mercedes, Lexus, and Cadillac.

Tradition, or what passed for tradition in a once reasonably secure upper class, both set and ruled over taste. The way the most revered members of that class dressed, furnished their homes, dealt with one another in public, amused themselves, and behaved generally was, ipso facto, good taste. Taste was what people in possession of social power said it was. But with the all but complete demise of Wasp culture and the steady erosion of the old class system, taste has fallen more into the realm of the professional tastemakers, those editors, designers, decorators, museum curators, critics, etiquette handbook writers, movie and television producers, and others who ignite fads, set trends, keep the rest of us — or those among us who have decided to care about such matters — guessing, hopping, and jumping.

The cliché had it that there was no accounting for taste, and the cliché, within limits, was often right. Except in particular instances, no one has really accounted for taste, at least not altogether persuasively. Instead people tend to argue over it. "You say there can be no argument about matters of taste," Nietzsche has Zarathustra say. "All life is an argument about taste." Some of the questions people argue about include: Whence does taste derive? Why does it seem to come so naturally to some people and to others not at all? How important is taste as a sign of intelligence, of character, of moral worth? Can taste be taught? And, not quite the same thing, can it ever be learned?

These are but a few of the questions about taste for which no one has managed to account. But one thing that is not in question is the centrality of taste to snobbery — and more and more so in our day, when there is perhaps more anxiety about taste than at any other time.

There isn't, in fact, taste, but *tastes,* several different tastes operating simultaneously in the culture and sometimes even in the same person. Far from being universal, taste is highly particular. To cite a wild example, cosmetic breast surgery in Brazil has preponderantly been in the direction of reduction of breast size, where too large breasts are thought to be "Negroid." In neighboring Argentina, breast surgery has been mainly in the direction of enlargement, because the fantasies of Argentinean men run to abundance. Taste — go figure.

Fashion has been said to be the motor force behind taste. Sometimes it is, but sometimes it is quite unconnected with it. Every age has its characteristic taste, often given names by art and other historians: Baroque, Empire, Biedermeier, and the rest. In time, the age itself grows tired of that taste. Boredom plays a role in the regularity with which taste seems to change. The roots of taste, Hilton Kramer has argued, "lie in something deeper and more mysterious than mere fashion." For one thing, its timetable can never be predicted. For another, as Kramer writes, "the denial of certain qualities in one period almost automatically prepares one for their triumphal return later."

People who pride themselves on the possession of taste are confident that they know what is beautiful. But what is beautiful is an extremely complicated question to which a major branch of philosophy, aesthetics, has for several centuries devoted itself without much success. Perhaps no more salutary exercise awaits the person who is confident he or she knows what is beautiful than the discovery — demonstrated with careful scholarship in such works of art history as Francis Haskell's *Taste and the Antique* and Gerald Reitlinger's *The Economics of Taste* — that entire ages have vastly undervalued individual works, often whole bodies of visual art, whose majesty is now thought to be beyond argument.

The painting of Vermeer is only one of many egregious examples. In the middle of the seventeenth century in Spain, mere casts and copies of ancient sculptures were more highly regarded than original works by Velázquez. In the latter part of the eighteenth century in England, Joshua Reynolds, the painter and first president of the Royal Academy, scored off Titian, Tintoretto, and Veronese as inferior painters, claiming that they were little more than decorators, chiefly interested in color at the expense of form. These are not instances of experts being put off by avant-garde or experimental works. They are instead glittering examples — and scores more could be instanced — of highly intelligent connoisseurs misapprehending beauty that now seems obvious to all.

Beauty and what passes for good, even exquisite taste are sometimes but not always congruent, and certainly they are not necessarily so. The range of the beautiful is broader than the range of the tasteful. A Praxiteles sculpture, a Limoges demitasse, an Arabian stallion, a noble act, an infant's smile — these are but a few from the uncountable immensity of beautiful things. Good taste is much narrower. It has to do with decorum in behavior and in things; it frequently has to do with preferences that grow out of social class; it is almost always influenced by the spirit of the times. Taste is a system — a not very systematic system, to be sure — of preferences. Taste often dictates what is beautiful, but is frequently proven wrong in its *diktats*. Taste has its limits, even

good taste. "Good taste," Jules Renard wrote, "may be nothing but a fear of life and of the beautiful." God, or, if one
prefers, Nature, creates beauty; men and women create taste.

To begin with its broadest division, there is good and bad
taste. Lionel Trilling, apropos of the photographs of Walker
Evans for the book *Let Us Now Praise Famous Men,* after noting their "perfect taste," went on to say that he was "taking
that word in its largest possible sense to mean tact, delicacy,
justness of feeling, complete awareness, and perfect respect."
Edward Shils, who edited *Minerva,* a magazine devoted to
science and higher learning, once accepted an article from a
contributor with the proviso that he remove the heavy jargon
from his writing. "Not a problem," said the man, "jargon or
no jargon — I suppose it's only a matter of taste." "Quite
right," Shils shot back. "It is only a matter of taste — good
taste or bad. Remove the jargon." In less clear cases, dispute
can be endless about what constitutes correct taste, and in the
hands of a snob taste can be wielded as a cruelly effective
weapon, used to keep all sorts of people outside the gates.

The domain of taste extends to things large and small, in
houses and cars, art and jewels, food and wine, and to a thousand other items that can result in someone's looking down
his or her nose at someone else. Where there exists the possibility of preference, there you will find taste. There is taste in
people, in behavior, and relativists would argue that there is
taste in morals. There is even a comedy of taste, which goes
by the name of Camp and which operates by standing what
normally is regarded as good taste on its head, deliberately
mocking the decorum of good taste in favor of the hideously
showy, garish, or otherwise vulgar. (Vulgar, a word with a long
history, today is mainly understood as a violation of what
passes for good taste.) There are, finally, people who pride
themselves on being everywhere and always in good taste. For
them, what are taken to be violations of taste are no mere ve-
nial sins. In this category are to be found many secret — and
lots of not so secret — snobs.

Taste can be tyrannous to those made nervous by it. And
those who are nervous about it include just about everyone

who is not absolutely confident of his or her preferences in possessions, culture, behavior. Perhaps the only people untouched by the tyranny of taste are those who haven't any notion that such a thing exists. Some people might consider it a badge of honor to be thought out of fashion, but fewer are prepared to be written off for being without taste. My guess is that most people would be less offended to have it said of them that they have bad judgment than that they have bad taste.

Taste is not by any means arbitrary. "The essence of taste is suitability," wrote Edith Wharton. "Divest the word of its prim and priggish implications, and see how it expresses the mysterious demand of the eye and mind for symmetry, harmony and order." Some things — generosity, courage, kindness — are always in good taste. "Taste is good sense," the aphorist Geoffrey Madan wrote. Something to it, but Reynaldo Hahn, the composer and Marcel Proust's dearest friend, widens the meaning of taste in a useful way when he writes: "By *taste* I do not mean that superior and transcendent ability to comprehend what is beautiful which leads to good aesthetic judgment. . . . By *taste,* I mean a wide-ranging instinct, a sure and rapid perception of even the smallest matters, a particular sensitivity of the spirit which prompts us to reject spontaneously whatever would appear as a blemish in a given context." Hahn continues: "A particular sensitivity of the spirit is necessary in this sort of taste, as well as emotion and a certain fear of ridicule."

For the snob, this fear of ridicule — or if the snob has the social whip hand, the delight in inflicting ridicule — is uppermost in questions of taste. Taste can be contentious. In many realms where taste seems significant, some people have inherently better equipment for making judgments, for demonstrating more intelligent preferences, than others: a stronger sense of color, a better feeling for design, a more sensitive palate. (In *Cousin Bette,* Balzac writes of the apartment of M. and Mme. Marneffe: "Yet there was no art or distinction in the furnishing, nothing of the effect which good taste achieves by intelligent selection of possessions.") But taste can also be composed of a fusion of assumptions, predilections, and simple prejudices. It can also be eclectic, a hotchpotch of borrowed bits from yesterday, today, and tomorrow.

Sometimes this fusion powerfully coheres to result in large, almost philosophical swings in taste, such as that in the early nineteenth century that brought about the change from Classicism to Romanticism, both in the arts and in human personality. Although not nearly so volatile as fashion, taste can sometimes take quick and radical turns. One year what is thought the best taste will be on the side of experiment and originality; two years later it will be on that of conservation and tradition. It is of course always easier to make out the taste of ages other than one's own. To ask what is the reigning taste of our age is to become acquainted with the difficulty of the exercise.

"Each to his own taste" is another of the towering clichés on the subject, but one usually says it confident that one's own taste is superior to the persons who, or the disagreements that, occasioned the remark. For a long while now taste has been more than an individual matter. It has become a social phenomenon. One's taste more than likely will betray one's social class, personal aspirations, conception of oneself. One's tastes — in food, in clothes, in culture, in politics and opinionation, in nearly everything — have become items upon which the world stands ready to judge one, and, as like as not, damn harshly. In some circles, to speak well of, say, Whittaker Chambers, Andrew Wyeth, Wayne Newton, nuclear power, or processed cheese, or even to commit a grammatical solecism, is considered a grave social lapse. "She is the kind of person," I once heard a woman say with deadly disdain about another woman, "who regularly misuses the word *hopefully*."

People began to be judged by their taste a long time ago. The Duc de Saint-Simon does it regularly in his memoirs of life at the court of Louis XIV at Versailles, and others must have done so well before him. Baldassare Castiglione, in *The Book of the Courtier* (1528), set out ideal behavior for Renaissance ladies and gentlemen, any breach of which would have constituted a lapse in taste. When H. W. Fowler's book *Modern English Usage* (1926) was first published, it sold fifty-five thousand copies in the United States, so worried were Americans about making errors in grammar, usage, and pronunciation, all once considered lapses in taste. Emily Post's *Etiquette in Society, in Business, in Politics, and at Home* (1922) was for years a strong seller whose message was that no false steps could be permitted in the respectable middle class, where life was a minefield of potential faux pas. Today we have the more sensible and wittier Miss Manners, but the need for someone to set up as an authority, even in our vastly more informal time, has not yet ceased.

Perhaps the only thing more chilling than too great an awareness of possible lapses in taste is a total unawareness of them. One of the socially saddest, even frightening scenes in American literature is that in William Dean Howells's *The Rise of Silas Lapham,* in which Lapham, a self-made man, decent enough and honest in his own way, disgraces himself when dining with the parents of his future son-in-law, who come from a family of considerably higher social rank than he. Lapham's discomfort is neatly built up by Howells, and it begins with his unfamiliarity with the most obvious details of the meal that is set before him: "It was not an elaborate dinner; but Lapham was used to having everything on the table at once, and this succession of dishes bewildered him; he was afraid perhaps he was eating too much. He now no longer made any pretense of not drinking his wine, for he was thirsty, and there was no water, and he hated to ask for any."

Meanwhile, Lapham has drunk too much, and now, alone with the men over brandy and cigars, he gases away confidently about things no one at table cares to hear about (his relatives, his employees, his business acumen). His confidence builds, and he begins to believe he is the equal, as he puts it to himself, "to their society, or to the society of any one else." He is, in fact, their equal, but he doesn't know how the game is played. He goes home flushed with the belief that he has scored heavily, that "it was a great time; it was a triumph." If one has any heart at all, one's flesh crawls at poor, socially

benighted Lapham, who has, in the realm of taste, committed
the sad sin of having gone too far, way, way too far.

Taste is often about knowing how not to go too far, lest one
expose oneself to the withering put-down or otherwise be
exposed to the cold eye of snobbery. "Being tactful in audac-
ity," said Cocteau, "is knowing how far one can go too far."
But Cocteau was a professional avant-gardist whose job was
precisely about going far enough. For almost everyone else it
will not do, for example, to appear to be spending too much
time thinking about taste. Nor will it do not to seem to give
too much thought to it. Even the freest spirits have feared
being caught on the barbed wire of taste. Lady Diana Cooper,
who as a young woman was counted among that smartest
of smart sets in pre–World War One England known as the
Corrupt Coterie, readily took morphia but refused to drink
either whiskey or gin. "To reduce oneself to a stupor with
morphia was risky, perhaps immoral," writes Philip Ziegler,
Lady Diana's biographer, "but to drink a whiskey and soda
would have been common — a far worse offense." An offense,
in other words, against that arbitrary construct known as
proper taste.

Some people believe that one comes into the world with
one's own natural faculty of taste, but that this is deflected by
one's education, social class, and fear of seeming outré and finally twisted into some proximation of the standard taste of
one's day. Strong character is required to assert one's true
taste. The philosopher Ludwig Wittgenstein makes a distinction between taste and originality. "Taste," he writes, "can be
charming but not gripping." Taste, in his view, "is refinement
of sensitivity: but sensitivity does not *do* anything, it is purely
receptive." He believed that "a great creator has no need of
taste; his child is born into the world fully formed." (Shakespeare, when you think about it, was weak in the line of
taste — thank God.) Taste refines and polishes, but creates
nothing. Wittgenstein's own fear was that, as a thinker, he
himself had taste merely.

But most of us are not Wittgenstein's "great creator," and
instead struggle to acquire such good taste as we can through

education and experience. Except for that infinitesimally small group of persons with unerringly true taste — with perfect manners, easy elegance of dress, an eye for the beautiful in nature and art, a penetrating instinct for judgment of people, and an independent spirit that accepts only those opinions learned in one's own heart — except for this small, possibly nonexistent group, most of us, however we might pride ourselves on our acquisitions in this realm, suffer at least a slight worry lest in one or another important division of life our taste will be found wanting.

If the possession of taste does not imply the possession of originality, neither does it usually imply the possession of moral worth. Taste can be a curiously amoral faculty. One can have the most exquisite taste and yet in every other wise be the dreariest of creeps. And of course one can have no taste at all and be wondrously good-hearted. The snob's error is to put good taste before a good heart — to put good taste before almost everything else. Clearly a fine thing to have, good taste can lend harmony, elegance, and graciousness to one's life. Yet to pride oneself on one's good taste is not only the beginning of snobbery; it is also unseemly and, in and of itself, a piece of certifiably bad taste.

In a mobile, some would say positively jittery society where one can rise up and fall down so quickly, the display of good taste can be decisive either to reach one's social aspirations or to hold on to one's place. Money can be important — no one, it has been said, has ever been kicked out of (capital-S) Society for having too much of it — but without a show of what passes for acceptable taste, no rise can be successfully negotiated, and in an earlier day specialists in the realm of good taste were hired by the newly rich to take the rough edges off them so that they could make an easier entry into Society.

When taste changes speedily, one usually finds, in the conduct and accouterments of that small band of select persons whom the rest of society has somehow or other decided to admire, clues to what passes for good taste. At different times these select persons have traveled under different ban-

ners: the Four Hundred, Café Society, the Smart Set, the Jet
Set, the Beautiful People, all of whom appear to be in possession of a magical combination of wealth, power, glamour, elegance, freedom. Admired or envied or secretly despised, in
the realm of taste they lead, and the rest of the populace that
can afford to follows as best it can. What makes it somewhat
confusing is that at different times the social atmosphere can
give off very different signals: tradition-bound conformity in
one period, an air of boundless liberation in another, will
be the hallmark of superior taste. One needs an inner radar
system in good repair to interpret the reverberations of this
accurately.

Unless one decides not to care in the least about what
passes for the good taste of one's age, and decides instead that
good taste really is good sense, which means that in friendship, it is represented by tact, generosity, and above all kindness; in possessions, by comfort, elegance, utility, and solidity; in art, by beauty, harmony, and originality; in culture
generally, by a discriminating tolerance for tastes at odds with
one's own. This is very different from that taste which is
determined by being around people thought tasteful, taking pleasure in cutting oneself away from the mass by the
criterion of ostensible good taste, and being supremely confident in judging — and thereby putting down — others by the
standard of what one takes to be one's own exquisite taste. All
of which is, of course, the way of the snob.

9

In the Snob-Free Zone

I s THERE a snob-free zone, a place where one is outside all snobbish concerns, neither wanting to get in anywhere one isn't nor needing to keep anyone else out, for fear that one's own position will somehow seem eroded or otherwise devalued? A very small island of the favored of the gods, clearly, this snob-free zone, but how does one get there?

To be wellborn is a start. To be blessed with ample talent cannot hurt. To have been fortunate in one's professional, marital, or personal life will provide a genuine boost. To have won the lottery on an $80 million payoff week would be a serious help. And the easiest way into this zone may be not to care at all, to feel no aspiration, envy, resentment, anger at social arrangements, to live contentedly within oneself and be shut of the whole damn social racket. Yet this last, the cultivation of sublime indifference, may not be the easiest but the toughest way of all into the snob-free zone.

Let me attempt to draw the portrait of a man (one could do something similar for a woman) who might have a chance for a life in the snob-free zone. I would begin by placing him on the lower edge of the old upper class. The poet Robert Lowell seems to have been in this condition, a Lowell but not one of the inner circle of Lowells — those Lowells who spoke only to Cabots, and of course we all know the only grand

party to whom the Cabots spoke. I imagine him, then, to
have upper-class family connections, but not be quite of the
upper class, lest he seem to share too completely in that
class's dreariness and likely snobbery. He should be slightly
of the upper class, in other words, but not enough to be
tainted by it.

His schooling ought to be mixed, public and private. All
private might make him seem too privileged, too lucky. A taste
of public schools — perhaps through grade school — would
show him not to have existed exclusively in cushy surroundings; it wouldn't do to make him look as if he's had too easy a
ride. Having gone to public school, too, will give him a democratic touch — in a democracy, not a bad thing to have. (Paul
McCartney and his wife sent their daughters to public — in
the American sense of the word — schools, which could be
interpreted as a brilliantly snobbish move.) He will have been
a respectably good student, but not a great, an off-the-boards
astonishing one.

I would have him go to Andover or Groton, thence to Harvard or Princeton, and put in a year at Oxford or Cambridge,
the last to Anglicize, cosmopolitanize, and polish him a bit. I
don't believe any of these places is so wonderful, please understand, but the world seems to believe they are, so if our man is
to enter the snob-free zone, he must do so in terms the world
recognizes. Besides, having gone through such institutions,
he will come to understand that the world, in its estimates, is
often stupid, and never more in recent years, when everything
has begun to break down, especially in education. Having
gone to what are thought very good schools, he will have
taken their measure and never have to think — yearningly, in
part snobbishly — as so many people seem to do, how different his life would have been had he only taken thought to have
gone to better schools. Unlike, say, poor Jay Gatsby, he will
not have to falsify an educational résumé.

He'll require money. "A man may be despised," says Balzac, "but not his money." Our man doesn't have to be a bil-
lionaire, but he ought to have enough to take him out of
the financial wars, so he need never do anything despicable

for reasons of money alone. Being in possession of serious money — "holding," as they used to say at the racetrack — will give him freedom in other ways, not least by cutting down on his longing, which in turn reduces his susceptibility to material snobberies of various kinds, from cars to summer houses.

He will have earned his own money. At . . . what? Something for which he has an inherent skill, or a craft he learned by sedulous application of his talents: he could be an artist of some sort, possibly an architect, or maybe he has begun a business, manufacturing or selling something useful and well made. His work gives him pleasure and no cause to believe his days misspent.

His wife, unlike him, is Jewish, a pediatrician perhaps, also happy in her work, physically attractive, a respectable money earner, kindly, large-hearted. They have two children, a son and a daughter, good enough at school, with no known hang-ups or other problems or disabilities.

The family is never put to any of the tests of snobbery. They are never excluded, everywhere thought to be winning and always wanted; and, because so confident are they of their own quality, they have no thought of excluding anyone else. Such clubs as they join — a tennis and swimming club, for their daughter is an ardent tennis player, their son a swimmer of promise — are joined for their utility and pleasantness alone. Status is never a first, nor even a last, consideration. Such judgments as they make about persons, places, and pleasures are made on the basis of intrinsic and therefore genuine merit, never on that of being the right social, professional, or political move. Happy family, I would say, lucky family. Let us hope there are a few such in America, while remaining free to doubt it.

Yet perhaps this is all wrong, and the person who is in the snob-free zone is more likely to be a half-black, half-Hispanic man in dreadlocks who is young, bisexual, and a painter of terrifying pictures of childhood abuse, from which he is known to have suffered but for which he is everywhere vaunted.

I can think of a man who lived in a snob-free zone in whom snobbishness, though never justifiable, might have been understandable. He happens to have been a cousin of mine whose name was Sherwin Rosen and who was an economist at the University of Chicago. He was supposed to have been in line for the Nobel Prize in economics before he died, of lung cancer, in 2001, in his sixty-third year.

At his memorial service and at a dinner afterward, I was impressed not only by the range of people who spoke on my cousin's behalf but by their varying personal styles. None seemed particularly elegant, handsome, suave. Neither, for that matter, was my cousin. He was instead immensely winning without any of these qualities, and in part because he didn't seem to care about status at all. He enjoyed owning sporty cars — a white Audi sports coupe was his last — and drinking good wine and listening to classical pianists and playing jazz piano himself, but he made no fuss about these things. He made no fuss about anything, in fact, except economics. He judged his colleagues by their skill at their discipline, and, apart from their characters, nothing else. My guess is that he judged himself by the same criterion.

He once told me that he was offered something called an Albert Schweitzer professorship in New York, which would have almost doubled his salary, but he said that, even though he could have used the money, he couldn't accept it. He couldn't because he needed the bruising intellectual combat that his colleagues at the University of Chicago Department of Economics gave one another. It wasn't pleasant, but, he felt, he needed it. When one of his best students did not land a job in one of the better-regarded universities, he told the student that it was a good thing, for it would take him outside all the worry about prestige and throw him back on his talent as an economist, which, if his devotion was such as to bring out his potential, would in the end result in his being made offers by better schools. Which, the student said, is exactly what happened.

My cousin Sherwin's way into the snob-free zone was simple enough: care only about one's work, judge people only by their skill at their own work, and permit nothing else outside one's work to signify in any serious way. View the rest of the world as a more or less amusing carnival at which one happens to have earned — through, of course, one's work — a good seat. Judge all things by their intrinsic quality, and consider status a waste of time. One of the reasons I liked him so much is that he brought all this off without any contortion of his essentially kind character.

Now in my seventh decade, am I, at last, anywhere near the snob-free zone? I think it fair to say that I haven't much interest in the social climb. When I think of people for whose company I yearn, I find the majority of them no longer alive. I have a weakness — a snobbish weakness? — for people who exhibit style, but style with the strong suggestion of substance behind it. From the previous generation, I should have liked to have known Noël Coward, Audrey Hepburn, George Balanchine, Marcello Mastroianni, Vladimir Nabokov, George Marshall, Edmund Wilson (when sober), Billy Wilder, of whom only the last is alive. Of people still in full career, I find that, among public figures, I admire Pierre Boulez, whom I met once and found both *haimish* and winning; Mikhail Baryshnikov, who surmounted the obstacles of being born to wretched parents in a miserable country to go on to become a prominent artist with a selfless devotion to his art; and Daniel Patrick Moynihan, who seems to me not only the most talented person in political life but the only one with whom I'd care to sit down to lunch.

On the other side — people with whom I wouldn't care to sit down to lunch — I include almost all current university presidents, present members of the U.S. Senate and Congress, most contemporary writers and painters, actors, athletes, and anyone vaguely known as a socialite. I came upon twenty-one men and women whom Absolut Vodka featured in an ad in a recent issue of *Vanity Fair,* all photographed by Annie Leibovitz, ranging in age from the architect Philip Johnson to the choreographer Mark Morris, and including Salman Rushdie, Gore Vidal, Spike Lee, Helmut Newton, Sarah Jessica Parker, and other of the usual suspects. They

were in this ad because they were supposed to be avant-
garde, hip, fascinating; add accomplished, revered, successful. And yet I find I do not long to meet any of them. (My
guess is that they can do nicely, thank you, without meeting
me, but that is another matter.) I feel about them as the Jews
of Russia once felt about the tsars: they should live and be
well, but not too close to me.

Does my list of people I'd wished I had known suggest its
own snobbery? Possibly. I prefer to think that I have a bias
toward people whose stylishness is informed by an unpredictable but subtle point of view, fine tact, and generosity of
spirit. In this line, I have always admired a man named Walter
Berry, who was the head of the United States Chamber of
Commerce in Paris and who shows up in the biographies of
such people as Edith Wharton, Marcel Proust, and Bernard
Berenson. Edith Wharton conceded that she ought to have
married Walter Berry: "He had been to me in turn all that
one human being can be to another, in love, in friendship, in
understanding." She arranged to be buried near him in the
same cemetery in Versailles. Proust immediately recognized
him as a man of quality, and Berry once wrote to Proust telling him that, when asked if he had read Proust's novels, he
always replied: "Yes, but they have a grave defect: they are so
short."

Not yearning to go socially any higher than I am now —
content, that is, with the friends I have — I am, in this regard
at least, in the snob-free zone. Not so, alas, in other regards.
Much as I like to think myself the democrat, I find myself doing a certain amount of snobbish looking down on,
in Lyndon Johnson's all too mortal phrase, "mah felluh
Amurikuns." On the Outer Drive in Chicago, I am behind a
car on whose back window is a decal reading "Illinois State
University." My view is that one oughtn't even to have a
sticker that reads "All Souls, Oxford," but Illinois State? Of
course the thought is a perfectly snobbish one. The guy driving the car is pleased to have gone to Illinois State; maybe he,
or his son or daughter, is the first person in the family to have

gone to college; possibly he completed his studies at great financial sacrifice. Still, I almost reflexively look down on that decal.

I do not look down on any of the current American pariahs: cigarette smokers, the overweight, the aged, the unhealthful food eaters. I rather cherish some among them and feel sorry for others. But I do look down on certain selected people, preferably, it's true, from a distance and until now unbeknownst to them; yet look down I do, usually with an uncomplicated feeling of satisfaction.

I am at a concert at the Ravinia Summer Music Festival, in Highland Park, on the North Shore outside Chicago. It is a Pops concert, with Eric Kunzel leading the Chicago Symphony Orchestra and a group, made up of six Englishmen, calling itself the King's Singers, since all were once at King's College, Cambridge. Normally, I shouldn't have gone to this kind of concert, but I had to miss another concert date, and in the exchange of tickets this was all that was open to me. I didn't think much of it. Listening to the great Chicago Symphony play the movie and television music of Henry Mancini felt to me like getting into a Rolls-Royce to drive around the block to take out the garbage. The King's Singers weren't much, either. Why, I wonder, am I here?

Bored, I look at the audience of which I am a part in the Ravinia pavilion. It is an older crowd, lots of comb-over hairdos among the men, a fair share of blue rinse among the women. Very suburban, I think: thick-calved younger women, men wearing pastel-colored clothes. They seem happy hearing this stuff, the musical equivalent of chewing gum, which left my mind wandering. The bloody snobbish truth is, I prefer not to think myself part of this crowd. I think myself, if you want to know, much better — intellectually superior, musically more sophisticated, even though I haven't any musical training whatsoever and cannot follow a score.

In part these feelings were justified: the music was terribly thin, leaving no residue, better listened to, if at all, while driving across town on an errand. But why did I have to establish my superiority to my (mildly) detested fellow listeners, even if only in my own mind. Why not simply note them and think about other things? Because, alas, the snob cannot bear to think himself a nobody, even in his own mind, and he certainly doesn't want to think himself included in an audience of what he sees as dull people, who have, as W. H. Auden once said to Nicholas Nabokov about a bureaucratic group in the U.S. Army, the "*wrong* ideas about everything and belong to that group of people neither you nor I can possibly like or condone." And rather than sit back and enjoy this concert, unmemorable as it was, I had to make plain, if only to myself, that I am a much more serious person than these people sitting around me, and serious in a way that deserves recognition, even if (again) only to myself.

Why do those thoughts play in my head at all? Why did I need to assert my superiority, even to myself, when no one was contesting it? Why cannot I, even so late in the day, grow into one of those admirable fellows — reasonable, tolerant, generous-spirited, honorable — that Jefferson called "natural aristocrats" and that a liberal arts education is supposed to form but almost never does?

Strange. And ridiculous. Snob-free zone? Haven't myself yet arrived anywhere close. Perhaps in the next life. Or possibly the one after that.

10

The High, Fine Nuttiness of Status

A SNOB, in one common definition, is anyone who thinks himself superior in a way that demands recognition. Samuel Johnson, speaking to the potential snob in us all, wrote: "There lurks, perhaps, in every human heart a desire of distinction, which inclines every man to hope, and then to believe, that nature has given himself something peculiar to himself." But how to gain the recognition mentioned in my first sentence, how to establish one's distinction mentioned in Johnson's? Each presents a problem the solution to which often comes under the heading of status.

Does one pronounce the word *stay-tus* or *stat-us,* and does either pronunciation suggest something about one's own (however pronounced) status? Unclear, but what is clear is that power and wealth often confer status, yet status is different from either power or wealth standing alone. Status is not in the possession of its holder but in that of its beholder. You cannot confer status on yourself; you are forced to look to others — equals, people above you, often people below — to confer it upon you. The trick for the seeker of status is to surround himself with visible evidence of his rank, or worth, or reasons for being highly regarded, so that he doesn't always — doesn't ever, really — have to announce it.

Status used inextricably to be lashed to class. One of status's chief functions formerly was to make plain — sometimes quietly, sometimes quite blatantly — a person's social class. In the bad old days of the Soviet Union, the world's most brutal attempt at imposing a classless society, many jobs entailed wearing uniforms that unmistakably indicated the standing of the persons who wore them. The social clarity this conveyed must have been something of a relief, removing all guesswork from social observation, rather like the colored belts worn in karate. Would something similar in social life — red belts worn by people with an annual income of more than $50,000, purple belts for more than $100,000, brown belts for more than $250,000, black belts for more than $500,000, suspenders for more than $1 million — be an aid and great convenience?

Or do we already have all the guidance we need in the clothes people wear, the houses they live in, the cars they drive, the subjects they choose to talk about and the selection of language they have at their disposal to do so? Is my man from the previous chapter with his Illinois State University decal all that different from the man wearing his Princeton tie? Both are advertising, and what they are advertising is their social class. The other night, coming out of a restaurant, I noted a man leaving his Jaguar with the valet parking attendant; the woman with him was twenty or so years younger than he. He looked to be in good shape — a heavy-workout man, no doubt — was wearing black shirt and trousers, the big wristwatch. He was advertising, too, advertising that he is a man with heavy money.

But these are easy cases. Nowadays the advertising is more subtle, complex, difficult to distinguish. Status calls are more complicated because many Americans prefer to play interesting games with their status. They wish, in part, not to come on too strong with it; at the same time, as with the ads for the American Express card, they aren't quite prepared to leave home without it. As status is lashed to social class at one end, so at the other is it lashed to fashion. One reads the now more than forty-year-old bestseller *The Status Seekers* by Vance Packard and notes how drastically the symbols of status have changed. In the time of Packard's book, having an air conditioner visible from outside one's house was thought to be a strong statement of one's arrival in the upper reaches of the middle class, and a television antenna on one's roof did something similar for the lower middle class. Closer to our day, William F. Buckley, Jr., wrote about having his limousine specially lengthened, which must have seemed a grand thing in its time; but today the height of vulgarity, surely, is arriving in a stretch limo.

At the upper reaches, status may consist of not being presented with a check at an expensive restaurant because it keeps a running tab for you, or of a woman's wearing short sleeves in public in winter, thereby quietly showing that a warm chauffeur-driven car awaits her. (Malcolm Muggeridge once said that you never want a job that provides a car and chauffeur; when the job ends, you'll miss the convenience sorely.) The only thing not now marked by status, near as one can make out, is the form of one's demise: the card one draws here — easy or painful death — seems to have nothing to do with one's status in life.

Exerting status is another matter. "This is Gene Siskel." I was sitting in the syndicated movie reviewer's Volvo station wagon when I heard him say, car phone pressed to his ear, "Have you a table for four?" Note the use of the name up front, before the request. The hour was late and the restaurant about to close, but apologies were extended and so was a not very heartfelt promise on Siskel's part that he would try the restaurant again. A nice reversal on this is the story told of Ira Gershwin and his wife and another couple about to go out to dinner at a fashionable Manhattan restaurant. Gershwin offered to call for a table. He returned to say none was available. "Let me try," said the other man. He returned to announce that they indeed had a table available at eight o'clock. Everyone wanted to know how he was able to accomplish this. "Simple," he said, "I told them I was Ira Gershwin."

People in America must exist who are utterly oblivious of their status, but I'm not sure that I have ever met one above the age of twenty-one. Contented with one's life, confident of one's success, one nonetheless cannot help notice that this phone call has not been returned, that e-mail went unanswered, the long letter filled with requests found no response. Whatever all this means, it cannot redound to certainty about one's own standing.

Major shifts in the status of people and things have been a regular part of the proceedings in America for the past thirty years or more. Fur coats, once a symbol of female glamour and *luxe,* became almost a political liability in the 1990s. The tweedy, Waspy male professor became nearly an alien presence in a university culture that preferred victims. Journalists, riding high during the Watergate era, saw a precipitate drop in their status by the late 1980s, when they once again came to seem camp followers, paid voyeurs, and slightly crummy. In Washington during the Reagan and then again during the Clinton administration, movie stars seemed to rise in status over lawyers and various rainmakers and power players.

In an ad for a special issue on status of the *New York Times Magazine* (November 15, 1998), five editors of the Hearst magazines division are quoted saying something stupid on the subject of jeans, the most piquantly silly of which runs: "I think jeans connote a new kind of status. When you wear them, you demonstrate that you have enough power to dress comfortably. It means you have the power to relax." I shouldn't have thought to read the deeper meaning of jeans this way — especially as a man who has not owned jeans for forty years and doesn't plan to acquire any between now and the grave — but then status tends to bring out the nuttiness in people.

Sometimes such things can be explained, sometimes not. The sociologist Alan Wolfe writes: "Revolutions in status give us all the excitement of rapid social change with little of the accompanying turmoil. . . . Status transformations have their victims and their costs, but if there is going to be rapid change, then let it be over symbols. No one knows who will be in America's status elite tomorrow. But we do know that just as we will have the rich and the poor and the powerful and the powerless, some will have more status than others." In our day, radical status shifts may have as much to do with making the world go round as money and sex.

While status can be sexy, it isn't always, or even usually, about money. A status system isn't a money system, as witness such status phenomena, mentioned earlier, as working-class chic. At a baseball game in Chicago, I pointed out to a friend from Los Angeles two large, bulky young men seated two rows ahead of us, remarking that such physical types either wouldn't be permitted in southern California or, perceiving how inelegant they were, would see the immediate necessity for taking their lives. My friend disagreed, saying I was missing something new on the contemporary scene: the human equivalent of the sport-utility vehicle. Men who were oversized and meant to seem menacing, like the SUV itself, represented a new California style. Thus can status, apparently, even alter body shape, or at least the way we are supposed to view it.

If all this makes the world seem goofy, it makes it goofiest of all for the snob, who often has to run fast just to stay in place — that is, if he or she wishes to stay in the game, the game being to get to, or at least somewhere near, the top of whatever social set is the object of his or her desire. But the difficulty with status is that it can make snobs of us all, for it is difficult wholly to ignore it, especially when, as now, status is no longer something one is born to yet isn't necessarily tied to one's achievements either.

Status is of course tied to prestige, itself a vague, airy, insubstantial thing, but crucial in the arrangements of any society. Prestige is, in *Webster's* words, "1: standing or estimation in the eyes of people: weight or credit in general opinion. 2: commanding position in men's minds: ascendancy." It also happens to be that thing the snob most reveres, wants, and almost always gets wrong. The snob requires prestige, cannot get along without it, thinks possession of it will eliminate his greatest of all fears — that of being nobody.

Such is the magic inhering in prestige that it can be aphrodisiacal: it is possible for a woman to persuade herself that she
loves a man when it is only his prestige she loves. (From
Samuel Johnson to Proust, social observers of some tren-
chancy have noted that it is difficult to find an ugly duchess.)
Everyone who encountered him remarked on Louis XIV's
grand manner of speaking, of walking, of gesture. He carried
himself as prestige incarnate. A veteran officer in the French
army of the time, finding himself atremble during an audience
with Louis XIV, said: "Sire, I hope your Majesty will believe
that I do not tremble thus before your enemies." In the hall
outside the Rothschild offices in nineteenth-century Paris, it
was claimed that a man took off his hat when the Baron de
Rothschild's chamber pot went past. Prestige can have that
kind of effect on people.

For prestige to have potency certain conditions must attend it. Possessors of prestige must live at a remove from the
masses: access to prestige must not be made easy. Nor ought
prestige to be too thinly spread through the population: the
greater the numbers who share in it, the more it becomes attenuated, dissipated, diminished. Exclusion is part of its cruel
magic. Any social circle, club, or university that allows everyone entry cannot hope to maintain its prestige. Here one sees
status, prestige, and snobbery all lashed together.

Although real enough, prestige is not quite rational. Even
the word is slightly insecure. Thomas Carlyle called it "a
newspaper word," and, though it has made its way into the
language, there are people today — language snobs? — who
refuse to accept the word *prestigious,* with its suggestion
of magic, sleight of hand, prestidigitation. H. W. Fowler, in
his *Modern English Usage,* remarks that the word *prestige*
formerly meant illusion or imposture. Wilson Follett, in *Modern American Usage,* preferred such words as reputable, re-
nowned, famous, illustrious, excellent, meritorious, notable,
respectable, praiseworthy, admirable, and glorious.

Prestige in the form of status attaches to universities,
teams, clubs, restaurants, the law, ancestry, religion, culture,
and the state. Sometimes the award of prestige is plain and

unarguable: the prestige that goes to superior courage or strength or intelligence, or talent or beauty. Sometimes it is somewhat mystical and highly arguable: the prestige conferred through heredity, or by fame or money, or through association with or imitation of other holders of prestige. When the reasons for prestige cannot be explained by logic, ethics, or aesthetics, it becomes unstable, shaky.

No complex society has ever done without prestige; in such societies, prestige splinters off into manifold forms of status. The social hope bound up in prestige is that striving to attain it will bring out the best in the society's men and women, driving them to higher and higher achievement. Then there is the hope that the attainment of prestige will itself make its possessors better. In the United States, the prestige of the presidency, the Congress, and the Supreme Court is habitually spoken of in connection with the hope that some of this prestige will, for reasons not quite explicable, rub off and improve the men and women who become associated with these institutions. But even where prestige has no uplifting function, it seems to find a place, as if fulfilling a human need. Rank according to prestige is said to obtain even in prisons, with men who have attempted big money crimes ranked at the top and child molesters at the very bottom.

A society can perhaps become too prestige laden, and also too respectful of prestige. The latter might well render its members too respectable, too uncritical, too cowed for the health of the society. A society with too few sources of prestige, on the other hand, is likely to have a paucity of strong traditions, causing it to float sadly adrift, with no greater goal than its members' individual betterment. When prestige is badly used — consider again how negligible honorary degrees have come to seem, after decades of being handed out to unserious people — it evaporates, and fairly quickly.

Ideally, that society would seem best ordered in which prestige most closely approximates merit. Of such societies where the distance between the two had been very close, only two come to mind: Athens in the fifth century B.C. and England in the middle and latter half of the nineteenth century. In those places during those times, the best people — the most capable, the most responsible, the most meritorious — had for the most part risen to the top. Yet even here, such is the uncertain nature of prestige, close inspection would doubtless discover a good deal of prestige wrongly placed.

Perhaps it is best that the distance between prestige and merit never close completely, that the two never become congruent. If it did, prestige would go only to the brave, the smart, and the beautiful. People who were born ungifted, unbeautiful, unlucky — that, I'm afraid, includes most of us — would have no opportunity to share in prestige. A properly arranged society is one that is somehow able to parcel out prestige, top and bottom, without depleting it and yet without making it so widespread as to lose its allure. From positions high in government to poet laureateships to bowling trophies, a complex society will find numerous ways to make prestige seem both available and laudably valid.

While it is a common occurrence to find, as Henry James once remarked, "imbeciles in very great places, people of sense in small," it nonetheless will not do, if prestige is to maintain some semblance of gravity, to have too many imbeciles in great places. If societies must have elites, establishments, hierarchies — and no known societies of any complexity have ever been without them — it is best that there be some substance to them. But whether there is substance or not, the machinery of prestige grinds on.

In fashion, in medicine, in art, Proust noted, there must be new names — by which he meant, of course, names to which prestige will attach — whether their bearers altogether deserve it or not. Literary prizes must be awarded whether books good enough to deserve them have been written or not; honorary degrees must be conferred whether there are people who deserve them or not; high government officials must be chosen and elected whether they are up to their jobs or not. Only every time a bad book wins a prize, an oaf is honored by a university, a mediocrity or worse serves in high office, prestige leaks away, never to return quite in full.

Prestige can disappear quickly. Four or five bad years and a reputable publishing house can lose its cachet. A decade of hiring inadequate professors and the same thing can happen to a good university or academic department. Three or four poor secretaries of state and the office seems depleted of gravitas. A wayward generation or two and a family with a long history of distinction is done in. Despite the (slightly twisted) pleasure that some take in the spectacle of the mighty fallen, the loss of prestige, when the prestige was solidly earned, is one of the sad events in the human drama.

Seeking deference, the snob believes it can be acquired through prestige. In the algebra of the snobbish mind, prestige equals deference. He reverences prestige, but he gets it wrong. He keenly senses its allure, yet the magic of it drives him a little mad. He hovers around prestige, and when any comes his way, he wallows in it. He knows prestige, knows its power. He can usually be counted on to know who or what has prestige, and to a fairly precise degree.

But the snob desires prestige and with it status in and for themselves. There is nothing he won't do to acquire them, and he doesn't want to hear any damn nonsense about merit, either. Still, though the snob knows everything about and surrounding and connected with prestige and status, his misunderstanding of both remains fundamental. What he fails to comprehend is that neither can be obtained, at least not successfully, as an end in itself. Prestige accompanies high achievement, is an accouterment of solid accomplishment. At the banquet of life, status is a side dish, never a main course. Prestige and status come *by the way;* they are not, in themselves, *the way.* So eager to be among the major players, the inner circle, the upper crust, the snob doesn't get it. He also doesn't understand that one of the best means of acquiring prestige and carrying status is not to give a damn about them, for the paradox of prestige and status is that the more one hungers for them, the more one is willing to do for them, the more elusive they become.

Part Two

*Everything painful and sobering in what psychoana-
lytic genius and religious genius have discovered about
man revolves around the terror of admitting what one
is doing to earn one's self-esteem.*

— Ernest Becker, *The Denial of Death*

11

To You, I Give My Heart, Invidia

Things — purchasable, visible, palpable things — ain't bad. I make this very obvious statement because I was educated to think that things really are pretty bad, that they are trivial, encumbering, ultimately corrupting. Although I grew up in a home where things were valued — not things I would later myself much value, as my tastes became, presumably, educated — it was at university that I first heard things attacked through the use of the word *materialism,* the scourge word for anyone interested in possessions. Materialism turns out to have all sorts of complicated meanings — in philosophy, in Marxism — but the rather coarse meaning it had when I first came across it was purely pejorative. To be a materialist was to be seduced by the world's goods. What was wrong with the world's goods was that they took one's mind off such lofty things as art, ideas, the good life. "Gaudy things enough to tempt ye," runs an old verse by John Banks, "Showy outsides, insides empty."

The secular hero of anti-materialism is Socrates, in many ways the most admirable man in human history. In his book on Alcibiades, E. F. Benson writes that Socrates "seems to have attained without effort that complete independence of material joys and pleasures at which the ascetic arrives only after years of discipline and struggling self-denial; to Socrates such indifference was natural." All such joys — including those of the flesh — were thought to be a drag on the spirit. The worthy spirit was interested in higher matters, in mind and meaning, in glimpsing truth, though Socrates's act — tighter than Noël Coward's at Las Vegas — was always to deny he had any special purchase on the truth. He was merely a bald, ugly man in a tattered cloak, come into the agora each day to investigate the pathetic suppositions of those who claimed to know the truth. Among the suppositions he was most easily able to rout was that material possessions could bring one the least scintilla of happiness. Happiness was available only with the acquisition of truth, itself the sole possession worth having.

Socrates was right: ultimately, of course, possessions cannot bring sustained happiness. But houses, cars, artworks, elegant clothes can nonetheless be amiable distractions until such time as one figures out how to attain the real thing, genuine happiness. And for those not in contention ever to receive happiness via truth at the Socratic level, they offer some of the best entertainments the earth has to offer. For those of us not operating on the Socratic heights, things can bring (forgive, please, the rhyming) that ting-a-ling that little else can bring. And even for those with pretensions to operating on the Socratic heights, possessions can rank high among life's pleasures. One thinks here of Allan Bloom, the University of Chicago Neo-Platonist who filled an apartment with Baccarat and Lalique, wore Charvet and Lanvin duds, paid out tens of thousands of dollars for stereo equipment, and who, when living in Toronto, was only half jokingly said to have single-handedly kept the local Georg Jensen shop in business.

I try to remember when I first recognized that the world contained superior goods and that I didn't possess them. I half suspect this sad knowledge came with leather. As a kid on the playground, I did not have one of the best baseball gloves, all of which were then, and apparently still are, made by a firm called Rawlings. I had a decent glove, mind you, but not a

Rawlings, and I also sensed that I probably could not persuade my father to spring for the extra money, perhaps ten dollars more, that a Rawlings glove cost — at least, so unlikely did I think my chances of succeeding, I never tried.

When I went off to college, I didn't have wretched luggage, but I began to run into people who had much better luggage than I. They had tan suitcases, smooth or grainy, often monogrammed (lest they forget their names?), with strong zippers and good locks, a pliant but solid feel. Such luggage hinted at good things within: soft fabrics beautifully tailored, swell colors, stylish clothes. I have read *The Catcher in the Rye* only once, in my freshman year at university — on the train down, in fact — but in my dim recollection of the book I remember a scene that had to do with luggage. I now discover that I misremembered it, thinking that Holden Caulfield, the book's hero, had poor luggage and that his cheesy roommate Stadlater had splendid luggage. But on rechecking I find J. D. Salinger gave Holden good luggage. (Could he not bear to send the kid off to school without those excellent Gladstone bags?) At another prep school, an earlier roommate of Holden's envies it, hiding his own ragtag luggage under the bed and claiming to people visiting the room that Holden's bags are really his.

When a graduate student named Irving Singer visited the by then aged George Santayana at the Hospital of the Blue Nuns in Rome, he noticed "two travel-weary suitcases under a table." Santayana, having detected his noticing them, remarked: "I know they're old and battered, but they've been all over Europe with me." Singer writes: "His caring about this diminished slightly my admiration." Odd, but it raises mine. To think that the elderly philosopher, who had perhaps thought more subtly about the large questions than any man of his generation, was still concerned that pathetic luggage might show him to be a man unmindful of the small things in life strikes me as impressive. I would myself expect Santayana to have old but distinguished suitcases. So, my guess is, did George Santayana.

I have never seen the luggage of Gerald and Sara Murphy,

friends of F. Scott and Zelda Fitzgerald, John Dos Passos, Hemingway, Picasso, Diaghilev, and others, American denizens of Paris and the French Riviera, charming hosts of Villa America at Antibes, but it must have been terrific. How could it have been otherwise, since Gerald Murphy's father owned Mark Cross, the high-line leather-goods company, selling everything from steamer trunks to key cases! Gerald Murphy's often quoted saying that "living well is the best revenge," by which he meant revenge against the fates, who (as you may have noticed) do not make a common practice of giving us precisely the lives we want. This proved to be so even for this rich and beautiful couple, who in later life were supplied with more than enough trouble to compensate for their early advantages.

Mark Cross is now out of business, but I can recall passing its shop in Manhattan when I was young, taking in its unmistakable feel and smell of deep tanned leather; it was pure swank, and then seemed awfully expensive. I now regret that I never went into minor hock to buy something there (a wallet perhaps, or a key case), but I never took the plunge. Living as life then forced me to do—responsible at the age of twenty-six for a wife and four offspring — provided no revenge at all.

Not much later, in Chicago, I became enamored of a cigarette lighter, a gold, pebbly-grained Dunhill that sold for $45, at a time when $45 represented close to half a week's salary. I was then a professional smoker, a two-pack-a-day man, punctuating everything in my life with a cigarette. I would take myself to Dunhill's, three or so blocks away from the office where I worked; inside, lifting the lighter, turning it over in my hand, I felt its texture, its heft. Flick it open and a spirited flame leapt before one's eyes. I must have thought about that lighter for the better part of two weeks — thought more about it than I did about world events, my family, my work, even my brilliant future. Enough, I thought, buy the freakin' lighter and get on with your life, friend.

And so I did. The lighter gave great pleasure. Every time I reached into my pocket to light a cigarette, I felt a minuscule but real jolt at the thought of my owning such a lighter, a small thing but the best and most elegant of its kind. I don't believe I looked down my nose at poor devils forced to use Zippos and other coarser instruments, not to speak of paper matches. But I felt a certain contentment knowing that in one department of life, the lighting of my cigarettes, I had achieved the untoppable sublime. Forgive me — do not turn away from me as irretrievably lightweight — if I say that, in some inexplicable way, this gave me a limited but quite genuine happiness.

After a year or so—try to hold back your tears here — I lost the lighter. But the pleasure its possession conferred determined me henceforth to be extravagant, in a selective way, in minor things. I could not and cannot now afford the grand things: the second home in Tuscany, the small but perfect Matisse over the fireplace, the $2,000 suit. But I have bought the $300 fountain pen, the occasional $70 bow tie, the cashmere jacket. A little voice within says "let 'er rip," and I do. Piker stuff to some, I realize, but the element of petty extravagance somehow lights my fire even now.

Why such things do so has its snobbish pertinence. Take the matter of clothes, an item that, beyond providing cover and warmth, oughtn't to matter in the least. Of course there are clothes many of us wouldn't be caught dead in, but if this is so, why oughtn't there be clothes we should most wish to be caught alive in? When I was in my last year at the University of Chicago—a place where no one seemed to care how one dressed — I discovered and bought a raincoat at the Wabash Avenue shop of Abercrombie & Fitch, which in those days could easily have outfitted one for a full-blown safari. It was an unlined single-breasted raincoat of a perfect tan, with a collar that fell just right and perfect tortoise buttons. The coat only seemed to get better the longer I wore it: it broke in beautifully, like a fine baseball glove, or a wallet, or a good husband. Its brand name was Macintosh, which is, I later came to realize, also the generic English name for a raincoat. It was more expensive than the general run of such coats, but not greatly so. I loved that coat. I felt I looked marvelous in that coat. ("Dahling, you look mahvalous, simply mahvalous.") The coat made me feel confident, which is merely another way of saying at home in the world. When it wore out, I tried to buy another, but the company had either ceased importing to America or had gone out of business. I never found another nearly as pleasing. Had I been able to acquire more Macintosh raincoats, I would today, I feel certain, be a distinguished United States senator (retired).

Complications can result if the thing or things you love become widespread, and through popularity lose their cachet. I liked to think that I had a special interest in design, in and for itself. But I see the subject of design is all over the *New York Times* and other newspapers, shops going by the name Good Design now exist, and my interest begins, just slightly, to wane. I was reminded not long ago by my son that, when I took him, as a boy of eleven, to buy a winter coat, the salesman took a coat off a rack and announced that here was a very popular coat this season. ("Nobody goes there anymore," Yogi Berra once remarked of a restaurant. "It's too crowded.") My response, my son reminded me, was that if it was popular we'd rather not see it. Snobbery — or, as in this case, reverse snobbery — never sleeps.

Things not only (rather obviously) have their allure, but (perhaps less obviously) they can suggest power and even be aphrodisiacal. "George always notices the aroma of Harold Mose," writes Kurt Andersen of a wealthy television producer, in his novel *Turn of the Century*. "Why hasn't Ralph Lauren bottled this fragrance? (Maybe he has.) It must be the daily haircut plus fresh flowers plus cashmere plus BMW leather plus the executive-jet oxygen mix plus a dash of citrus. That is, Mose smells delicious. He smells rich." That "dash of citrus" is a nice touch, but the fact is that I know that smell — it is the smell of serious money taking time out for superior grooming — and Andersen has it right.

There is scarcely any object, once turned into a commodity, that does not have its snobbish possibilities. Consider the wristwatch. Once a utilitarian object, an advance over the pocket or pin watch, the wristwatch has now become chiefly a piece of jewelry. The number of watchmaking companies is almost beyond counting; the various models, the range of prices, the sheer glut of watches are an amazement. Who needs, wants, wears all these watches? "Charlize Theron, Chloë Sevigny, and Courtney Love," reports *Talk* magazine, "have all been spotted sporting the new $4,000 Bulgari chronograph — which means you have about a minute left to get in on the trend." (Oops, too late!)

Watches used to be sold on the basis of accuracy, but now, with quartz movements, even the least expensive watches keep perfectly good time, and so that game is up. One wears the watch one does today because one likes its design; it has been given to one and thus has sentimental value; one wishes to show one can afford an expensive piece of jewelry. Patek Philippe, as of 1997, sold a watch in a limited edition for $44,500; presumably, the demand for it was such that it had to be put on back order. Safe to say that something very different from telling time is entailed in owning that watch.

"Your watch says a lot about you," a magazine ad for wristwatches not long ago stated. A great many things, evidently, among them how status-conscious, socially anxious, and finally foolish you are to spend the amount you did on an object that long ago passed beyond merely telling time. "The wristwatch remains the most powerfully symbolic accessory in a man's wardrobe," a journalist notes in the magazine *GQ*, and then goes on to quote a vice president from the watch dealer Tourneau: "A watch represents who we are in a society with fewer and fewer ways to distinguish ourselves. When you're in front of a maitre d' at a fine restaurant, he doesn't know what kind of car you drove up in, but he can see your watch." Can this be so? Is the maitre d', fiendishly clever fellow, really checking wrists? In my case, I have to wonder, will my André Knokovsky get me one of the better tables or put me just outside the kitchen?

Horses, coaches, and now cars have always held their snobbish cachet, serving as means of setting oneself above the next person. I was once in the garage of an expensive condominium apartment building in Hyde Park, the neighborhood of the University of Chicago, where every car seemed dull, some barely above the tired old cars known as beaters. When I queried the man who lived there why this was so, he answered, with a knowing smile, "Academic motors." Nice cars in such a setting would be thought more than a little vulgar. A university teacher is supposed to be beyond such things.

An acquaintance told me that he long aspired to own a Bentley, the understated version of the Rolls-Royce, but was discouraged when he learned that Averell Harriman was driven about in a ten-year-old Chevy with no heater (but, he added, with a mink lap robe in the back seat). The Bentley, however, strikes me as the wrong way to go. Better, in my current view, to adopt the go-for-it spirit of John O'Hara. He told himself that, if he won the Nobel Prize, he would buy himself a Rolls-Royce, but then decided, since it was becoming clear he wasn't going to get the Nobel, he might as well have the Rolls as a consolation prize. By phone he ordered a green Silver Cloud III with his initials painted on the door. "None of your shy, thumb-sucking Bentley radiators for me," he noted. "I got that broad in her nightgown on *my* radiator and them two R's, which don't mean rock 'n' roll."

From the time of Versailles, when many rewards were to be had for living in close proximity to the court of the Sun King, a good address has always given off a snobbish ping: Mayfair, London W1; the Faubourg Saint-Germain; upper Park Avenue; Brentwood. A few years ago someone paid $25 million for a penthouse in the Hotel Pierre in New York; I take it that person didn't do so purely for either the view or the eat-in kitchen. "Money," Balzac writes, "never misses the slightest occasion to demonstrate its stupidity." The right location in the Hamptons, Malibu, Georgetown, Princeton, the 900 block on Lake Shore Drive, the Back Bay, or Russian Hill will jack up real estate prices manyfold. "We find things beautiful," wrote Thorstein Veblen, "somewhat in proportion as they are costly." Perhaps nowhere more so than in connection with real estate, so much of which isn't intrinsically beautiful at all. Snobbery, Santayana writes in his one novel, *The Last Puritan,* is "love of a nicer prospect than one's own."

The other side of this is a desire to have things just a bit better than one's friends and neighbors. Robert H. Frank, an economist who wrote a book titled *Luxury Fever*, reports that most Americans would rather have a salary of $100,000 a year if others were earning $85,000 than have a salary of $110,000 a year if others were earning $200,000. We would, in other words, settle for less if we could be sure that others had still less than we. The point is nicely underscored, as Frank notes, by H. L. Mencken's definition of a wealthy man as the fellow who earns $100 a year more than his wife's sister's husband. Wealth, then, is not merely comparative, but the element of comparison can be crucial, especially to the snob.

Allowing for the exception only of extraordinary views — of mountain or water — the best places to live have traditionally been those where the best and brightest people live. In recent times (what are taken to be) the best and brightest people are often highly mobile, especially if one adds to the mix the youngest best and brightest, who move on to new neighborhoods faster than you can say TriBeCa. Allowing for differing temperaments, what one generally wants in the neighborhood in which one lives is safety, convenience, and pleasantness (if available), but many people are willing to forgo all of this to live in a place that gives them a sense that they are where the action is. Sorry to have to report psychological inflation in the realm of real estate. Pamela Fiori, editor in chief of *Town & Country*, reports: "If one is to be considered affluent, it is not enough anymore to own a house — even a big comfortable house with all the prerequisite contents. It is the second (or if you're lucky, the third) home that is now the symbol of success."

In the 1970s, Jason Epstein, a vice president at the publishing firm of Random House, wrote an article in the *New York Review of Books* in which he said that to live in Manhattan, one required an income of about $50,000 a year, which would perhaps be equivalent to $200,000 today. "It is possible to manage on less, perhaps on as little as half as much by living on the West Side," he wrote, "doing without this or that and thinking more or less always about getting by. But to fall below this level is to become not a citizen but a victim. . . . In

New York there are few respectable or comfortable ways of being poor or even middle class. To be without money in New York is usually to be without honor." Deeply snobbish though that passage is, it contains an uncomfortably high quotient of truth.

The East Side of Manhattan has traditionally been a place where the action is, but such places have a way of shifting around; and where the action is usually turns out to be where the richest, cleverest, most with-it, winning people happen to be. I have myself on occasion felt the longing to live in such places, but never have been able to do so. I have been either too poor or (now) too happily settled to live in the vicinity of the Sun Kings of my day. Instead of an exciting or inherently elegant neighborhood, I have chosen a pleasant and convenient one. In Evanston, just outside Chicago, I live two blocks from my office, a block from a swell public library, across the street from a supermarket, and within a hundred yards of seven restaurants and my barber, with two major bookstores just up the street. This great soak in convenience has dulled the excitement of a fashionable address for me. The only real estate I can today be said to long for I cannot afford to acquire: a splendid view of a body of water.

Of ample objects in the realm of things, now that prosperity has become so widespread, all that is left to excite the passion of the snob is ownership of waterfront property, works of visual art by famous artists, and private airplanes. The first-class section of commercial jets, though comfortable on long trips, seems, as you may have noticed, nowadays filled by people who do not themselves seem very first class. This is doubtless owing to frequent-flier programs that make first-class seats available to people who are always aloft on business: salesmen, middle managers, et cetera. Another snobbish possibility thus bites the dust.

Servants might once have been on this list, but the class system has changed, so that servants, were they to be available, which they mostly are not, provide as much complication as they do pleasure. Hence the delight people took in the simple loyalty of the servants portrayed on the PBS series *Up-*

stairs, Downstairs, showing that no nostalgia runs deeper than that for something one has never known and now cannot obtain.

Since waterfront property, costly artworks, and private planes are things only the very wealthy can buy, snobs must latch on to small advantages wherever they find them. Not that there is a paucity of things the possession of which doesn't permit one, properly positioned, to lord it over others. A friend who not long ago wanted to buy a croquet set learned, when visiting the International Croquet Association, that it refers to any croquet set under $300 as "a children's set."

The snobbery of things is seen at its highest power in certain shops in New York, Paris, Milan, and Los Angeles where extravagance itself seems to weigh in as an element in the game. In an article about a young woman and man involved in insider stock trading, the man, when caught, suggested that the young woman, though she suffered greatly, wasn't entirely innocent, and said that she enjoyed the style of living he called "Prada and two dogs." Prada is the shop where you might find a simple leather belt that costs $500 or a handbag for $5,000. Prada customers, working in movies or television, advertising or art galleries, the fashion or cosmetics business, think of themselves as a self-appointed cognoscenti and are ready to pay heavily for continuing to be able to do so.

Here we enter the snobbery of pure expenditure: the ownership of a Gulfstream V private jet for $41 million; a Rolls-Royce Corniche for $359,900; "the" Hermès Kelly Bag, between $3,200 and $8,000; and a prix fixe blowfish dinner at Ginza Sushi-ko in Beverly Hills for $250. "After seeing what the bourgeois crave," wrote Jules Renard, "I feel myself capable of doing without everything."

The "Prada and two dogs" remark is a reminder that dog ownership has long been an item with the smudgy fingerprints of snobbery all over it. Ten or so years ago, King Charles spaniels seemed the breed of choice for the dog owner with a social eye: Ronald and Nancy Reagan owned them, and so did William and Pat Buckley. Not long after,

King Charles spaniels were replaced by golden retrievers. I
knew a man, a fellow teacher at Northwestern University,
much given to the nuances of snobbery in his dress, manner,
and spirit, who owned not one but two golden retrievers. I
was only barely able to resist examining the chests of these
amiable beasts to see if they didn't bear the logo of Ralph
Lauren. Now I sense that there is yet another shift, away from
pure breeds toward mutts, half Lab, half you pick it.

If croquet sets and dogs have their separate snobbery
systems, so then of course does rose-growing, bowling, and
tattoo-wearing. A friend who once edited the London *Times
Literary Supplement* told me that he discovered that every
scholarly subject, no matter how minor, had its political divisions; in fact, the narrower the subject, the more intense the
politics. Something similar can be said about objects and
snobbery. Perhaps the best wisdom on the subject of possessions belongs to Montaigne, who wrote: "I attach too little
value to things I possess, just because I possess them." Very
smart. I would only add that such evidence as we have suggests that Montaigne, a nobleman, possessed, in his day, nothing but the best. Easy, then, for him to say.

12

....

A Son at Tufts,
a Daughter at Taffeta

A TOUCH UNNATURAL though the transition from possessions to children may seem, children, in a fundamental way, can be a person's proudest possession (but it is far from clear, in our day of nervous child-rearing, who, between parents and children, possesses whom). I hope it doesn't appear outlandish to suggest that children are used in the game of snobbery, because they are so used, and fairly frequently.

Apart from the modest project of continuing the human race, aristocrats historically had children to perpetuate their line, while the lower orders had them as a source of labor, mainly agricultural labor. Although they could prove useful in various ways, from making strategic alliances through marriage to caring for one in one's old age, children were under the obligation to be dutiful and, at a minimum, not dishonor their family. With the rise of the middle classes and the shift from primarily rural to almost wholly urban economies, the relation between parents and children altered decisively.

Pride in children is of long standing. The Yiddish word *kvell,* meaning to beam with pride and pleasure, is used most often in connection with the achievements of one's children. Another Yiddishism, *yiches,* meaning family pride or prestige, is also frequently invoked in connection with children. Finally, there is "family egotism," a term I first saw used in Tolstoy for which there is, so far as I know, no Yiddish word but for which there ought to be. Family egotism means not particularly caring if the rest of the world goes to hell so long as all is well with our little Kevin.

None of this will come as startling news, but in recent decades the phenomenon of investing pride in children seems to have been heightened, with children taking a larger and larger place in the psychic economy of the middle and upper middle classes. Among these classes, a vast amount of care is lavished on raising children. At times it seems our entire culture is arranged to see to the needs of children: preschools, private schools, lessons of various sorts, therapies, tests to diagnose learning disabilities, medicines to make up for little mental jiggeroos, parental attention of a kind no previous generation of children, in any land at any time, has ever had bestowed upon it.

Underlying this is a new assumption about child-rearing and human nature that holds that the right combination of genetic makeup and environmental control will produce hugely successful — happy, achieving, creative, sweet — children. As evidence of how much we believe in this, there now exists a vast body of prescriptives about treating the infant in the womb, running from not drinking wine when pregnant to playing Mozart pre- and post-delivery and through the toddler years. From conception till well after college, the child is coddled, cozened, cultivated as the precious piece of property he or she is. In an article titled "The Organization Kid," David Brooks, apropos of this intense concentration on correct upbringing, writes: "Your child is the most important extra-credit arts project you will ever undertake."

And a lot is riding, not only for the child but for you as a parent, on how he or she turns out. If you doubt this, ask yourself who in the current age is likely to be thought the greater success: the man or woman who has impressive achievements in science, public life, art, business, or athletics, or the man or woman who has been thought to have had a sig-

nificant influence in raising two or three swell children? Not
only are most people likely to choose the latter, but one can go
a step further to say that, should it become known that the
former has less than successful or otherwise troubled children, his achievement is likely to be thought not worth the effort. (Example: President Ronald Reagan is said to be currently much beloved by Americans, but the oddity of his by
now long grown-up children casts a slight doubt on him as, in
his time, a less than successful father.)

Parents who have had a university education, have advanced tastes, and feel the pull of futurity in their aspirations
know that their children are up against a new order if they are
to succeed. This new order goes by the name of the meritocratic elite, and it is restricted to those who make it not on
family connections but on sheer merit and includes those
young people admitted to the best schools, thence to the best
jobs, thence (the assumption is) to the best lives. A good deal
is felt to be at stake, and parents, rightly or wrongly, no longer
believe, as once they did, that they need only provide food,
shelter, education, and a model of responsibility for their kids
and let it go at that.

With so much psychic energy invested in children, snobbery could scarcely be precluded. The clue that there is a
snobbish element is first found in the naming of children.
Let's begin with Scott. Anyone who names a child Scott is, I
suspect, operating on a (perhaps unconscious) snobbish impulse. Nine times out of ten, perhaps more, Scott is a borrow-
ing from F. Scott Fitzgerald. As such, the first name Scott
speaks to a yearning for elegance on the part of the parents
who gave their sons that name. Nicole, another name Fitzgerald put into the snob hopper, through the female heroine of
his novel *Tender Is the Night,* speaks to the same yearning,
and so more recently does the name Jordan for girls. Gifted in
many ways, Fitzgerald was not least so in his ability to make a
certain kind of life, lived stylishly and amid great wealth, seem
the best of all lives. Nick Carraway may have been the narrator
of *The Great Gatsby,* but the *arriviste* Jay Gatz probably
comes closer than anyone in the novel, or in all of Fitzgerald's

work, to expressing the author's own deep desire for the elegant life. Fitzgerald was marvelous at understanding that desire, as only a man on the outside of things could be.

But let us not stop at Scott and Nicole. Think of all the names now out there, all those Brittanys and Tiffanys and Kimberlys, Whitneys and Tylers and Hunters, Saharas and Savannahs and Sierras, Camerons and Caitlins and Catesbys. In Nora Ephron's novel *Heartburn,* the chief male character claims to have dated the first Jewish Kimberly. Many Jewish Kimberlys in the world now, and not a few Kellys, Marins, Alisons. (The 1960s gave us such flower-child names as Moonbeam, Jagger, and, in one case I've heard of, Irony.) In his novel *Turn of the Century,* Kurt Andersen notes a family that named its son Max "twenty months behind the curve." Andersen offers the following paragraph on the naming of children among the parents of his generation:

> George has been amazed to discover that there were two Griffins in Max's class this year. . . . But Griffin is precisely the kind of name that's in vogue among parents who send their children to nonreligious private schools called St. Andrews, who buy forty-dollar-a-gallon Martha Stewart paint and fifty-dollar doll-size American Girl butter churns made of solid chestnut. One of Max's classmates is named Huck — not Huckleberry, Huck — and in Lulu's class there is a Truman, a Chester, a Sawyer, three Benjamins, two Coopers, a Walker, a Hunter (Hunter Liu), as well as multiple Amandas, Lucys, and Hopes, and even a Gwyneth.

What is going on here is the need to mark one's child off as different, unique, stylish, above and — why not come out and say it — just a little beyond the others. And why not? Our little Stefan, Sophia, Luc, Alyssa is, after all, the child of parents of exquisite taste. If not, he or she wouldn't carry such a special name, *n'est-ce pas?* These are children, let us face it, aimed at better places than, say, Michigan State or a job selling automobile insurance.

Caitlin Flanagan, a college counselor at Harvard-Westlake, a prep school in Los Angeles, believes that the silliness about getting one's children into the best schools is about "class anxiety." But isn't class anxiety merely snobbery put into socio-psychoanalytic language? She is charitable to parents, saying that they really only want the best education for their kids. But she adds that it is more than a bit difficult to understand what they mean by the best education. "It's the kind of education you get at certain places," she writes, "but not others — at Georgetown but not at the University of Washington; at Duke but not at Chapel Hill. It's the kind of education you can definitely get at Stanford, less so at Berkeley, much less so at Michigan, hardly at all at Wisconsin, and not at all at the University of Illinois." Miss Flanagan adds: "That kind of thinking has always bewildered me." It is called, she should know, snobbish thinking.

I first noticed the snobbish interest in children when my eldest son went off to college. I can recall meeting parents of roughly my own age who, when the time came to discuss children, would ask if my (then) nineteen- or twenty-year-old son was in college. When I replied yes, at Stanford, I felt I was holding a strong card. (I always wanted to say, "Yes, we have a son at Tufts and a daughter at Taffeta," but somehow restrained myself.) During such discussions, I felt I was in a card game, college-snobbery bridge, in which not suits but schools were bid: Brown, Duke, Princeton, Yale, Balliol College, the Sorbonne, École Normale Supérieure. Clearly, one didn't want to get into this game with a kid at Alabama A&M ("Our daughter is interested in performance studies, and it turns out they've got a really strong department there"), let alone at a junior or community college. To have to make such a confession — concession is more like it — is to cause one's table mates to wonder where you went wrong in raising this once precious but now hopeless child, and, by extension, what, exactly, is wrong with you.

It can get worse as one's children grow beyond school age, for one is apparently also responsible for the kind of work they do in later life. As there is college-snobbery bridge, so job-snobbery bridge follows. Are one's children doing what is construed to be OK work? What is thought OK will depend on the circles in which one travels. Among the enlightened classes, it is OK to have a child who is doing anything in the arts, in (however vaguely) "film," or is doing something in the line of social work; or is a chef or going to cooking school, is in medicine or science, is teaching, is in carpentry, or is building harpsichords or repairing violins. It's all the better if the kid is making tons of money doing any of these things, but distinctly not OK if he is making money in what is construed to be some grubby, unimaginative way — as a CPA, say, or running a useful store.

What has made this more complicated is that snobbery has had to make way for downward mobility, or the prospect, a real one for the first time in American life, that one's children won't do better than one has oneself done. In 1781 John Adams famously wrote to his wife Abigail: "I must study politics and war that my sons may have liberty to study mathematics and philosophy. My sons ought to study mathematics and philosophy, geography, natural history, naval architecture, commerce, and architecture, in order to give their children a right to study painting, poetry, music, architecture, statuary, tapestry, and porcelain." This probably has to be revised today by many immigrant grandfathers to read, "I must run a dry-cleaning shop so that my sons can go to medical and law school, in order that their sons may study sociology and communications, so that their children can run vintage clothing stores, act in avant-garde theater, and work in coffee shops."

For all that can be said about snobbery, it isn't finally all that rigid, but changes with the times. Snobbery might in fact be the best warning system going, foretelling how the times they are indeed a-changing. Snobbery can also be flexible and accommodating, if only to explain the changed situations into which the snobs' own children have landed them. Not a one-generation thing, snobbery. Sometimes a snob's children can cause him or her more awkward emotion than an anti-Semite might feel at a Hasidic picnic.

13

....

Dear Old Yarvton

SINCE ROUGHLY 1950 the great divide in American life has not (as I noted earlier by way of Tom Wolfe) been that between rich and poor, black and white, Jew and Gentile — though these divisions were all real enough — but between those who went to college and those who didn't. One saw this divide even in that most integrated of American institutions, the U.S. Army, where it seemed to surmount that between officers and enlisted men. But one began to see it in corporations, too, where the higher-echelon jobs were simply no longer available to people who hadn't gone to college, however bright they might be. Having gone to college suddenly became the key to so many things in American life. "Society in Los Angeles," Ethel Barrymore used to say, "was anyone who graduated from high school." No longer.

Increased college enrollments after World War Two had an immense effect in producing a more and more classless society in America. Still, after the war college became a sine qua non, indispensable not only in vocational life but in the life of the spirit. Intelligent people who hadn't gone to college began to feel a great hole in their lives, and those who had gone could usually be relied upon to hide from them what is all too sadly the truth: they really haven't missed all that much.

Paul Goodman, the 1930s radical who became something of a guru during the student rebellions of the late 1960s and early '70s, used to enjoy saying that all going to college meant was that in doing so a person showed how badly he or she wanted to succeed in society as currently constituted. Going to college entails a large expense, lots of useless work, and the acceptance of endless onerous, preposterous trivialities, all of which, Goodman liked pointing out, showed that any young man or woman who was willing to put up with this nonsense could be expected to put up with the even greater nonsense of boring and meaningless work later in life. College, in this view, functioned chiefly to turn out useful, moderately high-level drones, finely honed tools of capitalism.

This doesn't happen to be my view. But my respect for higher education is not much greater than Goodman's, at least in its nonscientific components. Considered purely as an institution for purveying information and imbuing culture, surely no other system can have been as inefficient as American education over the past hundred years. "If men made no more progress in the common arts of life than they have in education," wrote Sydney Smith, the wit of the *Edinburgh Review*, "we should at this moment be dividing our food with our fingers, and drinking out of the palms of our hands." Quite right.

As someone who has gone to a university and also taught at one for nearly thirty years, I have come to the depressing conclusion that education is mainly a matter of good luck: the luck to have had struck the divine spark of passion for things of the mind combined with the even better luck of discovering, amid the majority of mediocre university teachers, the one or two with the magic tinder to inflame that spark. Some young people are what are known as good students — that is, like good dogs of a certain sort, they fetch well, bringing back in their moist mouths the sticks they were thrown. "The significance of Anglo-Catholicism to T. S. Eliot — go get it, girl." "Was the Renaissance merely the Late Show of the Middle Ages or the Early Show of the Reformation — bring it back, boy, typed, double spaced, tidy footnotes at the bottom of the page." Woof, woof. Good student. Here's your Phi Beta Kappa key, now go get a good job.

Of course undergraduate education is only ostensibly about producing the sound paper on T. S. Eliot or the Renaissance or the Reformation. What it's really about, or at any rate is supposed to be about, is the development of young minds, teaching them how to think independently, how to combine common sense with proper skepticism, the whole given a fine texture by the attainment of an at first widened and later (after college, acquired on one's own) greatly deepened culture. But what percentage of the 65 percent of Americans who regularly participate in one form or another of higher education do you suppose derive anything resembling such things from their education? I would set it at somewhere between 1 and 2 percent, though that may be too generous. Most people come away from college, happy souls, quite unscarred by what has gone on in the classroom. The education and culture they are presumably exposed to at college never lay a glove on them. This is the big dirty secret of higher education in America.

This doesn't mean that their having gone to college isn't worth it. Not at all. On a strict accounting, a college education, expensively priced though it nowadays generally is, probably pays off as well as any investment. Endless studies show that young men and women who attend college earn hundreds of thousands of dollars more over a lifetime than those who, for one reason or another, do not go to college. Why should this be so? For the same reason that degrees in journalism, master's degrees in business, and other (shall we politely say?) not strictly necessary degrees make for success: because, that is, people who have already paid for these overpriced appurtenances wish others to do so, forming a (not so) little group of those who have already pledged the fraternity.

During recent decades it has become plain that education is the key to opportunity in America. Not only going to college but, as I have said, where one goes to college is crucial. In the nineteenth and early decades of the twentieth century, college was not considered essential to success. From Benjamin Franklin to Andrew Carnegie to John D. Rockefeller

to Henry Ford to Ernest Hemingway, so many of the great
American success stories were devoid of a pause for college.
H. L. Mencken, who also didn't bother to go to college,
thought it a comically, pathetically wasteful interlude, four
years spent listening to hopeless pedagogues and engaged in
inane social activities, and surely one that anybody who had
any choice in the matter would prefer to bypass. Mencken
had a choice — a career in journalism — and took it without
hesitation.

In recent years, many extraordinary athletes in basketball,
baseball, and tennis have forgone college for the large salaries
available to them in professional sports. Whatever else they
may be missing out on, no one, so far as I know, really thinks
they are missing out on the experience of a fine education.
Now it is reported that computer whiz kids are deciding to
take a pass on college, too. The money, the excitement of
business, and the lure of being in on the swell new things calls
them, and somehow it doesn't seem entirely a mistake to answer the call instead of going off to college, where they can
spend four years learning that the glorious culture of fifth century B.C. Athens was little more than a swindle built on a slave
society, that Shakespeare was a homosexual serving the interests of imperialistic England, and that women have gotten a
raw deal throughout history and up to twenty minutes ago.
With so much nuttiness being taught in the liberal arts and
social sciences, college, for people with exceptional talent, begins once again to seem less and less worth the time, trouble,
and expense.

Many of the privileged who went to the better colleges in
the first six decades of the twentieth century did so without
any vocational aim in mind; already well connected, they had
the businesses of fathers and fathers-in-law and uncles and
friends of classmates awaiting. Harvard, Yale, Princeton was
not for them a résumé item, an entrée, an open sesame. For
them the doors were already open. George Herbert Walker
Bush did not go to Yale College because he was hoping
thereby to gain a job. He went to Yale College because he
was George Herbert Walker Bush, and Yale — and Harvard
and Princeton and a few threadneedle Ivy colleges — was the

sort of place that families such as the Bushes (and Alsops, Achesons, Harrimans, Roosevelts, and the rest) sent their sons, with daughters going to Radcliffe, Vassar, Smith, and Wellesley.

They went there, as earlier they had gone to the various Choates, Grotons, Andovers, St. Paul's, and Exeters, as part of a general program in character building. At such institutions they were to learn, presumably, that wealth and privilege had their responsibilities. Intellectual brilliance counted at these schools for less than leadership, artistic understanding for less than the development of sound character. Athletic competition was considered part of this development. Public service was one of the primary ideals at these institutions — "To serve is to reign" was the motto established at Groton by Endicott Peabody, the school's founder and headmaster — and that ideal was by and large met in practice, as is attested by the endless chain of alumni who went on to become U.S. presidents, secretaries of state, and other cabinet officers.

These arrangements, resulting in an oligarchical American leadership class, might have gone on for a good deal longer but for World War Two, after which things began to change, with higher education providing the foot in the door. First among the things to help bring this about was the GI Bill, which extended the educational franchise by providing financial support to veterans to attend college; and a much greater number of them did take advantage of the GI Bill than had been expected. After the discovery of Hitler's Final Solution, anti-Semitism began to be less easily expressed and less openly enacted in, among other places, university quota systems. (Harvard's and Yale's admission policies called for allowing roughly 13 percent of Catholics and Jews among their student bodies.) A decade or so later, the civil rights movement worked similarly to integrate American Negroes — as African Americans then were — into schools they once would not have thought of entering. Jews, Catholics, and blacks became teachers in the same institutions that earlier had restricted their entry as students. What was loosely called "the women's movement" helped push talented women forward into places from which they were hitherto excluded, among them the formerly all-male Ivy League colleges, which became coeducational. Women now began joining the job market in positions of serious responsibility. In time many women were themselves part of the elite, becoming partners in leading law firms, chief executive officers of powerful corporations, entrepreneurs of a significant kind.

None of this would have been possible without the spread of testing, specifically of the widespread use of the Scholastic Aptitude Test — the famous, scarifying, utterly crucial SAT. In *The Big Test,* Nicholas Lemann recounts in impressive detail the development of the SAT, which got a big push from the need for testing large numbers of people for the armed forces during World War Two. The installation of the SAT into admissions procedures changed the nature of the college population.

Its immediate effect was to turn American higher education away from its former basis in recent ancestry, in which the children of alumni were given first shot at entry into the best-regarded colleges and universities. After the arrival of the SATs, it was no longer sufficient for a boy or girl to have gone to one of the handful of elite prep schools and have a father or mother who preceded him or her there to gain almost automatic acceptance into Harvard, Yale, Princeton, Dartmouth, and the rest. The standard now became more nearly meritocratic, with grades and test results having increasingly greater import than family or the judgment of headmasters about a youth's good character. No more of the best and the brightest; now only the brightest would go forth, those kids who, when asked to supply three reasons for the Renaissance, came up with seven.

One might think this, on the face of it, a solid blow against snobbery: down with the old oligarchy, up with the new (at last genuine) merito-democracy. What it did above all was put pressure on children to perform well academically from an early age so that they could gain entry into one of the small number of colleges that would give them a substantial jump-start in life.

Allow me to name, in alphabetical order, what I think those top twenty or so colleges are: Amherst, Brown, California at Berkeley, Chicago, Columbia, Dartmouth, Duke, Georgetown, Harvard, Johns Hopkins, Michigan, Northwestern, Princeton, Smith, Stanford, Virginia, Yale, Wellesley, Wesleyan, and Williams. (Interesting that whenever one of the elite women's colleges — Vassar and Radcliffe most notably — became coeducational it lost its prestige, with Radcliffe losing its identity in the bargain.) Get your child into any of these schools, it is felt, and he or she is well on the way to . . . a superior graduate or professional school, making the right connections, getting the best job interview, crashing — make that dancing — into the good life.

Whether or not this is so, people tend to believe it, which goes a long way toward making it so. James Fallows, writing in the September 2001 issue of the *Atlantic,* suggests that it may not be so and cites a study that found that "the selectivity [that is, the number of applicants a school turns down] of a school made no significant difference in the students' later earnings." He mentions that the four richest men in America currently are "a dropout from Harvard, a dropout from the University of Illinois, a dropout from Washington State University, and a graduate of the University of Nebraska." He tosses in for good measure that during the past fifty or so years, presidents of the United States, along with one from Harvard, two from Yale, and two from the service academies, have come from "Southwest Texas State, Whittier, Michigan, Eureka, and Georgetown," and adds Harry S. Truman, who never went to college at all.

But none of this is likely to quiet all those middle- and upper-middle-class parents who are so agitatedly concerned about their children's education, and from the earliest age. In New York, Chicago, San Francisco, and Los Angeles, getting one's kids into one of the better private schools begins at preschool. The better private grade and high schools, in the major American cities, are all usually oversubscribed. A lot — from a parent's point of view, it must sometimes seem everything — is riding on these little acceptances. The latest figure on the cost of such private grade schools in Manhattan was $17,000 a year.

One sees the fight to gain entrance into what the world reckons the best schools in an upper-middle-class public institution such as New Trier High School on Chicago's suburban North Shore. Students at New Trier are tracked — that is, placed according to their presumed potential — upon entry as freshmen. They themselves, cheered on, not to say aimed, by their parents, do all they can to achieve success during their four years at the school. And success is measured clearly enough by the schools to which they are accepted. Among the highly motivated at New Trier, the unwritten program is known as Preparation H, standing not for the hemorrhoid relief salve but preparation for acceptance at Harvard. All efforts are bent toward the goal of getting into the superior college: extracurricular activities, summer jobs, charitable works, ambitious reading. One question is behind everything a bright kid at New Trier does: How will this look on my application to Duke (Brown, Princeton, Williams)? Students who put themselves through this torture no doubt emerge more disciplined young men and women, yet it does seem a sad way to surrender one's adolescence.

I have seen intensity of this kind in my own family. Without much encouragement from me, my eldest son, at Evanston Township High School, fell in among a group of fast-track academic kids who revved themselves up into a high lather of expectation. I was pleased by my son's ability to master academic skills: he taught himself to write, got nothing but A's in Latin, became editor of the high school paper. All the while I said not a word about wanting him to go to any particular university. Senior year he applied to Harvard, Virginia, Stanford, Michigan, and Chicago (the last a backup school, since he wanted to leave the city of Chicago). When his letters came in from the various offices of admission, he was rejected by Harvard, put on a waiting list at Virginia, and accepted by Michigan and Chicago. "You know, Dad," this then earnest and always good son said to me, "if I have to go to the University of Michigan, I guess my life is effectively over." "Do you truly feel that way?" I asked. "I do," he replied without hesitation. "If you do," I said, "then I think I shall not pay for Michigan, for if your life is *effectively* over, why waste the money on tuition?" The next week's mail brought a letter of acceptance from Stanford, which I suppose makes it a story with a happy ending. But the larger meaning of the story is the pressure that children put on themselves.

I do not know if my son received a good education at Stanford. As someone partially in the business of higher education, I have my doubts: he was able to pass through the place without any foreign language courses; he took no ancient history or philosophy. He did meet some bright kids; he made some good friends; he came out much more worldly than he had gone in. He had a good time. He was elected one of the school's student-body presidents. Stanford, which has prestige in the state of California, helped him land a job with a large investment firm. It worked; it paid off. Stanford has to have been considered a good deal, worth every dime.

"Go with the snobbery," I tell the occasional student who asks me where he or she ought to go to graduate school. "Why go to the Harvard [Law School]?" asks a member of the class of 2001 in a letter in response to an iconoclastic article on that school in *Esquire.* "It's the name, stupid!" The world, that great doofus, respects certain schools, even if you, after the experience of having gone there, if you are a person of any critical acumen, will probably learn not to. Still, most people are not going to know how thin it all is. Snobbery, ignorant snobbery, cannot but work to your advantage.

I have always felt fortunate to have gone to the University of Chicago because, first, it allows me to know with a certainty that I didn't miss out on anything; and, second, it suggests to people that I am, somehow or other, brilliant for having gone there. I also happen to think it was a better choice for me than Harvard-Yale-Princeton — or, as I think of them in shorthand, Yarvton. At Yarvton I would have been exposed to social snobbery of a kind I might not then have quite grasped, not to speak of possible anti-Semitism, which was freer and easier on the draw at those schools in the middle 1950s.

The intellectual snobbery of Chicago was at least based on something real — knowledge, brilliance, erudition — and my being Jewish cost me no discomfort.

The notion of "hot" colleges had not yet come into being when I was of college age. A hot college is one that suddenly becomes greatly desired by the young. In the late 1970s Brown became such a college; in the 1980s Duke became another; and both have remained, in this snobbish sense, hot. Brown seems a case of snobbery combined with a curriculum of such flexibility as almost not to exist. At Brown students needn't take any mathematics or foreign languages; they can construct a flashy major of their own devising in what is the intellectual equivalent of a salad bar; grades are amorphous, with failure scarcely a possibility. Everything, in short, is arranged around the notion of the student as customer or consumer. To this may be added what might be called a Studio 54 (after the once fashionably excluding dance club) student body, with lots of children of celebrities on campus. John F. Kennedy, Jr., went to Brown; so too did President Carter's daughter Amy. Diana Ross, Jane Fonda, Jordan's King Hussein, Calvin Klein, Ringo Starr, Ralph Lauren, Itzhak Perlman, Louis Malle, Giovanni Agnelli, and Marlon Brando sent children to Brown. Hey, yo, go for it!

Then there is New York University, good always new NYU, to which one's children go for theatrical, film, and other less than sobering studies. Holding classes in a number of midrise buildings in and around Washington Square, it has been able to attract a glittering faculty because of its location in Manhattan. NYU has an oddly ambiguous status. It's all right for one's kids to go there, though it's understood that it is nowhere near so presentable as Yarvton. NYU has somehow brilliantly positioned itself outside the mainstream in American high education, and yet it remains cozily in the snobbery rivulet by offering itself as something resembling an advance-guard institution. "Versace University," after the expensive and deliberately outré designer, I have heard it called, which, for accuracy, isn't too far off.

None of this is to say that there aren't superior teachers in all these various universities — I think of the historian of early America Gordon S. Wood at Brown and the literary critic and scholar Denis Donoghue at NYU, to name two teachers at the schools I have just mocked — but such teachers are isolated, seem almost accidental figures. Outside science and mathematics, good departments and solid liberal arts programs are rare to the point of being nonexistent. One hears that Carleton College still offers a strong education, or that Kenyon College, which has a bookstore that stays open twenty-four hours, is a serious place, but who really knows? Best, I think, to judge all contemporary American universities, with the exception of Cal Tech and MIT, as shoddy until proven good.

I have a friend, a political philosopher, who spent a year as a visiting professor at Harvard. "What was it like teaching there?" I asked him. "The students prefer you to be amusing and, if possible, brilliant, rather like a good movie," he said. "But both they and I know that main event in their lives has already taken place — that is, they were accepted at Harvard."

The journalist Murray Kempton long ago said that intellectual contentment in America consists of not giving a damn about Harvard. I would extend it to Yarvton generally and toss in the so-called hot colleges. But most university teachers never come close to achieving contentment on this point. For the snobbery at universities is not restricted to students and their parents and an outside world that doesn't know any better. I know this from teaching at Northwestern University, a school, as I think of it, at the crossroads of snobbery.

In the perfectly unpersuasive *U.S. News & World Report* surveys on higher education, Northwestern usually comes in fifteenth or sixteenth — close, you might say, but no cigar. A preponderance of its faculty has at one time or another studied at Yarvton or, on the West Coast, at Berkford (Berkeley-Stanford). I have always thought that, with the appropriate stationery from these schools, I could write letters offering Northwestern's teachers jobs and clear the joint of faculty in under a week's time. Apotheosis for the vast majority of Northwestern's nonscientific faculty would come with a beseeching letter offering a job at Yarvton. At Northwestern there was a teacher locally reverenced because, *mirabile dictu,* he actually turned down an offer from Harvard. Snobbery of the kind that goes on in universities allows for no loyalties, to either colleagues or institutions. You take the better offer and — not exactly run — prance.

I once had a student tell me that he was the only one among his acquaintances who was happy to be at Northwestern. Everyone else he knew had hoped for Yarvton or Brown or Duke, with Northwestern as the fallback school. Not a great high school student, he felt himself lucky to have been admitted and seemed to have made the most of it. But the larger point is that it is impossible to be unaware of the intricate hierarchy of colleges and universities and the snobbish ranking that results from this hierarchy. The sociologist Pierre Bourdieu, who sees society as an organized competition in which status is the main prize, has always considered universities as decisive in this competition.

Tell me that you went to the University of California at Santa Barbara, and while envying you the lovely scenery upon which you were permitted to gaze for four years, I also note that you apparently weren't good enough to get into the University of California at Berkeley. Pity. Tell me you went to Michigan State, I think much the same about your not being able to cut it at Michigan in Ann Arbor. Of course, if you're at Michigan, why weren't you good enough for dear old Yarvton? More's the pity. It's a mug's game, really.

Snobbery often resides most comfortably where substance is absent, and for a long while now snobbery has deeply infected higher education, among faculty and students and parents alike. In its way the university scene may be the place where snobbery is more pervasive than anywhere else. One of the lessons of a fundamentally sound undergraduate education, one might have thought, would be to tell the difference between appearance and reality. In American higher education, it doesn't quite work that way. As in snobbery, so in education: appearance is reality. Like the man said, "It's the name, stupid."

14

Unclubbable

I F I AM CORRECT about the degraded quality of American colleges and universities, they should probably, with a few exceptions, be considered as clubs of a sort, the more highly regarded among them being expensive, difficult to join, and exclusive (which is also of course to say, excluding), as the best clubs always have been. Like clubs, too, some are better than others: Harvard is a better club than the University of Minnesota, Princeton than Purdue, Stanford than Maryland.

Clubs are as much about keeping people out as joining them together, which is why they have always had a central place in the history of snobbery. Tocqueville early caught the force and significance of what he called voluntary associations in America, that vast variety of groups from citizen-run fire departments to professional organizations, but that youthful genius failed to stress that many of these, in their exclusionary function, also entailed compulsory disassociation.

In the old days of service clubs — when every town of ten thousand or more had a Rotary, Kiwanis, Lions, Elks, Moose, and the rest — there was an unspoken hierarchy, with one of these clubs having a higher standing than the others. College fraternities and sororities operated on the same principle — the principle, that is, of attempting to establish superiority over others in the field. Kappa Kappa Gamma, Kappa Alpha

Theta, Pi Beta Phi — and it didn't take a young woman at any college in America long to know which was the best, the most desirable sorority, though these would vary somewhat from campus to campus.

One joins a club for fellowship, but one of its perks is, inevitably, the quiet pleasure of knowing — or at least hoping — that not only can't everyone join, but one's own club is just a touch better than others of its kind. Even with the best intentions and histories of good works behind them, clubs are snobbery organized. Create a concept and reality leaves the room; create a club and pretensions to democracy disappear. It was ever thus; it can never be otherwise.

I grew up in clubbish surroundings, and superficial though I know them to be, I have never quite got over them. Not always but often enough when I encounter a public figure, I measure him by my old high school standards. When I see Senator Joseph Lieberman on television, for example, I say he looks to me no better than a Gargoyle, a member of a club of reasonably high-achieving Jewish boys who weren't good athletes, hadn't much style, were untouched by strong humor or brilliance. And please understand, I don't dislike Joseph Lieberman. This may be a stronger judgment on me than on him, but there it is, and I seem to be stuck with it.

The most famous remark about clubs is Groucho Marx's: "I don't care to belong to any club that will accept me as a member." Amusing as it is, containing a grain of insight as it does — how good, after all, can any club be that would accept so obvious a schlepper as deep down I know myself to be? — its truth quotient isn't finally all that high. However low our opinion of ourselves, most of us nonetheless would be pleased to have been found acceptable in certain quarters. Although I don't go to Paris, nor play golf, nor travel much to England, still, if money weren't a concern, I would accept membership if offered in the aristocratic Jockey Club in Paris, the tony Augusta National Golf Club in Georgia, the Atheneum on Pall Mall. *"J'y suis, j'y suis,"* gleefully wrote the young Henry James to his family when accepted as a member of the Reform Club in London. I am here, I have arrived, I am established, he was saying. And being there, having a sense of arrival, of establishment, is of course the principal lure of clubs.

I belong to only one club, the Tavern Club in Chicago, a dining club with a fine view of the city. A generous reader of mine arranged to have me accepted as an honorary member. (I was asked to undergo an interview with two older members, perhaps to show that I wore no ponytail and ate with a knife and fork.) Honorary membership means not having to pay monthly dues, which is pleasing. (I do pay for my and my guests' food and drink.) The Tavern Club was founded, in the 1920s, by a few Chicago drama critics and architects, though its membership today is made up more and more of lawyers and various corporation characters. I go there for convenience, not for prestige. Near its entrance is a photograph of Carl Sandburg and Frank Lloyd Wright, former members. "Note that photograph," I sometimes say to people I take to the Tavern Club. "Just goes to show the joint wasn't very distinguished in the past, either." I hope they realize I'm not kidding. I do not use this club very often — perhaps five or six times a year — and suspect that if I had to pay the monthly dues of $150, I should probably drop out.

A friend some while ago offered to put me up for an out-of-town membership in the Century Club of New York. I demurred. I take pleasure in the look and feel of the Century Club, with its grand Stanford White building on Forty-third Street, off Fifth Avenue. I've been taken to it many times by friends, and an editorial board on which I sat for many years had its biannual meetings and dinners there. Two of the most pleasant intellectual meetings I have known — with the novelist Ralph Ellison and with the journalist Joseph Mitchell — took place there and make it the setting of delightful memories for me.

A swell place, the Century Club, but I get to New York too seldom to make the fees for an out-of-town membership — $1,000 for entrance, $895 annually — worth it. The club has no sleeping rooms, so my membership would wind up costing me roughly $450 per meal. (The nice thing about this kind of math is that it allows me to know with some precision

how much the kind of prestige of belonging to particular
clubs is worth to me, which usually turns out to be not very
much.) There is the additional problem that, though once
mildly pleased to encounter famous people from the arts,
publishing, journalism, and government among its members,
I now find I'd rather not see most of them. ("Joe, you know
Edward Albee, don't you?" Groan.) The personal moral of
the story is not the Grouchoesque one that I wouldn't care to
join any club that will accept me as a member, but instead that
when it becomes possible for me to join such clubs, my interest seems long since to have departed.

My first memory of clubs is of a certain plushness. Neither
golfers nor athletic in any way, my parents had no interest in
city or country clubs, and their joining one was never a real
possibility. The first club I was taken to was a country club
north of Chicago called (with no sensitivity to cliché whatsoever) Green Acres. I was sixteen. The father of a friend of
mine belonged, a physician who golfed and whose medical
specialty I once cited as real estate. It was exclusively Jewish,
and its membership was made up of physicians, lawyers,
owners of car agencies, borax men, and other *nouveau riche*-
making businesses.

My memory here is of heavyset men freshly emergent from
showers and the *shvitz*, beclogged, swathed in thick towels,
eating blood-red watermelon and playing gin rummy while
young Filipinos, a cadre of valets in white shirts and blue
pants with a gold stripe along the outer leg, rushed about seeing to the small comforts of these men. In the dining room a
buffet served the pinkest beef, the largest prawns, and fruits of
Edenic quality. The overwhelming impression was of opu-
lence unrestrained by any foreign (or domestic) notions of
elegance, which was, as we used to say in Chicago in those
days, fine by me.

I was also taken to the Covenant Club, a Jewish city club,
by friends whose parents belonged. We played basketball or
handball in the gym, swam, took the steam, had a swell steak
sandwich in the men's grill. The most notable, and just
slightly notorious, member of the Covenant Club was Sid

Luckman, the quarterback of the Chicago Bears in the forties and early fifties, who would pocket himself away with a few rough-looking pals for what one assumed were high-stakes gin rummy games.

Although I didn't then understand the force of this distinction, the Covenant Club's membership was composed of Jews of Eastern European background, which are my own origins. Another city club, the Standard Club, only a few blocks away on Plymouth Court, was in those days made up chiefly of Jews of German background, who held themselves as grander than their Eastern European coreligionists. If the former thought the latter coarse, the latter thought the former stuffed shirts. (In Yiddish, a German Jew is known as a *yekke*, which means jacket, and derives from the stiffness of the German Jews in never taking off their suit coats. An old joke asks what is the difference between a virgin and a *yekke*, to which the answer is "A *yekke* remains a *yekke*.") There were also German-Jewish country clubs, such as the Lakeshore, whose golf course was laid out by Frederick Law Olmstead, designer of Central Park in New York.

(A digression here on the snobberies among and between ethnic groups, some of them historical. I recall in the early 1960s coming upon a copy of *Jet*, the African-American magazine, that someone had left in the seat next to me in the IRT subway whose cover story was "New York's Puerto Rican Problem." I was once going to rent a house from its Greek owner in Babylon, on Long Island, who, when picking me up, asked if I was Jewish. When I said I was, he averred: "Before we begin, Mr. Epstein, I think you should know that it takes four Syrians, three Italians, and two Jews to cheat a Greek." Ethnic groups, I have sometimes thought, are merely the largest clubs of all.)

I had no friends whose parents were members of the Standard Club, and my distant sense of its membership in those days was of small, stern-faced men — Jewish bankers, lawyers, and investment counselors playing with big numbers — in dark gray suits and neckties with quiet patterns who were not so much proud of as resigned to making the

best of being Jewish, though among other requirements for
membership was the extent — it was assumed to be high —
of one's giving to Jewish charities. Members of the old Standard Club prided themselves on their solidity, and were
probably correct to do so.

If the Covenant Club excluded by money — the initiation
fee and dues were not small — the Standard Club excluded
by both money and ancestry. Some might see a harsh justice
in the fact that in those days the respected members of the
Standard Club couldn't get into the Chicago Club, the Illinois Athletic Club, and other city and country clubs from
which all Jews were relentlessly restricted.

Which recalls the story about the two successful New
Yorkers from the garment district, Lou Shapiro and Irv Rabinowitz, standing in front of the Union League Club on Fifth
Avenue. When Shapiro asks Rabinowitz what the building is
they are standing in front of, and is told that it is a club,
Shapiro says, "Great. Think I'll join. I could use a *shvitz* and
some herring after a day on Seventh Avenue." When Rabinowitz tells him that he has no chance to get in, a Jew hasn't
been a member of the Union League Club since its founding,
Shapiro, stirred by the dare in his friend's voice, bets him
$100,000 that in three years he will gain membership. Rabi-
nowitz ups the stakes to a quarter of a million. Shapiro proceeds to have a total makeover: undergoing plastic surgery,
changing his name, taking voice lessons to alter his accent,
inventing a new résumé. With thirty days to go, beautifully
tanned, in a Savile Row suit, Lou Shapiro walks into the office
of the executive secretary of the Union League Club and an-
nounces that he would like to apply for membership. The
secretary, looking him over approvingly, informs him that he
need answer only a few questions on the application, which
he himself would be delighted to fill out for him.

"Name?"

"Townsend Birmingham Baxter," says Shapiro, brandish-
ing his newly changed moniker in his newly acquired mid-
Atlantic accent.

"Schools attended?"

"Groton. Yale. Balliol, the latter as a Rhodes scholar."

"Law firm that handles your legal business?"

"Sullivan and Cromwell."

"Financial firm?"

"J. P. Morgan."

"This is all excellent. Only one more question. Religion?"

"Ah," says the former Lou Shapiro, "*goy,* of course."

In a real-life variant of this joke, Sol M. Linowitz, the former chairman of the Xerox Corporation and ambassador to the Organization of American States, used to take me to an elegant club in Washington called the F Street Club. Understated, out of the way, it had a dignified maitre d' and pleasant Irish waitresses. No menu was presented; a single dish was served to all, but the food was always delicious. Often we had a room to ourselves, in which we traded one Jewish joke after another. The one I just told may have stimulated Sol Linowitz to tell me that when Ambassador Ellsworth Bunker put him up for the F Street Club, informing him that it was a place where one could have a lunch meeting where privacy was guaranteed, he, Sol Linowitz, checking the membership list, noted that his was the only Jewish name on it. He went forthwith to report this to the club's manager, saying that this felt awkward; it made him feel, don't you know, as if he might be something like a token, don't you see. No more was said. Within a few months, other Jewish names appeared on the membership list. Nicely handled all around, I'd say.

In my youth, as it does today, the Standard Club had the best kitchen in the city of Chicago. The club hasn't been able to maintain its German-Jewish exclusivity, for the *yekke* line has long since been broken by intermarriage — to Eastern European Jews, chiefly, though not to them alone. One goes into the place now and encounters brash lawyers, commodities traders, real estate operators with expensive haircuts, gaudy wristwatches, and overpriced designer clothes, and women with money but no interesting secrets of the kind once held by the wives whose husbands had been members there. Except for its food and possible convenience — if one has an office nearby, say — there is no compelling reason to join, and I am told that, with more and more people living in the suburbs, the Standard Club worries about its membership dropping precipitously.

Ten or so years ago I was asked to speak to a dinner club in Chicago called the Wayfarers, whose members constituted the city's cultural and educational establishment: presidents of local universities, the chairman of the PBS station, local publishers, successful architects, foundation executives, a small selection of presentable academics, a few cultivated physicians and businessmen — an attempt, in short, to approximate in Chicago something akin to the Boston Brahmin tradition. The Wayfarers met one Tuesday a month (excluding the summer months) at the old Chicago Club to have a few drinks, eat a decent dinner always beginning with oyster chowder, and hear a talk not to exceed half an hour on a subject of cultural or civic interest. The annual cost was $250, which paid for a year's dinners.

After my talk, I was invited to become a member of the Wayfarers. Why not, I thought, membership would get me out a bit more, perhaps give me a better sense of the city in which I live. The club had a number of members for whom I had genuine regard. I joined. I attended meetings. I met a few impressive people, including a physician named Henry Betts, who was the head of the Rehabilitation Institute of Chicago, which treats patients who have been in terrible accidents or who have intractable physical disabilities.

One evening at dinner, Dr. Betts introduced our table to two young physicians training under him at the institute whose names I didn't catch. In the interlude between dinner and that evening's talk, he sent one of these young men with a $10 bill down to get him a cigar. When the young man returned, with a Macanudo cigar, Betts said, "Thank you, Willie, but didn't you forget my change?" As the young man dug into his pocket, I came out of my daze to realize that this Willie was William Kennedy Smith, who had been prosecuted for alleged rape in Florida and whose Kennedyness obviously didn't phase Henry Betts. Good man, Dr. Betts — the kind of man I'd invite to join my club, if I had one, any day.

But I would have needed at least one incident of this kind each month to keep my interest in the Wayfarers even marginally engaged. Dutifully, I went to the club's meetings for a few years. I even put up a friend, a brilliant jurist, for membership. I drove to meetings with a man named Raymond Mack, a sociologist who had been the provost of Northwestern and whose company I much enjoyed. Moments occurred when I felt a touch of that snobbish satisfaction that membership in even mildly distinguished groups can bring. Rank has its privileges, and I suppose I am still sometimes pleased that others assume I have middling rank and thus deserve minor privileges.

The problem, though, was that among the Wayfarers I found myself bored a very dark navy blue. The talks, I understood, were meant to be a bit dull, but most of them pushed the envelope into the thin air of dullness where one gasped for mental oxygen. The best parts of the evening for me tended to be the drives up and back with Ray Mack. Whenever I missed a meeting I felt relieved, like taking off a raccoon coat in August. After three years, I resigned, and it hasn't since occurred to me to regret it.

I have to conclude that I am unclubbable. Unlike John O'Hara, who kept embossed seals of his various clubs on his gold cigarette case, I apparently take no continuing pleasure in clubs nor any real satisfaction in the thought that I have been asked to join a few of them. Might this be because my snobbery is of a different order than that which membership in even moderately exclusive clubs stimulates? Might it be that, unlike Groucho, I am convinced that I am too clever to take the pretensions of any club altogether seriously? No, my snobbery is of a different kind, the kind I think of as intellectual snobbery.

15

....

Intellectual Snobbery, or
The (Million or So) Happy Few

S<small>NOBBERY</small> has traditionally been founded on birth, access to power, fame, in some quarters wealth, and (on occasion) knowledge. But if knowledge doesn't register on the snobbery scale for everyone, among people in what one might think of as the knowledge business — among people, that is, who fancy themselves, in the loosest sense of the term, intellectuals — snobbery runs more rampant than bacteria through the kitchen of a Tijuana slow-food restaurant.

Nobody is born an intellectual, or with intellectual interests, or even with much in the way of a natural propensity for those things of the mind that most excite people who think themselves intellectuals: ideas, art, and culture. A high intelligence quotient may help, but it isn't an absolute requirement; many people with stratospheric IQs — among them people doing high-level science — have little interest in things that absorb the thoughts of intellectuals. Intellectual interests have to be learned, acquired, cultivated. They are in some sense artificial, a construct of a sort, and chiefly the work of previous intellectuals.

An intellectual is a man or woman for whom ideas have a reality that they do not possess for most people, and these ideas are central to the existence of the intellectual. Because of this extraordinary investment in ideas, the intellectual is occasionally admired for a certain purity of motivation, but he or she is just as often thought of as unreal, out of it, often a comical, sometimes a dangerous character. Historically, the intellectual has been guilty of all these things.

Intellectuality is the quality of being able to talk about ideas — political, historical, artistic ideas — in a confident, coherent, or (best of all) dazzling way. If not everyone admires intellectuals, intellectuality tends to garner praise, especially from the social classes that think themselves educated or enlightened, among whom I include most but far from all members of the vast army of Ph.D.s now roaming the universities.

Whenever intellectuality is on display, an air of edginess, contention, one-upmanship, put-down, or general nervousness I won't say pervades but usually hovers over the proceedings. All this provides fertile ground for snobbery. Most intellectuals I have known have had at least a tincture of snobbery; it seems almost to come with the job. Sometimes the snobbery is intramural, or among other intellectuals exclusively; sometimes it looks down on all who make no claim to intellectuality; and sometimes much more than a tincture is entailed: "The melancholy thing about the world," wrote V. S. Naipaul, an authentic intellectual, "is that it is full of stupid and common people, and the world is run for the benefit of the stupid and the common." Sometimes, as I say, much more than a tincture.

In certain pockets of intellectual life, traditional snobbery crops up in high relief. In American publishing there has always been a strong strain of traditional snobbery. Publishing is a business that attracts people with a disdain for business and a yearning for culture. Book editors tend to be paid low but lunch high, taking agents and authors to expensive restaurants. Some of the most impressive restaurant snobbery I've seen has been at lunches to which I have been taken by editors, including one at which an editor asked the maitre d' at a French restaurant why, oh why, did they leave the cheese out of refrigeration for so long?

The tradition of snobbery among those in publishing perhaps begins with the oenological pretensions of Alfred Knopf, founder of the firm of Alfred A. Knopf, Inc. The story is told that Knopf's brother, being well aware of these pretensions, invited Alfred over for dinner and laid in an expensive bottle of wine. When Knopf failed to react to the wine, his brother asked him what he thought of it. "How can I tell," Knopf is supposed to have replied, "drinking it out of these glasses." I once heard Clifton Fadiman, a longtime judge of the Book-of-the-Month Club, say with a sigh that all that remained of interest in life for him were a "few wines and certain cheeses." He was sixty-three at the time and had thirty years yet to live; let us hope that those wines and those cheeses were available in sufficient supply to see him off the planet. Michael Korda, of Simon & Schuster, who likes to be photographed in jodhpurs, wrote a book called *Power! How to Get It, How to Use It*, whose impulse seems to have been how to encourage a feeling of hopelessness in others and make snobbery work for one's profit in a corporate setting. (His uncle, Alexander Korda, the movie director and producer, was known in London as a snob of the highest power.) Jason Epstein, for years a vice president at Random House, states in a recent memoir that he doesn't keep a paperback in the house, and has elsewhere reported on his pleasure in buying rare Chinese herbs for his gourmet cooking and acquiring only the best culinary equipment.

In academic life, snobbery is stronger in some places than others. In her novel *The Mind-Body Problem*, Rebecca Goldstein posits the notion that the further an academic's subject is from the truth, the more snobbish he or she is likely to be. In this amusing scheme, mathematicians and physicists care least about clothes, wine, food, and other such potentially snobbish refinements, while people in English, history, and modern language departments, whose subjects put them so much further from the solid ground of unarguable truths, care a great deal, since their reputation for being cultivated is really all they have going for them. Quite nuts, or so it might seem, if lots of evidence didn't support it.

The snobbery of intellectuals may be owing to the uncertainty behind the mask of authoritativeness intellectuals feel the need to wear. Snobbery also insinuates itself in intellectual life in ways far from purely intellectual. The novelist Jean Stafford once remarked that "the greatest snobs in the world are bright New York literary Jews," by which she meant the crowd of intellectuals around *Partisan Review* and *Commentary* in the 1940s and '50s, almost all of whom, born to immigrant parents, came from insecure social positions and were thus perhaps more susceptible to snobbery than most people.

But then a general nervousness has always been present in America when it comes to intellectual attainments. With the large increase of Americans attending colleges and universities after World War Two, anyone who had been to college was almost required to show an interest in culture, which meant in novels, painting, plays, serious music. (Pierre Bourdieu has written that "nothing more clearly affirms one's 'class,' infallibly classifies, than tastes in music." He also notes that one's taste in sports tends to identify one, the range running from hockey to polo.) Russell Lynes, an editor at *Harper's Magazine* in the 1950s, wrote what was to be an essay that divided people on the basis of their tastes in culture into highbrows, middlebrows, and lowbrows.

All this would change toward the end of the century, but when I was coming into intellectual consciousness, the highbrow, middlebrow, lowbrow distinctions were important, even crucial. There wasn't much room for negotiation, either. To be called a middlebrow was to be more roundly condemned than to be called a lowbrow, though highbrow, like first class, was the only way to go. Real as they were, and remain, these distinctions nonetheless inevitably bring snobbery in their trail. Even among political radicals, these cultural markers had their snobbish currency. "Stalinists were middlebrow, the Trotskyists were highbrow," Irving Howe, himself a Trotskyist in the 1930s, remarks in the film *Arguing the World.* "We prided ourselves on reading Joyce and Thomas Mann and Proust . . . whereas they were reading palookas like Howard Fast." Which only goes to show that,

even among Communists and socialists, room was found, in
the domain of the intellect, for snobbery.

I cannot be certain when, precisely, I determined to become an intellectual. But the notion first took hold at the University of Chicago, where the intellectual life was made to
seem tantamount to the good life. In my desire to present myself to the world as an intellectual, I labored under a little
technical difficulty: I didn't know anything. The great benefit
to me of the University of Chicago in this endeavor was that it
provided many important clues about where to go to learn a
few essential things, which, forthwith, I set out to do.

A few decades later, much of this time spent reading, I
emerged with a broad if somewhat sketchy knowledge of
Western history and culture. I learned a few things about the
literature of America, England, France, and Russia, and
rather less about those of Italy, Germany, and Spain. I listened
to lots of classical music, went occasionally to the ballet,
viewed a respectable amount of visual art, and I read a vast
quantity of criticism on all these subjects, informing myself
about what others had thought about them.

Since I was fortunate enough to arrange my life so that
this acquisition of knowledge became almost a full-time job,
my cultural hunting and gathering were fairly widespread,
though always tending toward the general, as is the way of the
intellectual, who is often more interested in the ideas behind
the subject than in the subject itself. How far did my culture
go? To name names: in literature it ran, roughly, as deep down
as Philip Guadella and Lord Berners; in music to Corelli
and Reynaldo Hahn; in visual art to Caillebotte and A. M.
Cassandre — with, let me admit, vast Gobi-like stretches of
ignorance in between.

Not that there need be a direct competitiveness about such
things, but no matter how informed I became, there were
always people who knew much more than I. Confident of
my own possession of culture, I would nonetheless lapse into
occasional error, sometimes late in my life. As recently as a
few years ago, I was blithely pronouncing the modern Greek
poet C. P. Cavafy's last name Cav-a-*fee*, with the accent on

the last syllable, until a friend with many foreign languages took me aside to let me know it was properly pronounced Ca-*va*-fee, with the accent on the second syllable. ("The mnemonic device, Joe, is," he said with a sweet and unsnobbish smile, "You're the Kareem in my Cavafy.") The other day another friend, also no snob, told me about an acquaintance of ours who recently took over a gallery-shop selling paintings, prints, and lithographs in a swank hotel and that he didn't know how to pronounce the word *genre* or the name Seurat. I cringed before saluting him on the beginning of a great new career.

In intellectual life, everyone begins as a novice. Some have the slight advantage of being brought up in bookish homes, although in America, for some reason, the most impressive intellectuals seem to have been brought up in homes where culture played almost no part; perhaps it was the absence of culture that increased their hunger for it. But turning oneself into an intellectual is all on-the-job training. From learning correct pronunciation to acquiring cultural literacy to becoming adept at playing with ideas to discovering which ideas, personages, issues are more important than others — for all these things there are no schools, no self-help booklets, only one's own mental energies, love of the life of the mind, greed for that loose collection of knowledge that comes under the baggy-pants category known as the cultural.

As admirable as all this sounds, how does snobbery get into the game? It gets in because American intellectuals, real and aspiring, generally feel themselves on shaky terrain. The reasons for this go back a long way. When I was at the University of Chicago, while vast quantities of names and new forms (new to me, at least) of knowledge flew in at me, one point emerged with perfect clarity: in matters intellectual and cultural, Europe was superior. Europeans had history on their side: they lived among the great monuments of art; theirs were the countries that gave birth to the towering geniuses of thought and art; they had direct historical experience of Communism and Nazism, the dark political events of the century. Orwell, Camus, Sartre, and de Beauvoir; Silone,

Koestler, Arendt, and Jaspers; these were among the leading
European intellectuals, and next to them American intellectuals seemed slight, yokels really.

The philosopher Sidney Hook once told me that he didn't
think Hannah Arendt all that intelligent, but that American
intellectuals were cowed by her German education (she knew,
among other languages, ancient Greek) and European outlook. He may well have been correct: as improbable as it is to
think of Arendt as anything other than the German intellectual she was, if one imagines her as American born, her intellectual luster immediately falls away.

More recently, American academics have gone well over
the top in their upward-looking snobbish reverence for the
intellectual phenomenon known as Bloomsbury. Effete, elite,
and themselves impressively snobbish in their view of the
world, the more the Bloomsbury writers and artists — Virginia Woolf, Lytton Strachey, Vanessa Bell, E. M. Forster,
Roger Fry — get written about by Americans, the thinner, almost to the point of disappearing, they seem. Yet academics
of a certain kind never seem to tire of them.

Much of the snobbery of American intellectuals, then, has
its roots in the cultural inferiority that Americans have felt in
comparison with their European counterparts. The sad irony
is that the United States for some decades now, has been the
main site of contemporary artistic and intellectual interest; in
painting, literature, music, and film, America is where the action is. Yet American intellectuals continue to feel, somehow,
inferior. And those among them who play what I think of as
the European game, if they play it well, win, for their efforts at
superior simulation, the world's prizes and adulation.

Consider through the lens of snobbery the career of Susan
Sontag, whose fame is greater than her achievements and out
of proportion to the amount of pleasure her essays, stories,
novels, and films have given the people who have troubled to
read or see them. Her prose lacks personality; it reads, as
the English novelist John Wain once said, like "translator's
English — the sort of composite idiom one gets from great
Continental novels one first meets in translation during ado-

lescence." Edmund Wilson referred to her style as "far-fetched, pretentious, esoteric." Susan Sontag's message, though not always easily made out, would appear to be one of (unearned) desolation, like Samuel Beckett's but with less talent and on a higher budget. The only thing that appears to run really deep in her is her humorlessness. And yet among the enlightened classes (you will pardon my leaving the quotation marks off the word *enlightened*) Sontag is nearly as well known as any writer in America. What is the attraction? How to explain it?

The explanation is to be found, I believe, in a winning combination of snobbery and self-promotion that have gone into her career. (The latter is set out in impressive detail in Carl Rollyson and Lisa Paddock's *Susan Sontag: The Making of an Icon*.) Sontag was carefully packaged by her publisher as broodingly beautiful, avant-garde, Frenchified, grimly serious. She also happened to have been a writer of perfectly acceptable radically chic views — when young, a knockout American woman who did a fairly decent impression of a European intellectual.

Outside America, interesting to note, the Susan Sontag act never quite took flight. Her first English publisher dropped her because of low sales. She never caught on in France. And why, after all, should she have, doing as she did an imitation of a French intellectual when the French had more than enough of the real thing on hand. Her left-wing politics — very late in the day, in 1982 in fact, she recanted and came out against totalitarian Communism — would have made her a laughingstock among dissident Soviet artists and intellectuals. She wasn't sufficiently stylish for the Italians. Only in America, where both a snobbish interest in European culture and a lingering feeling of cultural inferiority still reigned, could she have succeeded as she did. "Susan," as Yoram Kaniuk, an Israeli writer remarked, "has used America better than anyone."

Susan Sontag was for many years a contributor to the *New York Review of Books*. If one wanted to study intellectual snobbery in America through a single institution, one could scarcely do better than peruse the contents of and contributors to that biweekly journal of politics and culture. One

sensed when the journal began, in 1962, at the time of the
New York newspaper strike that shut down the *New York
Times* and its *Book Review,* that it had a large snobbish com-
ponent. Its first contributors included W. H. Auden, Edmund
Wilson, Robert Lowell, Mary McCarthy, Isaiah Berlin, and
Igor Stravinsky (usually being interviewed by Robert Craft).
These men and women represented not only culture at its
pinnacle but culture with a cachet — the cachet here residing
in their international, cosmopolitan, in good part English feel
and connection. If culture can be said to have a social class,
the *New York Review* clearly traveled upper class.

The poet Robert Lowell, one of the founders of the *New
York Review,* is another example of how snobbishness can
work in American intellectual life. A large, disheveled man
with a genuine mental illness — he was a manic-depressive
who fairly regularly flipped out in horrendous ways, one of
them being his stating the belief that Adolf Hitler was no
fool — Lowell was far from talentless and possessed real literary culture, all acquired by hard work. But much of his prestige, one couldn't help notice, was owing to his ancestry,
which was impressive as American ancestry goes and practically royalty among American intellectuals, whose own social
origins tend to be middle and lower middle class. Lowell
didn't hesitate to play what I suppose we should now call the
ancestor card. *Life Studies,* the book that made him a great
figure, had a clearly upper-class accent and setting, being in
good part about his family and upbringing, which was of
course the world he knew. Still, his poem "My Last Afternoon
with Uncle Devereux Winslow" wouldn't, let us face it, carry
quite the same glow with the title "My Last Afternoon with
Uncle Sammy Shapiro."

Norman Mailer, in his Vietnam protest book, *Armies of the
Night,* compared his own grubby social condition to that of
Lowell's elevated one: "What do you [Lowell] know about
getting fat against your will, and turning into a clown of an arriviste baron, when you would rather be an eagle or a count,
or rarest of all, some natural aristocrat [Lowell again] from

these damned democratic states." Poor Norman Mailer, always behind his times, was still smarting under the old Wasp model of snobbery.

Writers are among the greatest of snobs, and during its great days — roughly from 1963 to 1984—they longed to write for the *New York Review*. If there is guilt by association, glory is available by the same route. The prospect of having one's prose appear between an Igor Stravinsky interview and an essay by the art critic E. H. Gombrich was sufficient to cause many American academics to quiver and swoon. The Anglophilic role in the magazine was large; some issues had more English than American contributors, including intellectuals who had been made lords (among them H. R. Trevor-Roper, Noel Annan, and Solly Zuckerman); a joke went the rounds that when one of the journal's two principal editors went to London, he was treated as if he were the Viceroy of India home on furlough. So successful was all this that the English actually devised a journal, the *London Review of Books*, modeled on the New York version.

No journal was ever so successful as the *New York Review* among American academics. Every two weeks a fresh issue would arrive, fill up campus pigeonhole mail slots, and be brought home by university teachers eager to be instructed on what they ought to think about art, literature, music, and above all politics. The *New York Review* made the snobbishly brilliant connection between high culture and radical politics, making left-wing views seem integral to highbrow culture. Along with the powerhouse names — Stravinsky, Auden, Wilson, Lowell, and the rest — others scored heavily by appearing in the journal: Gore Vidal, Susan Sontag, Elizabeth Hardwick, Christopher Lasch. The left-wing iconoclastic journalist I. F. Stone made a comeback via the *New York Review*. None would have had quite the renown they did without their appearances in its pages. To be sure, it published many useful, brilliant, even grand things. It is perhaps the only journal of its kind in America to have run in the financial black since soon after its founding, owing to American publishers' eagerness to place their ads in its pages. But its reputation derived from its snobbishness as much as from its intellectual dazzle.

Academic jobs opened up at Harvard, Yale, Princeton, and Chicago for academics whose work appeared in the *New York Review,* whose intellectual validation also meant professional and even social validation. It was not a place where new talent was discovered, but publication there was the mark that a young writer — Bruce Chatwin, Julian Barnes, Robert Stone — had really arrived, after testing his mettle elsewhere. It would never attack the sacred cows that it had let loose on the lawn — Salman Rushdie, Gore Vidal, or Susan Sontag — no matter how goofily, gloriously, incredibly wrong-headed they might be.

Although it is beginning to slip now — with no Auden, Wilson, Berlin, Stravinsky et alia on the scene — for years the *New York Review* remained academia's house organ, the spiritual home of people who pretended they were all out for the powerless without ever for a moment being able to envision themselves outside that utopia where good taste and intelligence, intellectual and social power combine. It was the journal of choice for those happy few (hundred thousand) left-leaning, right-living intellectuals, happily safe atop a cloud of nearly celestial snobbery.

16

The Snob in Politics

MAN, " said Aristotle, in perhaps his most memorable phrase, "is by nature a political animal." And so perhaps in a general sense man, and woman with him, is. But not all or even most of us are very political, at least not in modern life. Politics is about power, and while no one wishes, or can stand for long, to be or even feel absolutely without power, most of us don't think at great length about it — about how to acquire it, how to take it from someone else, how to use it for our own benefit, how to advance our own ideas concerning how society ought to be organized, or about much else in the realm of the political. Aside from wanting those people to hold office whose views seem to us congenial or roughly congruent to our own, or appeal to our special interests or social-class tastes, politics is not the route through which we seek or expect to find happiness. Megalomaniacs apart, politics is for most of us about something very different from power. I happen to think that this something has a lot to do with snobbery.

"Impotence and sodomy are socially O.K.," wrote Evelyn Waugh, "but birth control is flagrantly middle class." Now there is a sentence that gets a person's attention. One of the things it means, of course, is that much behavior, the most private behavior, is conditioned by social class and has to do

with taste. In a letter to his friend Nancy Mitford, Waugh lists
a number of other things that made one, in his view, seem
middle class: to decant claret, not to decant champagne, certain kinds of notepaper, saying *luncheon* instead of *lunch,* and
more. Middle class is clearly not a thing that Waugh ever
wished to be, once he had acquired some money and set himself up as a squire.

In a more rigidly stratified society than America has long
been, a snob, which Evelyn Waugh most assuredly was, might
separate himself in one of a thousand ways, from claret to
notepaper, from impotence to sodomy, most having to do
with social class. In America, we have found other ways to
separate ourselves, and none perhaps more insistent in recent
years than through political opinions. Political opinions here
sometimes tend to be worn as proudly as Savile Row suits
and as subtly as a wafer-thin $5,000 Omega wristwatch with a
plain brown leather band. Opinions tend to become ways of
identifying a person not only politically but socially. Not to
be a practicing Catholic and yet to be against abortion, for
example, is to risk tossing oneself in with all those terribly déclassé Christian fundamentalists, not to speak of the loonies
who shoot up abortion clinics and other assorted antedilu-
vians. At least it is to risk seeming so in many circles. "Style
is class," said Trotsky, "not alone in art, but above all in
politics."

In a thin political culture, political opinions are one more
way — for many people a significant way — of setting oneself
apart from, and, more important, above the next person.
Apart and above is, of course, where the snob wants to be.
Politics in its contemporary phase is certainly one way to get
him or her there. There are various political paths to this sim-
gle goal, but all entail establishing oneself as deeply enlightened and morally superior. Politics in America, in its nonpro-
fessional, un-smoke-filled-room aspect, sometimes seems to
be about little other than establishing the fineness and ultimately the moral superiority of one's views.

A way to establish one's moral superiority in recent decades has been to situate oneself firmly in one of the country's

victim groups, and there has never been a larger stock from which to choose than now. At one time or another these groups have included African Americans, Jews, women, homosexuals, Third World immigrants, the handicapped, and just about every ethnic group going except the poor old Wasps. As everyone knows, there's been a bull market in victims, making them appealing candidates for jobs in government, universities, large corporations, and other institutions. For one thing, along with giving one's life an element of drama — one is oppressed, unjustly treated, a permanent underdog, and the rest of it — to present oneself as a victim allows one to cut the ground out from others who make an appeal on the basis of their own victimhood. For another, it gives one a special moral status, so that one can live grandly without giving up one's claim to suffering: once a victim, it turns out, always a victim. The larger point, though, is that if one carefully sets oneself up as a victim, one is in a position of moral superiority to anyone who cannot make the same claim.

I have felt this small pleasure myself as a Jew in America. Although I've not suffered a jot of oppression and very little discrimination in a lucky life, I have held in reserve — never yet called upon — the historical oppression of the Jews. It gives me a small leg up over white-bread-and-mayonnaise Americans, who cannot hark back to historical troubles. It is a smug feeling, entirely unearned of course, giving one a slight moral edge over the next fellow, from which it can be easily transferred to social (or snobbish) superiority, where it seems to work very nicely.

Yet in the realm of political snobbery even victimhood can be trumped by what passes for that set of perfect political opinions possessed by one of those persons I have come to think of as virtucrats. The virtucrat is any man or woman who is certain that his or her political views are not merely correct but deeply, morally righteous in the bargain. The virtucrat is in no doubt that virtue is on his side. What he believes to be the goodness of his political views fills him with a sense of his own intrinsic goodness. He is a prig, but unlike the prigs of other days, he isn't sniffy about your private life but only your public one. The old prig was contemptuous of the drinker or of the person thought to be sexually promiscuous; the new prig, the virtucrat, will nail you for not having his opinion on Israel or the environment. He is a moral snob.

I once found myself in a mild political disagreement with a middle-aged physician. I cannot now recall the matter we argued about, but when it became apparent that, as in most political arguments, no winner was going to emerge, he said with a complacent smile, "Oh, you may be right, but all I know is that I care deeply about people." (*Esprit de l'escalier:* how I wish I'd had the good sense to reply, "I guess that leaves me with only small buildings and strip malls to care about.") The virtucrat is dedicated to showing you that, no matter their rightness or wrongness, his or hers are morally the finer positions.

The virtucrat takes the high ground, leaving you struggling down below on the gravel with the rabble. He cares about the earth, children, the economic condition of women, the aged, and he cares in the only way that counts, with all his heart. And the main point is that he cares a lot more than the rest of us — great-souled, large-hearted, perhaps unconscious but nonetheless very real snob that he is.

Of course, there is a sense in which all politics is about virtue. The national conventions of the two major political parties, viewed as a game, might be called Steal the Virtue. Republicans or Democrats, each party claims to be in possession of knowledge of the good and where it might be found. The Democratic Party cares about the downtrodden and the defeated. The Republican Party wants to get back to the old verities, insisting that our straying from them is what led to the large number of downtrodden and defeated we seem nowadays to have on hand. Virtue resides with us, each party insists; we are the light and the way.

Still, it's not difficult to spot a virtucrat, from whichever side he comes. Whatever he may ostensibly be saying, the subtext is that he is fundamentally a superior person (". . . all I know is that I care deeply about people"). And within every virtucrat, not having to struggle at all to get out, is, be assured, a snob. He may like to think himself a member of E. M. Forster's little "aristocracy of the sensitive, the considerate, and the plucky," open to the new, hospitable to the young, caring about the underdog, a steadfast justice lover, a terrific guy really. But what especially pleases him is knowing that his opinions are finer than ours — and because of this he is rather better than you and me. This is what makes the virtucrat at heart a snob.

Virtucrat snobs are to be found everywhere in American life, but they infest some places more than others. The generation that came of age in the late 1960s and early 1970s carries a strong virtucratic strain. They tend to think of themselves as the generation that broke down the national hypocrisy of middle-class mores, got America out of the disgraceful Vietnam War, and represented the United States in its highest idealism, imbuing even the smoking of pot and easy fornication with social significance. Anti-abortion, which is to say pro-life, forces — and what a virtucratic word *pro-life* is — have something of the same sanctimoniousness, only coming from the other side of the political spectrum.

Just now in our history, more virtucrats are to be found on the left than on the right. The left has always styled itself the side of the heart, leaving the right with the liver, that bile-producing organ. Conservatives and those on the right are usually willing to settle for thinking themselves correct on political issues; those on the left have always needed to feel not so much that they are correct but that they are also good. Disagree with someone on the right and he is likely to think you obtuse, wrong, sentimental, foolish, a dope; disagree with someone on the left and he is more likely to think you selfish, cold-hearted, a sellout, evil — in league with the devil, he might say, if he didn't think religious terminology too coarse for our secular age. To this day one will hear of people who fell for Communism in a big way let off the hook because they were sincere; if one's heart is in the right place, nothing else matters, even if one's naive opinions made it easier for tyrants to murder millions. The main thing, once again, is that one's heart should always be in the right place. The rest is moral small beer.

What makes the virtucrat a snob is that not only is he smug about the righteousness of his views but he imputes bad faith to anyone who doesn't share them. Upon this imputed bad faith he erects his own superiority. The virtucrat's is an easy snobbery, too, in that he doesn't have to act on his lovely opinions. He is for art, the environment, the oppressed, and against violence, hunger, war, the big corporations. What makes these opinions virtucratic instead of merely earnest is that one doesn't have to do anything more than hold them; they are good cards in a game with no real stakes. Not that there aren't good and bad causes in the world; there are plenty of both, of course, but the difference between the virtucrat and the men and women who take politics seriously is that, for the latter, politics is about how society ought to be organized, and it isn't so personal, so much about making oneself feel good by setting oneself apart from the swine who aren't as sweet-natured as oneself.

The virtucrat was given a boost with the advent of political correctness. You can always detect him, happy chap, showing his heart is in the right place, whether addressing a letter "Dear Gentlepersons" or writing sentences that keep an eye out for the pronoun police: "every economist knows that *she* has to factor in GNP," "no construction worker feels right entering a fight for which *she* hasn't union backing," and so forth. He glows as only an alrightnik can when he shows once again his heart is in the right place when calling a waitress a "server," or tapping out "he/she" in a report, or attending a diversity conference in which white men can get in touch with their negative identity feelings about gender, race, homosexuality, and finding other ways to show he is a real pussycat, a multicultural kind of guy. Much of this political correctness is about snobbery — about, that is, making one feel above the unenlightened.

The victim and the virtucrat nicely meshed during the *fatwa* ordering that a death bounty be placed on the novelist

Salman Rushdie. A Third Worlder, an artist, and now a true potential victim, Rushdie — from many accounts a difficult and unpleasant man — became a grand object of snobbery. Virtucrats among the cognoscenti slavered over him, gaining points through his genuine victimhood. One sees this highlighted in *The Year of Reading Proust,* by Phyllis Rose, a literary critic of some personal wealth, who was told by the novelist Robert Stone that he wanted her to give a dinner party at her Key West winter home for fifteen people, including a guest of honor whom he couldn't just then name but who, he promised, was a figure of importance. Professor Rose holds back the name of the mystery guest — it was, of course, Salman Rushdie — till the last moment, to get the most pop from her story. But it's not a story that edifies. Poor Professor Rose worked fiendishly hard on her dinner, acquiring all the best food, trying to put together the best mixture of people, but it turned out rather flat. Not so flat, though, that she can resist recounting it in her book, where she reveals herself a Mme. Verdurin of our time — Proust's social-climbing hostess in *Remembrance of Things Past,* who is unaware of her own deep snobbery.

If snobbery is the art of demonstrating, blatantly or subtly, one's own moral superiority, politics offers many opportunities for doing so. One may do so through political name-dropping, a kind of snobbery by association. ("I play golf a lot with Tip O'Neill," an old high school acquaintance of mine who has made lots of money in real estate once told me.) Or one may do so through the purity one claims for one's political views — something that went on a great deal, often in a literally murderous way, under Communism, both in Europe and in America. Or one may insist that one's political views, in their measured nonpartisanship, are not necessarily purer but finer than anyone else's: here one suggests that the motives behind one's political views are more disinterested in a way that makes everyone else's political views seem coarse in their base mundanity. Or one may suggest that one's political superiority derives from one's deeper insight into the way the game is truly played.

This last is the form Gore Vidal's political snobbery takes. Vidal's is different from the standard literary man's political snobbery. He works both sides of the street — the one place you will never catch him is in the middle of the road. An upper-class radical, a cynical leftist, a critic of capitalism who has made capitalism pay through the nose, deeply contemptuous of the country he professes to want to save, Vidal has it every which way. For the snobographer, his has been one of the most amusing performances of the past half century.

Gore Vidal regularly reminds his readers of his upper-class connections — a grandfather who was a United States senator from Mississippi, an Auchincloss stepfather shared with Jacqueline Bouvier Kennedy Onassis (about whom he has been comically contemptuous), a father who taught aviation at West Point — which is to say, of his place on the edge of the Waspocracy. Or, as Ned Rorem puts it in *Lies,* the most recent published installment of his diary, Vidal is always thrusting forth "his upper-crust lineage (the only dull thing about him, but which he pushes)." Vidal's act is to play the patrician trying to save a country so dreary as scarcely to be worthy of his efforts, though against his own better judgment he continues to try. His move some years ago to Ravallo, in Italy, where he appears to live in the way of the old Roman patrician class, gives a nice twist to the act. Fiercely ambitious while seeming to mock ambition, requiring vast attention while mocking the publicity culture in which he thrives, he is, as the British writer Karl Miller remarked, "a *seigneur* who was also a leftist," "a left-wing lord."

Vidal has written about politics in plays and novels (many novels, in which the most admirable figures are remarkably like — here's a shocker — Gore Vidal), has run for Congress, been a friend of Eleanor Roosevelt, been a Joseph Alsop of the *Nation* and the *New York Review of Books* but without the anti-Communism or the need for taking responsibility for his opinions, and been a television commentator of only the loftiest views about the folly of his countrymen — that is, the rest of us, swarming below, so many navvies shuffling about with brooms in the heat of the sun. He has made a career out of hard work in the service of hauteur.

Gore Vidal is no virtucrat. His feeling of superiority requires no mediation by trying to look sensitive in the eyes of his audience. He thinks us all one form or another of naif, simply too obtuse to see the grand swindle of politics that he views with shining and amused lucidity. His condescension is unrelieved. A reviewer in the *Times Literary Supplement* wrote of *The Golden Age,* the final novel in Vidal's series about American history, that "having someone talk down to you for 500 pages grows tiresome." But Vidal doesn't court the love of critics or anyone else. Self-love, which in him never goes unrequited, is sufficient for this remarkably confident snob.

Jonathan Swift once remarked, apropos of politics, that you cannot reason people out of something to which reason hasn't brought them. But politics nowadays tends to be less about reason than ever; it is much more often about making us feel good at the expense of those who aren't as kind, generous, and sensitive as we. La Rochefoucauld wrote that "our virtues are, most often, only our vices disguised," thus formulating with perfection the character snobbery takes in politics.

17

Fags and Yids

IN AN EARLIER CHAPTER, I mentioned tastemakers — designers, decorators, curators, magazine editors, movie and television producers, art, literary, and dance critics, and others — but neglected (quite on purpose) to mention that a large number of them are homosexual or Jewish, and not infrequently both. "I liked this business better," I not long ago heard the television comedienne Brett Butler joke at a roast for the movie director Rob Reiner, "when it was run by straight Jewish men." A fairly complicated joke, this, it turns out.

The reason so many Jews and homosexuals (chiefly, though far from exclusively, homosexual men) have been involved in the formation of taste, and hence in the changes and twists in the character of snobbery, is that Jews and homosexuals have always felt themselves the potential — and often real — victims of snobbery, and of course much worse than snobbery. "Whom do you call a kike?" a vicious old joke runs. "The Jewish gentleman," the answer is, "who has just left the room." "What do you call an Irish homosexual?" a three-cushion joke asks. "An Irishman," the answer is, "who prefers women over booze."

Some of the great snobs in literature are portrayed as homosexual or as Jewish. Proust's great character the Baron de Charlus is perhaps the most notable example; Somerset Maugham's character Elliott Templeton in *The Razor's Edge* — played nicely over the top by Clifton Webb in the 1946 movie version of the novel — is another strong example, an American living in Paris who "took no interest in people apart from their social position." Ernest Hemingway, in a touch of anti-Semitism, in *The Sun Also Rises,* mocks his character Robert Cohn for being both Jewish and an upward-looking snob.

And of course Marcel Proust, himself half Jewish and fully homosexual, was the supreme portraitist of snobs, starting out in life a pure snob himself and ending as the greatest of all anatomists of snobbery. "I don't think Proust was [a snob]," said George Painter, his biographer. "He began as a snob partly because he was a Jew and a homosexual. If he could be accepted in the place where it was most difficult to get in at all, then that would make him feel better, feel more at home in the world. When he found that [the aristocrats he encountered] had very similar failings to everybody else in his own middle classes or in the working classes of his servants, he was partly relieved, and perhaps a little disappointed. He often says how similar the bourgeois, the working classes, and the aristocracy are in their ways, except that the working classes are much kinder and more intelligent. He became an anti-snob."

"In the first place," said W. H. Auden, himself a make-no-bones-about-it, very-early-out-of-the-closet homosexual, to Alan Ansen, a man recording his conversation for a slender book called *Table Talk of W. H. Auden,* "all homosexual acts are acts of envy." Auden does not expand on that impressively large, provocative, and risky generalization, but it is a reminder that the toughest critics of homosexual foibles have tended to be, for a complex of reasons, homosexuals. (Just as, in some ways, the most cunning anti-Semites have been Jews.) Auden might have meant that behind every homosexual act is envy of the family, or child-making, possibilities of heterosexuals. But what he may also have meant is that homosexuals, up until recent years, have been in a potentially degraded position of extremely tenuous social insecurity. The envy Auden may have had in mind is for the comparative social ease of life for people who are not homosexuals.

One of the best methods for allaying this insecurity on the part of homosexuals has been not to hang back but to step out in front — but carefully, not too far in front — of society, from which position one can change taste and possibly the most basic social arrangements. Arthur Gold and Robert Fizdale, themselves homosexual, in their book *Misia,* about Misia Sert, the Polish patroness who kept a salon in Paris in the early decades of the twentieth century, placed Jean Cocteau in this regard when they wrote: "Always a little behind the avant-garde but ahead of society, Cocteau in the twenties was the epitome of the advanced artist as homosexual hero."

The linkage between the social insecurity of both Jews and homosexuals is perhaps nowhere better established historically than in the year 1895, when in France Captain Alfred Dreyfus was falsely charged with being a spy and sent to Devil's Island, and when, five months later, in England, Oscar Wilde was sentenced to two years of hard labor for homosexual offenses under the Criminal Law Amendments Act of 1885. Both trials showed, among other things, the vulnerability of Jews and homosexuals, however well integrated into French and English society they might have thought themselves, though neither really did. The situation was not all that much better in the United States, where the Jewish Leo Frank was lynched outside Atlanta in 1915 and many states kept laws against homosexuality on their books until recently. Crimes against homosexuals, many brutally violent, continue to turn up.

Some Jews were so grand — the Rothschilds, the Warburgs — that they were unsnubbable and hence outside the range of injury by snobbery or even virulent anti-Semitism: inside a snob-free zone made possible by immense wealth. Others had the combination of wit and perspective — maybe the two are the same quality — to laugh it off. "Fancy calling a fellow an adventurer," said Benjamin Disraeli, in the face of what were anti-Semitic attacks on him, "when his ancestors were probably on intimate terms with the Queen of Sheba."

Yet the vulnerability for both Jews and homosexuals has never been completely eliminated. "I find much more anti-Semitism among Americans than among Europeans of a corresponding class," Auden noted. Anti-Semitism has historically taken two forms: one in which the Jews are castigated for being inferior, and another in which they are resented for being superior. Philo-Semitism, where it turns up, tends to be found among the European upper classes. "I like Jews," the Princess Elisabeth Bibesco said, as recorded in the journal of the Romanian writer Mihail Sebastian. "I like them passionately. Not because they have had an unhappy time of it — no. I like them because they move the horizon forward." But this view is of course exceptional. Anti-Semitism has a much fuller history than philo-Semitism, for the former, as Sebastian, who was Jewish, noted, "covers up many disappointments."

A friend of mine, a successful painter and Jewish, upon telling me that she had moved to Darien, Connecticut, couldn't resist adding, half jokingly, "I guess I'm now just another Aryan from Darien." Otto Kahn, the successful New York financier, whose assimilationist efforts caused him to be described as "the flyleaf between the Old and New Testament," once told a friend, "You know, I used to be a Jew." "Really?" the friend is said to have replied. "I used to be a hunchback," making the point that, even with vast financial and social resources, it is not so easy to de-Judaize oneself.

Some homosexuals have been, or at least felt themselves, in a position of unassailability comparable to that of very grand Jews. These have been homosexual artists, chiefly, especially those who positioned themselves as above and beyond and thus invulnerable to society in its drab quotidian social concerns. Yet despite all the outward changes in attitudes in American life toward homosexuality, despite all the new enlightenment and heightened tolerance, when it comes to the crunch a person's homosexuality may still be used like a lash against him, even by people who happily go about wearing

red ribbons on their lapels in support of the fight against
AIDS.

To the best of my knowledge, I have never been held back
for being Jewish, but I shouldn't be shocked to learn that,
a time or two, I myself may have been the gentleman who
just left the room. Much of my Jewish education — apart from
the three years of sketchy training in Hebrew in preparation for my bar mitzvah — was in the form of my father's
regular warnings about the always lurking prospects for anti-
Semitism, especially for someone carrying a last name like Epstein. Growing up in a part of Chicago and going to public
schools where Jews were roughly half the population, I never
sensed any strong animus against myself as a Jew. The first
time I felt uneasy was when, as a boy, I began playing tourna-
ment tennis in and around Chicago. Tennis was mainly a
country club sport in the early 1950s, and the clubs where
tournaments were played were usually restricted. This was
the first time I had stepped out of my predominantly Jewish
world in any significant way. In tournaments, I suddenly ran
up against kids named Vandy Christie and Gaylord Messick.
When asked one spring by my high school tennis coach to be
a ball boy for a tennis exhibition at the Saddle and Cycle Club
in Chicago—also restricted — I agreed. The players that afternoon were Bill Talbert, Tony Trabert, Hamilton Richardson,
and Antonio Palafox, who played for the Mexican Davis Cup
team. From that afternoon, I remember what seemed to me the
easy generosity of spirit of Bill Talbert, the good nature of
Palafox, the intensity of Trabert, but a certain edge to Hamilton Richardson. I am perhaps doing him an injustice as I
write about this now, but I sensed that I had to be wary of
this man, who set my Jewish radar atwitter. Nothing untoward
happened, but I recall feeling a palpable relief that I had
gotten through the afternoon without Richardson — Ham,
as the other players called him — yelling at me, complaining
about me, somehow or other humiliating me. Pure paranoia,
no doubt, but there it was, a case of Jewish nervousness I had
not hitherto felt and hoped not to have to feel ever again.

In the realm of snobbery, then, Jews and homosexuals tend to be more alert to the snubs, or even the potential for snubs, that can be rendered them in the wider society in which they operate. The more delicately attuned among them, if they have strong and sensitive social antennae, tend to get out in front of the loop and sometimes to lead it. Others hang back, too cautious to engage the world in a fully open way. But real social security may finally not be available to either.

As for feeling socially secure, one day I found myself sitting in a concert hall in Jerusalem, awaiting a performance of Shlomo Mintz and the Israel Chamber Orchestra, thinking that it may well be that everyone in this hall is Jewish. I had only to say this to myself than to realize that, for strange reasons, I prefer to be part of a minority. I liked my status as a Jew in the United States. Being part of a small though active minority, I felt that I had an interesting angle on the larger society of which I was a part. And more and more a secure part: thirty years ago, for example, it would have been unlikely for a Jew to have attempted a book on the subject of snobbery, except possibly from the standpoint of being a victim of it. You've come a long way, Izzy.

Truman Capote, who in some ways, *mutatis mutandis,* may have been the American Cocteau, had for a number of years been running with what passed for the smart set in Manhattan, becoming especially close to the women who comprised the heart of the set: Babe Paley, Nan Kemper, Slim Keith, and others. Then Capote made what turned out to be a (socially) fatal mistake by publishing, in *Esquire,* "La Côte Basque, 1968," a chapter of a book he planned to call *Answered Prayers.* The mistake was that he exposed in print many of the dirty secrets, little and large, of these women and their husbands. With that single stroke, Capote was permanently banished from the friendship of all of them. Perhaps rightly, he was viewed as a betrayer, though he always claimed not to understand how this could be. When one among them, Princess Lee Radziwill, sister of Jacqueline Kennedy Onassis, was queried by the gossip columnist Liz

Smith about a dustup in print between Capote and Gore Vidal, she remarked for publication that she was "tired of Truman riding my coattails to fame. And, Liz," she added, "what difference does it make? They're just a couple of fags."

Not, to be sure, that homosexuals and Jews don't have impressive snobberies of their own — as, doubtless, do African Americans, Romanians, and prisoners on death row. In his memoir, *The Sorcerer's Apprentice,* John Richardson speaks of *la haute pédérastie,* a phrase that speaks to hierarchies within homosexual life. In America, Jews live on the ample ground between worry about being found inferior and absolute certainty of their superiority. The Hebrew word *goy* is used to mean stranger, but it also conveys the notion of barbarian, in the sense in which the Greeks of the fifth century used the latter word: a stranger and someone whose ways are not only not ours but inferior to ours. In Yiddish, *goyishe kop,* meaning Gentile-brains, is no compliment. Doubtless homosexuals, so many of whom specialize in irony, have similar intramural put-downs — "straight-thinking," if not already in use, might serve as one among them.

In doing this, Jews and homosexuals are only doing what has for so long been done to them. No one in recent times has captured this point better than the novelist Dan Jacobson, in an essay on his boyhood as a Jew in the town of Kimberley in South Africa:

> Of course, not even the most self-hating Jew believes that all Gentiles lead happy and unproblematic lives or that he would himself do likewise if only he were released from servitude to his Jewishness. But anyone who has been the object of racial hatred knows that it is so wounding to its victim — more wounding than personal abuse directed against him as an individual — precisely because it denies his individuality. To every member of the spurned race it says: to me you will never be a person with a life and interests of your own, but always a representative of a species. Whatever you do will reveal only your speciesdom; and if you try to escape from it, that too will reveal the species you belong to.

Much snobbery is about denying the next person his individuality, or, when allowing it, permitting it only inferior standing.

Because of this background, Jews and homosexuals are not of the stuff out of which social establishments are best made. Owing to their not (for the most part) having children, homosexuals lack the sense of futurity, the sense of passing things on to the next generation, that society requires to continue. Owing to historical memory, most Jews, including those with a genuine taste for social climbing, tend to feel more than a little uneasy thinking of themselves fully part of society. "Jews are the only people," Milton Himmelfarb wrote many years ago, "who live like Republicans and vote like Puerto Ricans." By this amusing remark Himmelfarb meant that because of the experience, or even the fear, of anti-Semitism, Jewish identification with those who feel themselves oppressed remains strong — as it does today when anti-Semitism seems happily in abeyance. A true patrician class doesn't worry overmuch — or at all, really — about such things as the oppressed.

At the same time, when all this social prejudice visited upon Jews and homosexuals in America hasn't caused major tragedy of the sort the Nazis brought about, it has made for wild social comedy. "Let's face it, sweetheart," says the character Mel Brooks plays in the movie *To Be or Not to Be*, apropos of Hitler's race laws at the German invasion of Poland, "without Jews, fags, and gypsies, there is no theater." Exclude the gypsies, and the theater might also be taken as a larger metaphor for contemporary American society in its more sophisticated aspects.

For today Jews and homosexuals, far from everywhere being excluded from American society, seem at the dead center of it. *Town & Country*, once the exclusive preserve of Wasps, in its Weddings section now regularly shows wedding photographs of Mr. and Mrs. Jordan Michael Klein, Mr. and Mrs. Scott Michael Weinberg, and Mr. and Mrs. Joshua Bloch Rubin. In an article in *Talk* magazine about the want of interest in older notions of Society on the part of the new Silicon Valley super-rich, among the "old-line" names cited are those of Zuckerman, Bloomberg, Tisch, Perelman, Gutfreund, Kravis, and Steinberg, *Yiddles* all. Until the retirement from the presidency of Harvard of Neil Rudenstine, the presidents of Harvard, Yale, and Princeton were all Jews, and, significantly, quite as undistinguished as other university presidents of our day. Jews have generally made something like a long march through American cultural institutions: academia, journalism, publishing.

The infusion of homosexuals into society is seen most obviously in the prominence now accorded clothing designers, few of whom are in the least equivocal about their homosexuality: Valentino, Armani, St. Laurent, Calvin Klein, and others. (The journalist and former movie producer Dominick Dunne noted an earlier phase of this with the advent of hairdressers as significant players in Hollywood society.) Once perhaps thought of as dressmakers and tailors, and as such just a tad above servants, the designers, along with running hugely prosperous businesses, are now considered major tastemakers. The rich once told them how they wished to dress; things are quite the reverse now, and it is the designers who instruct the rich on how they shall be dressed. Clothing designers are among the great figures of the age, vaunted in the pages of *Vanity Fair, Talk, The New Yorker, Town & Country, People,* and the *New York Times.*

But it is not the wealthy designers and notable hairdressers alone who have broken through the old barrier, but homosexual artists, curators, performers, and others who have a vast deal to do with setting tastes for the larger culture. In America, what has traditionally passed for (capital-S) Society has tended to be controlled by women. Returning to lecture in the States in 1904, Henry James noted that his audience was composed preponderantly of women. He went on to write that women were the cultural representatives of their husbands, who were "seamed all over with the scars of the marketplace," while they, the wives, attended concerts, galleries, lectures, imbibing culture in heady draughts. This tends still to be so, and the professional tastemakers make their appeal most successfully to women of social and cultural aspiration, which has given them, the tastemakers, not only a front-row seat at the show but an unusually strong hand in directing the show.

The barbarians (for which read: Jews and homosexuals) are no longer at the gates; they are eating canapés and drinking champagne in what used to be called the drawing room. In any accurate chronicle of what passes for Society in our day, Jews and homosexuals, in Virginia Woolf's coarse trope, swarm. Proust, had he seen what lay ahead, would not have been astonished. Prescient fellow, he wrote, in *The Captive:* "The day may come when dressmakers will move in society — nor should I find it at all shocking." Whether he would also have been delighted is more difficult to know. The social scene and situation seems so much more fluid now than in his day. Yet Proust also knew that "snobbishness, in changing its objects, does not change its accent."

18

....

The Same New Thing

T HE NEXT NEW THING" is a phrase currently going the rounds, which, along with suggesting the promise of further innovation also suggests the ephemerality, the imminent passing, of whatever is now in fashion: in clothes, in children's and adult toys, in large-scale commercial ideas. Don't go away, the next new thing implies, because a newer thing is on its way. I myself prefer "the same new thing," which has more economy, and suggests the notion of *plus ça change, plus c'est la même chose.* "The same new thing," in fact, aptly serves as an all-purpose gloss on the history of fashion.

Fashion implies transience, but transience regularized, almost as regularized as meter in verse. A mistake, though, to conclude that because fashion is transient it is also trivial. Fashion speaks to two widely different but apparently not contradictory human impulses: the first toward being in, with, and part of things; the second toward being distinctive, apart, and above things. When it succeeds, fashion allows one to feel both with-it and above it — with the right people and above the rabble — the heavenly condition to which the snob aspires, though perhaps not the snob alone.

"Thus fashion lives," wrote William Hazlitt, "only in a perpetual round of giddy innovation and restless vanity." He added that fashion is "one of the most slight and insignificant of things." The temptation to moralize about fashion, with its sad ostentation and shoddy egotism, is difficult to resist. "You cannot be both fashionable and first-rate," wrote Logan Pearsall Smith, who himself tended to be closer to the former than the latter. "The best dressed of every age," a handbook of 1859 called *The Habits of Good Society* noted, "have always been the worst men and women." Dreary to be caught up in fashion, little doubt about it. And yet . . . and yet . . .

Exhibit A: My old Burberry. I owned a tan, single-breasted Burberry raincoat, in good condition. One day I put it on and discovered that it was no longer, well, quite right. I hadn't outgrown it, but suddenly this excellent coat — not inexpensive when I bought it four or five years before — seemed a bit tight, skimpy, slightly yet definitely inadequate. I hadn't changed — grown no heavier, surely no taller — but fashion had, and raincoats, including newer Burberry raincoats, had grown longer and fuller, giving the look and feel of greater amplitude. My old raincoat felt somehow off, wrong, and because of this — you'll have to take my word on it — uncomfortable. Not long afterward I bought another raincoat, not a Burberry this time around but an Aquascutum. Does this make me a slave to fashion? Probably.

The modish, the voguish, the *au courant,* these are not among the things that serious people ought to take seriously. Panting devotion to fashion is in itself deeply vulgar. Yet if not entirely hostage to fashion, most people do go along with it, or at least don't wish to be caught too far behind it. Certainly not many of us wish, except perhaps deliberately, to outrage decorum: to show up for an IRS audit in a bikini, or at a Lake Forest wedding in a bowling shirt (though the latter, come to think of it, might nowadays work just fine). It is fashion that, in a rough way, establishes decorum. In my own dress and manner, I would like to think myself existing in a permanent state of ironic conformity to the decorum of the day. But I sometimes wonder if the conformity isn't much greater than the irony.

"It is the bourgeoisie, the respectable people," wrote James Laver, the English historian of fashion, "who decide what a fashion shall be, though they very rarely inaugurate it." Proust refines this point when he writes that "in society (and this social phenomenon is merely a particular case of a much more general psychological law) novelties, whether blameworthy or not, excite horror only so long as they have not been assimilated and enveloped by reassuring elements." Closer to our time, the novelist Harold Brodkey wrote: "We want to be dressed, and we want others to be dressed somewhat similarly, partly for the democracy of it, and partly so that we are speaking a halfway common language — so that we are not isolated inside our own heads, trapped in the babble of madness or in fears of obesity or whatever, but are part of a dialogue about acceptable or exciting appearances."

Common enough though fashion is, no one has formulated a truly useful definition of it. The English novelist Frederic Raphael has written that "fashion is a way of redressing the invariable in an air of novelty." Neatly put, but not quite, I fear, a bull's-eye. Kennedy Fraser, who wrote well about fashion for *The New Yorker* for more than a decade, remarked that she still hadn't found a definition of fashion she would enjoy defending. Teri Agins, who covered fashion for the *Wall Street Journal,* has written that "by definition," fashion "is ephemeral and elusive, a target that keeps moving."

Academics, those most unfashionable of people, have now got hold of fashion as a subject. A quarterly, *Fashion Theory: The Journal of Dress, Body and Culture,* professes to provide an "interdisciplinary forum for the rigorous analysis of cultural phenomena ranging from footbinding to fashion advertising." It has opened its pages to semioticians, gender theorists, social historians, feminists on political fire. Articles in its pages not infrequently attempt to show that fashion is associated with "social construction of identity" and the reactions to the political and social changes of the day, in all their subtle nuances. How like the very reverse of amusing all this sounds!

Easier to say what fashion is associated with than what it actually is. Fashion is bound to custom, style, changes in taste; it has to do with emulation and, often but not always, with social class. It hasn't to do with clothes alone, of course, since there are also fashions in furniture, food, music, literature, and ideas. Although fashion can feed off the past and feel itself (usually falsely) of the future, it really lives only in the Now. The problem with my not so old Burberry was that — sigh — it was more than a touch too Then.

Not everyone strives to be fashionable. I don't, and I believe I succeed. But like most people, I tend to fall in with it and don't wish to expend the energy required to be determinedly unfashionable. Nor is it altogether clear that fighting fashion is a strong key to individuality. Georg Simmel, the trenchant German sociologist, has suggested that the individual who takes a stand against fashion may do so out of personal weakness, fearful that "he will be unable to maintain his individuality if he adopts the forms, the tastes, and the customs of the general public."

Fashion operates under its own, not always easily decipherable laws. It swerves off in new directions regardless of dissidents or even adherents. Fashion fades of its own success; as it spreads it loses appeal, and hence strength; in its accessibility lie the seeds of its own death. Without a feeling of exclusiveness — the snobbish element — fashion isn't successfully fashionable. Nothing can do a fashion in quicker than unselective appreciation. Fashion requires a safe and selective originality. Once this originality becomes too widespread — the supermarket checkout girl wearing a T-shirt with *Gucci* across its front — the game is up, and people who pride themselves on being fashionable are gone, hot on the trail of fresh fashion newly created.

"After all, what is fashion?" asked Oscar Wilde. "It is usually a form of ugliness so intolerable that we have to alter it every six months." Like many an Oscar Wilde witticism, amusing but not quite true. It doesn't take in the odd way that what seemed smart and chic today can seem boring and vulgar tomorrow. Nor does it take in the compulsory character of shift in fashion, which is not finally about ugliness but about the need for change, for some people to cut themselves off from the herd, to set up as that select group once referred to as PLU, or People Like Us. "Fashion," as Tom Wolfe rightly says, "is the code language of status."

The origins of fashion are in status, and in status, too, are to be discovered the mechanics of fashion. The kinds of status that one's clothes can reveal are obvious: one's wealth, one's rank in society, one's age or generation, one's aspirations, and not least one's interest in fashion itself. Fashion was once fixed by law — the so-called sumptuary laws, promulgated by Charlemagne early in the ninth century — which prescribed that a person's dress match his place in the social hierarchy. As a carryover of this, in the court of Louis XIV only certain men were allowed to wear certain ribbons. The Duc de Saint-Simon, that careful chronicler of status at Versailles, complained that nobles at the Sun King's court were kept near bankruptcy by trying to outfit themselves at the level of splendor set by the king — an instance of fashion setting an economic tyranny.

The trick is somehow to find a place between being fashionably stupid and stupidly unfashionable. The aim is to avoid vulgarity yet never join that world, which Balzac speaks of in *Lost Illusions,* "where the superfluous becomes indispensable." If one can arrange all this, there is no reason why fashion cannot enliven existence, infusing it with an ever-refreshed lilt, with change in dress, manners, and styles of living lending life a witty, zany, breezy, lyrical, charming feel. Not to know the fashion of one's time is to keep oneself ignorant where really so little is required to be informed. In his journals, Ralph Waldo Emerson reports a woman saying to him that "a sense of being perfectly well dressed gives a feeling of inward tranquility which religion is powerless to bestow." That may be pushing it, but to feel oneself in fashion without feeling enslaved by it can give one a sense of living in harmony with one's time.

The snob's problem is that he allows himself to make judgments based on fashion, to let the competitive edge that lurks about fashion gain sway, to find being out of fashion veritable hell. For the snob, fashion becomes a standard of judgment, a means of gratification, a method for acquiring self-esteem, an ethics, something akin to a religion, and of course a stick with which to beat on those who fall behind or get it wrong. Once, at a meeting of the National Council on the Arts, a wealthy and well-turned-out woman, a fellow council member, regarding the new chairman of the Endowment, whispered into my ear, "He really is off the rack, isn't he?" Cruel SOB that I am, I laughed.

Yet one doesn't have to be a snob to want one's own tastes in life's superfluities not to become too widespread, to want to keep one's minor passions from becoming too popular. Especially in a democracy one needs to feel one is not always traveling with the herd. But which way the herd is traveling is getting to be a more complicated question than it once was. Once it was thought to travel from the top down. Thorstein Veblen was the authorized guide on this trip: "Emulation occurs," he wrote in *The Theory of the Leisure Class* (1899), "where social groups become strong enough to challenge the traditional patterns of society, in fact in those places where a strong middle class emerges to compete with the aristocracy and, at a later stage, a strong proletariat emerges to compete with the middle class." The notion here is that the upper classes set the fashions, which percolate down through the *nouveaux riches* to the middle classes and thence make their way merrily on down. How efficient! Unfortunately, no longer very true.

Georg Simmel, writing only five years after Veblen, felt that the fulcrum of change in these matters was the middle class. "The higher classes, as everyone knows," he wrote, "are the most conservative, and frequently enough they are even archaic. They dread every motion and change, not because they have an antipathy for the contents or because the latter are injurious to them, but simply because it is change and because they regard every modification of the whole as suspicious and dangerous. No change can bring them additional power, and every change can bring them something to fear, but nothing to hope for." The middle classes, Simmel felt, were in control of changes in fashion, giving them their peculiar tone and rhythm. True, the upper classes have seldom supplied the artists, designers, editors, curators, interior decorators, and other arbiters of taste; the middle and even the working classes largely have. Often they have produced fashions in clothes, literature, and home decoration that attempt to convey their sense of upper-class life — see here Ralph Lauren, John O'Hara, Martha Stewart.

For a time, this general line veered off and the spirit, if not the actuality, of the avant-garde seemed to prompt changes in fashion. Whatever was new was the fashion. The great cliché — in clothes, in art, and in ideas — was "cutting edge," and particular clothes and styles came to be called "edgy." People who practice the profession, as the Austrian novelist Robert Musil put it, "of being the next generation" have been on the scene for centuries. "There are people," wrote the eighteenth-century German aphorist G. C. Lichtenberg, "who possess not so much genius as a certain talent for perceiving the desires of the century, or even of the decade, before it has done so itself." Alma Mahler, who married, *seriatim*, Gustav Mahler, Walter Gropius, and Franz Werfel, was such a person; she captured the spirit I have in mind when she said: "For me the only thing that exists is tomorrow's truth." This spirit calls for one to be the first in and the first out; another word for it is "trendy."

For people caught up in the trendy life, the true and the new are the selfsame; the new is the word and the way. Trends, though a part of fashion, are even less stable. Fashion magazines run small sections of help to their readers, letting them know what's in (thin belts, red vodka, the novels of Arturo Perez-Reverte) and what's out (shearling coats, kiwi fruit, David Letterman). Under the regime of the trendy life, as Kennedy Fraser has written, "clothes will never make you fashionable. Friends, thoughts, face, and life must match." And all these must conduce to make one seem to belong among the right people, the happy few. A pretty damn grim business it can be.

People who work in advertising, public relations, sometimes journalism, what generally goes by the name communications, have nonetheless to keep up with this business. David Brooks has caught something of their spirit in an essay called "The Clothing of the American Mind," in which he writes of the type in communications: "He is a protean figure, constantly changing in surprising and contradictory ways in order to win attention. He has a short time horizon, because the great blizzard of messages quickly obscures anything that has happened as long as a few months ago. . . . He has a great tolerance for flux and insecurity. He has a genius for reading cultural signifiers, knowing how to behave with the cowboy hat crowd and another way with the counterculture set. . . . He has a great rhythmic sense for when people are sick of a cultural trend and ready to hop on a counter-trend." Why do people bother, one wonders? It all sounds rather like the man who, after years of cleaning up after the elephants in the circus, when asked why he doesn't go into some other line of work, exclaims: "What — and leave show business?"

Trendiness and fashion have by now become so intermingled that they can scarcely be separated, with the only thing uniting the two being marketing, which is, not to put too fine a point on it, money. Money has now invaded fashion as never before. According to Teri Agins, the great couturiers were more snobbish than greedy. Christian Dior rated aristocrats much higher than movie stars, she reports, and would not design clothes for a Brigitte Bardot movie. Fashion was once defined, if by nothing else, by its exclusiveness. But in our day it has sought to become inclusive, attempting to sell everyone.

T-shirts, jeans, and underwear with designer logos have become, and remain, big moneymakers. Designers licensed all sorts of manufacturers to make everything from socks to perfume for them, with perfume being the biggest moneymaker of all. Something known in the trade as "lifestyle merchandising" came into play. Styles of living were now designated by the designer clothes one chose to wear. And for the first time people wore the labels, or at least the names or logos, of the designers on the outside of their duds. ("Once upon a time," noted *Esquire,* "labels were worn only on the inside of clothes — those were better times.") Teri Agins

notes that, in this new social calibration, a wealthy man's
wife might wear Armani, his mistress Versace. At the same
time Ralph Lauren stood for vanished Waspishness, Calvin
Klein for what-me-worry-about-kinky? sexiness, Tommy Hilfiger for a vague kind of all-American good time. Other hot
designers — Jil Sander, Marc Jacobs, Antonio Berardi, Tom
Ford, Helmut Lang — gave off their own messages, all per-
ceptible to people who perhaps care a little too much about
such things.

So pervasive has this designer culture become that, in the
July 19, 2001, issue of *Winnetka Talk,* the newspaper for an
upper-middle suburb on Chicago's North Shore, the following item appeared in the police blotter: "A Coach purse containing a Gucci wallet and Louis Vuitton change purse valued
at $800 was reported stolen Sunday from a black Jaguar
parked in front of the Winnetka Golf Course. Two cell
phones and $200 in cash were also missing from the car."
Strange, said a friend to whom I read this item, one doesn't
feel an immediate rush of sympathy for the victim.

The goal in this new mass merchandising was to give people clothes that they felt were somehow cool and sexy, and
that conferred status upon them — with the status having a
good deal to do with what constituted the cool and sexy.
Thus Ralph Lauren told a reporter from *GQ* about Purple
Label, his high-line menswear: "I was trying to say this isn't
about fashion; it's about aspiration. Now I know about aspirations. What do you want to be? What do you want to have
in your life? Purple Label has an aspirational quality to it. It
says you have money, you are chic, you have arrived." Perfect
clothes, you might say, in which to look down on people who
either can't afford them or, sadder still, haven't the freakin'
good taste to acquire them.

Earlier, socially prominent figures became known for wearing the clothes of specific designers: Jacqueline Kennedy
Onassis wore first Oleg Cassini, then Halston, for example.
On the male side, the basketball coach Pat Riley became
known as an Armani man. In a curious reversal, people once
thought to be part of capital-S Society went on the payroll of

designers: Princess Lee Radziwill worked for Giorgio Armani as something called his "special events coordinator."

More interesting, as the country went bonkers for youth culture, with the new ideal being not to grow into an adult as soon as possible but instead to stay youthful as long as possible, another shift took place. As mentioned earlier, black youth took the lead in fashion design among the young, with white middle- and upper-middle-class kids following the lead of black kids in clothes — in gym shoes especially, but in style generally. Part of the success of the Tommy Hilfiger operation was that rap singers began wearing Hilfiger clothes. Shoe and clothing manufacturers, wanting to pick up the custom of these kids, sent people into inner-city neighborhoods to find out what the kids thought cool. Other people made their own fashions by main force. "My job," remarked Isabella Blow, a (at the moment) hot fashion consultant, "is to make bad clothes look good." Of Miss Blow, a fashion director for Max Factor reports: "She feels trends in the ether, as it were." A strange world, volatile, febrile, explainable only after the fact.

Before the fact, however, there loomed an odd, slightly ghoulish figure, a commercial artist, a man a little nutty about women's shoes, best known for saying that everyone would be famous for fifteen minutes, though he himself held the limelight for more than a decade and, dead since 1987, hasn't completely faded from prominence yet. Andy Warhol, pop art painter and maker of mesmerizingly boring films, is in many quarters thought a serious avant-garde artist; in others, a man without whom the culture today would have been in a good deal better shape. I wonder if he isn't best considered a fashion leader, perhaps the most significant of the twentieth century, and all the greater for having no real products for sale.

Born to Czech parents in Forest City, Pennsylvania, in 1930, awkward, shy, pale nearly to the point of being albino, Andy Warhol, during a childhood in which he was often picked on, fell back for solace on reading movie fan magazines. Given to fantasy, he had an early fix on stardom. Enrolled as an art student at Carnegie Tech, he thought he might like to teach art in the public school system. Instead he moved to Manhattan, where he shared an apartment on St. Marks Place with a classmate, the painter Philip Pearlstein. Before long he was getting jobs from advertising agencies and second-line women's magazines; his specialty was drawing shoes. Unassuming and passive though he might seem, he was excellent at ingratiating himself with the people whom he needed to advance his career.

Warhol graduated from movie to fashion magazines, which he studied with great care. Glamour, aura, chic, such things had an endless fascination for him. Soon his own work as a commercial artist began appearing in the toniest of these magazines. He moved from St. Marks Place to a townhouse he bought on Eighty-ninth and Lexington. While still in his early twenties, he dyed his hair white. With his pale skin, white hair, and red-rimmed eyes, he looked, as a friend later described him, "like a super-intelligent white rabbit."

Star-struck Warhol may have been, but he was no naif. He was very sharp about status and, in the world of Manhattan advertising and art, knew where it was to be found and how to work his way close to its most fashionable sources. He was highly perceptive about the world of contemporary art and the mechanics of promotion within it. Contemporary visual art had long had an element of fashion, but Warhol knew how to combine the two, art and fashion, and manipulate them in his favor.

Not yet a celebrity himself, Warhol remained hung up on celebrity. He was of the species of upward-looking snob. Truman Capote reported that Andy Warhol used to write to him daily and hang out in front of his house. One day Capote's mother let him in. "As far as I knew," Capote said, "he was a window decorator . . . let's say a window-decorator type." (Nice piece of downward-looking homosexual snobbery here, I'd say.) Capote later revised this view. Warhol, he said, wanted fame. "I can't put my finger on exactly *what* it is he's talented at, except that he's a genius as a self-publicist."

Warhol soon enough became famous, hugely famous, on his own: through his Campbell's soup can paintings, through the filmmaking at the Manhattan studio he called The Factory, through the rock group got up in S-M garb he called the Velvet Underground, through being shot and critically wounded by a madwoman named Valerie Solanas. In his journal he recounts how he had become too well known to use a public washroom; at the Vatican, awaiting an audience with the pope, nuns asked for his autograph. Yet he bemoans not being invited to Arnold Schwarzenegger's party for the Statue of Liberty or to Caroline Kennedy's wedding. At his own parties amazing human combinations were found, the most zonked-out acidhead next to Judy Garland, Montgomery Clift next to a transvestite, Tennessee Williams next to the wife of a wealthy Jewish New York state assemblyman. So many worlds came together under his roof and auspices: that of the watered-down New York avant-garde, of drugs, of homosexuality, of the beautiful people (so called), the worlds of publicity and money and show business, all orchestrated by a once bashful boy with a bad complexion and a sense of fashion of the highest power.

But fashion and an upward-looking snobbery were always at the center of the Warhol enterprise. At one point, Warhol told a friend that he thought of opening a store that sold the used underwear of the famous — $10 a pair of washed, $25 if not. Today those prices seem way too low, though the difference in price between the washed and unwashed items still seems just about right. If anyone could have made a go of this particular business, Andy was the man.

19

Names Away!

Name-dropping is the act — as performed by some people, the art — of using one's connection to famous people to establish one's own superiority, while at the same time making those who are without such connection feel the hopeless want of glamour in, the utter drabness of, their own lives. As such, name-dropping is almost always an act, however indirect, of snobbery. "I really must put an end to this name-dropping," an old joke has it, "as I was saying only the other day to Queen Elizabeth and the Pope."

I am a bit of a name-dropper myself, and once wrote an essay on the subject called "A Nice Little Knack for Name-Dropping." In that essay I recorded a few significant "drops" from my childhood years. These included two champion boxers of the day, the welterweight Barney Ross and the middleweight Tony Zale. I had a neighbor whose cousin was Morey Amsterdam, a comedian whom I don't think it would be imprecise to describe as a third banana. Everyone in the neighborhood in which I grew up seems to have known Shecky Greene, a comedian once higher on the banana bunch than he is today, though I somehow missed meeting him.

My name-dropping fell off after that until I became an editor of a scholarly magazine that had an editorial board with some highly droppable names from the worlds of art, intellect, and scholarship: Lillian Hellman, Jacques Barzun, and Diana Trilling are a representative sample. Later I was made a member of the National Council on the Arts, which caused business in this line to pick up substantially. At quarterly meetings in Washington, I met and spent a fair amount of time with Celeste Holm, Robert Joffrey, Roberta Peters, Martha Graham, Toni Morrison, Robert Stack, Helen Frankenthaler, and other men and women who are, as the English say, rather namey. Some I came to like, some I thought greater bores than are to be found on a howitzer, some I had no feeling about at all. By now, most of those still alive probably have little or no memory of me.

I had a three-year friendship in the late 1970s with Saul Bellow, who during that time won a Nobel Prize. I was once taken to a Chicago Bulls basketball game — in the $350-a-seat front-row section — by Gene Siskel, whose fame came from his television show on the movies with Roger Ebert. Before the game he introduced me to Oprah Winfrey, who seemed, like many another early-middle-aged woman, tired after a tough day at the office. I had coffee and dessert with Dick and Lynne Cheney at the Four Seasons Hotel in Washington, and Lynne Cheney at another time had a light dinner at my wife's and my apartment before giving a talk at Northwestern University. I was once the only guest on *The Phil Donahue Show,* in connection with a book I wrote about divorce, a ninety-minute show that felt just a tad longer than a bad fiscal quarter. In connection with the same book, I was the subject of a most unreal article in *People.* I've dined with five other Nobel Prize winners, three in economics, two in physics. I once had dinner with the television actress Barbara Eden. I went to high school with the film director Philip Kaufman, who remains a friend. One of Monica Lewinsky's attorneys is another friend of mine. I had a whitefish dedicated to me and Pierre Boulez by a great though too-little-known chef named Ben Moy. I occasionally receive nice notes from Senator Daniel Patrick Moynihan. I've never, alas, slept with, or known anyone who slept with, Rita Hayworth.

With that, I believe I have got most of the name-dropping

out of my system, except to add that a while ago someone told me that a woman had dropped — of all names — my own with him, which was all right with me. And more recently a friend in publishing told me that his dropping my name with a young woman who liked my writing helped him, as he put it, "to score" with her. Hearing this made me happy. Better to be dropped than to resort to dropping. Still, I feel that my roster of names is, among heavyweights in this line, rather pathetic.

If one wants to see serious name-dropping on display, one can scarcely do better than consult the earlier mentioned *Sorcerer's Apprentice,* the memoir of his life among artists and collectors of art by John Richardson, the biographer of Pablo — not to be confused with, shall we say, Bob — Picasso. "Many years later," Richardson writes, "I told Princess Margaret the story of Picasso's quest for her hand." Attending a music festival in Aix-en-Provence, Richardson was longing for sleep, but, "unfortunately, Segovia, most revered of classical guitarists, had the room above mine, and was practicing for a concert later in the week." When Jacqueline Kennedy Onassis attempted to visit Château Castille, the house in France that Richardson lived in with his friend Douglas Cooper, Richardson is able to report Cooper's delight in telling friends: "The Onassis woman tried to invade my house, but I sent her packing." Now here is prime-quality name-dropping.

The art of name-dropping requires that one match up name to audience, and the practiced name-dropper is likely to feel immense frustration when the match isn't there. The playwright Alan Bennett, so far as I know no name-dropper, illustrates the point in an anecdote he told about trying to explain to his mother, the wife of a butcher, that the daughter of one of their customers married T. S. Eliot. "The thing is," Bennett said to his mother, "he won the Nobel Prize." To which Mrs. Bennett, not overly impressed, replied: "Well, I'm not surprised. It was a beautiful overcoat."

Sports, show business, art, intellect, commerce: different games call for different names. A name that has real bounce in

Washington, D.C., may not leave the pavement in Los Angeles. Proust says that in art, fashion, and medicine there must always be new names, by which he meant that even if there aren't people worthy of being "names," someone must be chosen to play the role of significant personage in the field. The Anglo-American world is without a great poet just now, but according to Proust's dictum that cannot be permitted, so a name must be found and of course one has: the Irish poet Seamus Heaney, a quite good poet yet nowhere near the scale of the great poets of even the recent past, among them Eliot, Wallace Stevens, Robert Frost, W. H. Auden. Yet someone must be called upon to accept all those grants, awards, prizes, praise. Fashion as much as poetry dictates it, and so the modest Mr. Heaney, lucky man, has been chosen. For now, if one wishes to drop the best of living poetry names, Seamus Heaney's is probably untoppable.

In one of his journals, Edmund Wilson likens the persistent name-dropping of the writer Paul Horgan to that of rain pattering on a tin roof. To get in a quick drop here of my own, I knew Horgan, chiefly through telephone calls and correspondence, and he seemed a very decent man. Why, then, this robust propensity to name-dropping? My guess is that Edmund Wilson may have done more than a little to bring this out in Paul Horgan. Between the two men, Wilson was the more important writer, the more admired, powerful, influential, with a reputation as something of an intellectual bully. Perhaps Horgan, in Wilson's company, was trying to make up some ground. He was a friend of Igor Stravinsky, and must have tossed that name into the conversation a fair amount. He'd had dealings with T. S. Eliot, and that, too, might have made for useful ammunition. He must have tossed in whatever else he had at hand, poor fellow. Meanwhile the pattering of all those names on that tin roof proceeded, and one's heart goes out — at least mine does — to Paul Horgan in his use of name-dropping as a defensive measure in the attempt to preserve his own standing.

Sometimes one feels the name-dropper is operating on purely snobbish grounds. Janet Malcolm, in an article in *The*

New Yorker, claimed that "[psycho]analysts are the worst name-droppers in the world." Julian Symons remarked, of the published journal of the critic Cyril Connolly, on "its snobbery, that passion for the right people and the right places that never left him." One feels something of the same quality in the published diaries of Robert Craft, the junior partner of the firm of Stravinsky & Craft, whose name-dropping, persistent though it is, has the quality of a small boy still slightly astonished to have been invited to the party with so many intellectual and artistic celebrities present.

Big names have been known to drop names on their own. Or, on occasion, to drop people when their own social fortunes have risen. I not long ago read, in a biography of John Sparrow, the warden of All Souls College, that he used to save the letters of the poet Edith Sitwell, though she never saved his. But once he became warden of the prestige-laden All Souls, Miss Sitwell began saving Sparrow's letters, at which exact point John Sparrow ceased to save hers. The story is one that shows with a fine perfection — and a fearful symmetry thrown in at no extra charge — how the seesaw of social power and status can work.

Many years ago I met a man who ran a drugstore in Chicago who told me that he used to acquire all sorts of pills and other illegal substances for comedians, singers, and jazz musicians who played the city's Near North Side nightclubs. With great pride he recounted how, when in town, they would gather at his house — the names came burbling out of his mouth like froth from champagne, those of Lenny Bruce and Miles Davis most prominent among them — which was known as "the shooting gallery." What exactly did he get out of this? The right to claim an intimacy with the talented that his own less than bedazzling charms minus the drugs would never have earned. Sad, I thought, the chronicles of this happy pusher to the stars.

What's in a name? Quite a bit; enough, in fact, that being a mere relation to a name is sufficient to unhinge people. Eleanor Coppola, wife of the movie director, in her journal for

June 26, 1976, notes: "When I am cashing a check or using a credit card, people often ask me if I am related to Francis Ford Coppola. Sometimes I say I am married to him. People change before my very eyes. They start smiling nervously and forget to give me my package or change." That's partly what's in a name; if it is the right name, it can turn almost everyone else into a fluttering, pathetic upward-looking snob.

Sometimes one doesn't mind name-dropping because it seems so genuine in its enthusiasm. The two brothers John Gregory Dunne and Dominick Dunne are impressive name-droppers, but among the two I much prefer Dominick, the older brother, for his forthrightness at the game. Some while ago John Gregory Dunne, asked by the editors of *Esquire* to name a woman he admired, chose Katrina vanden Heuvel, the editor of the *Nation* and granddaughter of the powerful Hollywood agent Jules Stein. Mr. J. G. Dunne reports first sighting Katrina vanden Heuvel at parties at her grandfather's, where "one mixed with Gregory Peck and Warren Beatty and Jennifer Jones," and later, in Manhattan, at parties "where all the nobility of arts and letters regularly congregated" and where one encountered "William Styron and Norman Mailer and Gore Vidal and Lillian Hellman and Robert Rauschenberg." Note, please, those breathy "ands," and note also the admirable indirection of the name-dropping that allows Mr. Dunne to drop — bombs away! — without making too great a display of his own presence among those glitterati. This is art.

Indirection in name-dropping is not to be confused with the "secondary name-drop," said to have been perfected by the public relations man Ben Sonnenberg, who claimed to, and probably did, know everyone: "I know the difference between Irving Berlin and Isaiah Berlin, and I know them both," he said. Asked if he knew George Gershwin, Sonnenberg, in a deft secondary drop, replied, "Know him — I used to play gin rummy with his mother!"

Dominick Dunne plays no games with his name-dropping. He tells you straight out that he is thrilled to have been in the company of the famous. In a recent book, *The Way We Lived Then*, to which he appended the subtitle *Recollections of a Well-Known Name Dropper*, Dunne gives us the background to his passion for what might euphemistically be called exclusive company. The background, as in many another case of American snobbery in the twentieth century, was Dunne's Irishness.

Dominick Dunne was born in 1925, and his father was a successful heart surgeon in Hartford, Connecticut. "We were the big-deal Irish-Catholic family in a Wasp city," he writes. "We were venerated by the Catholics of the city but only tolerated by the Protestants." The situation is reminiscent of that of John O'Hara, whose father was a physician in Pottsville, Pennsylvania, but whose Irishness kept the family outside the first circle of the town's social life. Though Dr. Dunne sent his children to boarding schools, belonged to the right golf and tennis clubs, and was a powerful money-maker, none of this cut perfectly square ice cubes with the important families in Hartford. "Irish Catholics didn't come into social respectability," Dunne writes, "until after Jack Kennedy married Jacqueline Bouvier and became the 35th president of the United States."

Dunne allows that he had "always been star struck," and tells about having been rendered speechless when spoken to as a boy by the bandleader Eddie Duchin. Of an early meeting with the diarist Anaïs Nin, he writes: "I was also a natural-born star-fucker even then, before I'd even heard the term." After Williams College and a tour in the army during World War Two, Dunne became a stage manager during the early days of television. From there he moved to Hollywood, working his way up to become a producer, though along the way he married, wisely and well, a woman whose family had made the wheels for all the railway trains in America before the advent of air travel. Soon after his arrival in Hollywood, fortified by his wife's money, he was invited to a party given by Humphrey Bogart — a graduate of Andover and, Dunne reports, a bit of a snob himself — at which he met Spencer Tracy, David Niven, and Judy Garland; Frank Sinatra sang, Lana Turner appeared latish, and the then Mrs. Henry Fonda did a knockout imitation of Joan Crawford. "I thought to myself," Dunne writes, "This is how I want to live."

And for a long while he did. Katharine Hepburn, Kirk Douglas, Claudette Colbert, Jack Benny, Gloria Vanderbilt, Rex Harrison, Mia Farrow, Oscar Levant, Vivien Leigh, Merle Oberon, Steve McQueen, Natalie Wood, Bette Davis, such was the company in which he found himself: the names whir by, usually accompanied by photographs of these people, most of them taken by Dominick Dunne himself. "There was never anything quite like Roddy McDowall's Sunday brunches in Malibu," he writes. "Strictly hot dogs and beer, and everyone you ever heard of came." Dunne and his wife were mentioned in Joyce Haber's gossip column in the *Los Angeles Times,* he reports, as "members of the A group in Hollywood society."

"Beverly Hills was a very glamorous place," where one found the best furniture, jewelry, and art during "a very glamorous time." "Once we'd lived in Harold Lloyd's and Louis B. Mayer's beach houses," Dunne writes, "and President Kennedy helicoptered in for Sunday brunch, and Marilyn came and Judy came, and you knew that where you were was the best place to be at that moment in time." So open is Dunne's exultation in the surroundings in which he has landed himself that one feels he has stepped beyond and above mere snobbery into very heaven itself. A rare bird, Dominick Dunne, the happy snob.

Dunne comes across as a heterosexual Truman Capote, whom he much admired, but without the guile. But even happy snobs cannot seem to stand the heights they have long sought; they grow dizzy and totter and eventually fall. Like Capote, Dunne, too, would crash. One night, at a fashionable restaurant of the day called The Daisy, Frank Sinatra, who viewed Dunne as a social climber who had attained a position he didn't deserve, paid the captain of waiters $50 to punch him in the face — an act of true malevolence. ("I'm so sorry, Mr. Dunne," the waiter whispered before letting fly. "Mr. Sinatra made me do it.")

This marked the beginning of the end for Dunne. His

drinking, already well under way, picked up; later he would do a fair quantity of cocaine. His wife eventually left him, and then died an early death from cancer. (He would also be tested by the death, through murder, of his daughter.) Dunne brought himself back and returned to reality, but it took real character to do so. An extreme case, Dominick Dunne's, of name-dropping and social climbing, but one with what I suppose must be thought a (relatively) happy ending. While retaining his fascination with glamour, he shook his utter dependence on it.

Most of us don't turn a nice little knack for name-dropping into a way of life, the way the young Dominick Dunne did. But few among us can resist the casual drop, which doesn't always have to be of a name. One can drop an address (Kensington in London), a town (Princeton, Jackson Hole), a restaurant (Ducasse, Le Cirque), or a hotel (George V in Paris, Brown's in London). I sat a dinner some while ago at which a woman couldn't seem to complete a sentence without a good school in it: "My son-in-law, whom my daughter met at Oxford . . . my other daughter, who began at Princeton, the same year my son started his first year at the Yale Medical School . . ." ("Daddy," I wanted to say to her, "was at Leavenworth.") Name-dropping of this kind is the reverse of guilt by association; it is glory and glamour by association, though the glory and glamour can scarcely be thinner.

Name-dropping is also a form of social climbing — social climbing on the cheap. It's social climbing because it suggests to people on whom one uses it that you are in a higher, more exciting world than you probably really are; and it's on the cheap because, unlike a serious social climber, one hasn't had to pay out much in the way of effort to get to the sacred city suggested by one's easy dropping of names that have the magic of fame, achievement, or great wealth attached to them — the exclusive city on the hill inhabited by only the best people. If the upward-looking snob exists in a state of nearly perpetual envy, through the device of name-dropping he hopes to garner, at least a little, the pleasure of being envied.

Still, one likes to think that there is benign name-dropping — one's own, naturally. Sometimes famous people really are among one's friends or acquaintances and say or do things worth reporting to other friends. Sometimes, too, there are stories in which the famous are wonderfully foolish, and these stories seem especially worth recounting, in the spirit of "See? The famous are as (cheap, spiteful, unsophisticated, peevish) as you and I."

I have been known to begin a story by warning the people I am about to tell it to that it contains a fairly heavy dose of name-dropping. Yet if the names are good, even with my mild disclaimer, I suppose I am reaping some of the easy rewards of name-dropping. Perhaps the only check on this minor snobbish vice is to ask oneself, Would I tell this story anyway, even if it didn't involve an excellent name, which, through this flimsy association, makes me look good? Am I, in other words, using the fame of others for my own aggrandizement? Not always an easy question to answer.

Perhaps the only way out of the silly game is for oneself to have a name of such thumping grand distinction that, after dropping it upon introduction, none other need be mentioned and everyone can settle down to an evening's enjoyable conversation, name-free and beyond all this fiddle.

20

The Celebrity Iceberg

NAME-DROPPING is closely and naturally connected to celebrity. And celebrity is crucial to snobbery in its new, post-Wasp-dominated American setting. Certainly it is if I am even roughly correct in the following one-sentence history of social power in the United States: It used to be who you were, then it was what you did, then it was what you had, then it was whom you knew — and now it's beginning to be how many people know you.

The odd condition of being well known called celebrity has become a key element in contemporary American social life, one that cuts across and often transcends wealth, culture, and class. Somewhat different from fame — which goes back to ancient civilizations: in Rome it was known as *fama* and was closely connected to civic virtue and later to personal achievement — celebrity is usually more detached from pure achievement. I, for example, believe I have modest fame but no celebrity whatsoever. "You're slightly famous, aren't you, Grandpa?" my then seven-year-old granddaughter once said to me. "I am slightly famous, Annabelle," I answered. "It's just that nobody knows who I am."

The celebrity, in Daniel Boorstin's formulation, is "a person who is well known for his well-knownness." The old categories for fame were rigid and quite clear: one could become famous as a prophet, martyr, monarch, poet, artist, scientist, or warrior, and, much later, banker or merchant. The first famous man was Alexander the Great, the first famous woman Joan of Arc. How different from today, when one can acquire celebrity for committing murder, winning money on a quiz show, or performing the act of fellatio on a (admittedly high-level) public servant!

In the contemporary world, the snob's interest in celebrity is, first, in acquiring it; and if that is not possible, second, getting close enough to it to have some of its magic rub off and adhere to him. Where once the snob wanted to get into Society — no easy thing — today he can consider himself having arrived if he finds he is among the well known. Not that this is an entirely new phenomenon. Already in the eighteenth century, G. C. Lichtenberg wrote, "The journalists have constructed for themselves a little wooden chapel, which they also call the Temple of Fame, in which they put up and take down portraits all day long and make such a hammering you can't hear yourself speak." In late-nineteenth-century Paris, the Abbé Arthur Mugnier, a man known for his sweet nature who shows up in the memoirs of Edith Wharton and other people of literary interests, wrote in his journal: "What I like in society is the setting, the names, the beautiful homes, the reunion of fine minds, the contact with celebrities." The snob likes the same things, but if need be, he can make do without the fine minds.

Contact with celebrities does lots of things, and not only for snobs. Lord Reith, the founding director general of the BBC, noted in his journal: "I do not enjoy parties unless there are people bigger than myself present." Being with people the world reckons as notable gives one the feeling that one is living a little closer to the center of the universe. "We are all in the gutter," Oscar Wilde has a character in *Lady Windermere's Fan* say, "but some of us are looking at the stars."

The stars, from the standpoint of celebrity, aren't what they used to be. They come increasingly from show business, but of an order of magnitude much lower than that of Fred Astaire and Ingrid Bergman, Grace Kelly and Louis Armstrong.

Stars in our day are television news readers, quiz-show hosts, talk-show Johnnies and Janes. In America at this time, perhaps no greater celebrities exist than Oprah; the three major network anchormen (Dan Rather, Tom Brokaw, and Peter Jennings); Regis Philbin, a quiz-show man; and maybe Donald Trump, who builds gaudy hotels, marries slightly gaudier women, and manages to stay on the covers of the grocery (or gutter) press. The best-known American singer must be Madonna, though I am unaware of any songs she has sung, and because her hair and makeup change so frequently, most Americans, having glimpsed a best-selling book of photographs of her naked, perhaps have a clearer mental picture of her bottom than of her face. No business, it is truly said, like show business.

Celebrity consists mainly of having oneself talked about and mentioned frequently in public places. As for how one knows one has achieved the condition of celebrityhood, this is not always so easily divined. In the ancient world, having one's face on a coin was firm evidence of renown. Today I suppose that finding one's name as a clue in a crossword puzzle might be one indication, though having a crazy person imagine he is you would be a stronger one. Celebrity has its own hierarchy. In his diary, Alan Bennett notes that, in the audience at his play one evening, the singer Barry Manilow is disconcerted to find the press and paparazzi desert him when Prince Charles and his great good friend Mrs. Camilla Parker-Bowles enter the theater.

Being recognized by strangers is another measure of celebrity. Perhaps this paragraph belongs in my name-dropping chapter, but during the few years that I went out fairly frequently with Saul Bellow, I felt he used to check the room in restaurants and other public places to see if anyone recognized him, and was faintly disappointed when (too often) no one did. He was also, poor fellow, sometimes confused in good old philistine Chicago with a powerful defense attorney around town named Charley Bellows. On the other hand, I was taken to dinner by George Will, at the Cape Cod Room of the Drake Hotel in Chicago, and everyone seemed to recognize him: the maitre d', the waiters, lots of fellow diners, two of whom sent up (by way of the waiter) slips of paper asking for an autograph. As we left the restaurant, two couples entered the hotel, and one of the women actually screamed, "My God, it's George Will."

The difference between the celebrity of Saul Bellow and George Will here is that the latter regularly appears on television, and, with the exception of major scandal on the Monica Lewinsky level, television and the movies are perhaps the only ways to acquire serious celebrity in America. I once gave a talk at California State University at Los Angeles that was televised on C-Span, which I thought no big deal. The reaction to that was wider — I do not say better — than to any piece of writing I've ever published. Thirty or so acquaintances, channel surfing, reported catching my talk. A number of letters and notes came in, and more than a hundred e-mails. One day three or four months afterward, I was crossing a street in Baltimore when a man in a red Mazda Miata, about to make a right turn, stopped midturn, lowered his window on the passenger side, pointed a finger at me, couldn't bring up my name, and finally exclaimed, "C-Span, right?" Only television confers this kind of goofy renown.

People's propensity for excitement when around celebrities is apparently never to be underestimated. I have a friend who had the misfortune to have a minor stroke in Los Angeles. At Cedars-Sinai Medical Center, he was told, with something like civic pride, that he was being put in the same room in which Sammy Davis, Jr., died. The next morning, on the way to take neurological tests, he was asked by the attendant pushing his gurney if he'd like to go the long way down to neurology because doing so they might see Olivia Newton-John, who was reported to be in the main waiting room.

The snobbery connected with celebrity runs at least two ways. First, and more obvious, is that in which upward-looking snobs seek to attach themselves to celebrities, in the hope of improving their own (presumably) shaky status. Second is that in which the celebrated themselves suffer their own status anxieties about slippage in their celebrity. Neither tends to bring out the best in people.

For the celebrity who enjoys his fame, there is only one thing in the world worse than being talked about critically, and that is not being talked about at all. This is especially true for celebrities who sense their own notability on the slide, if not altogether dissipated. I was once introduced to Marshall Goldberg, the (1937–38) All-American football player from the University of Pittsburgh (and, later, with the Chicago Cardinals), who, it was impossible not to see, was delighted that I knew who he was — or should I make that who he had been. A nice man, Marshall Goldberg, but clearly a man of deeply diminished celebrity, in the sense that few people under sixty were likely to know what he had done.

Celebrity may seem terribly superficial, yet it is not without its pleasures. Leo Braudy, in *The Frenzy of Renown,* remarks that "the spiritual glow conveyed by being recognized means finally not having to say who you are." How much more comfortable a room seems when there are people in it who have some notion of your proximate worth. Even historical figures have felt the allure of fame and celebrity. "Why, upon the very books in which they bid us scorn ambition philosophers inscribe their names," wrote Cicero, who was an impressive self-promoter in this line. Montaigne, a great realist, thought it hopeless to expect people not to seek every recognition for themselves.

Yet something different, and more than merely wanting one's quality recognized, is going on in the desire to be celebrated. It is one thing to wish to be distinguished from the ordinary. But people who worry a good deal about celebrity — about not having it, or about not having enough of it, or about losing it — are contending with essentially snobbish emotions. They wish to be above the ruck, the sweaty riff-raff struggling down below. Intent on finding a way to arrive at this elevated position, they must themselves sometimes be shocked at the lengths to which they will go to achieve this simulacrum of achievement.

The job is the more difficult for people who have nothing to offer other than the desire itself. I think here not only of the people who hang around the celebrated but who eagerly put themselves out for them in the hope of somehow sharing in their celebrity. One hears endless stories about women falling, quite literally, before athletic stars: the toughest thing about playing in the National Basketball Association, it has been said, is not smiling while kissing your wife goodbye when your team is going on a road trip.

Richard Ben Cramer's biography of Joe DiMaggio shows the phenomenon of the celebrity hanger-on in extreme form. DiMaggio was the greatest all-round player in the history of the game of baseball, but off the field his intrinsic charms were not, to put it gently, immediately or universally evident. Yet, owing to his celebrity, a long list of people were always ready to put themselves at Joe DiMaggio's service: to run interference, to serve as gofers, to arrange his financial, sexual, and quotidian needs. Not a few left their families to keep Joe company at odd hours. Some had their own motives — among them, wanting to use him to make money off his name — but most found it thrilling enough just to be around Joe.

What they got out of it is complicated, I'm sure, but part of it had to do with the right it conferred of telling others of one's connection to a man who, in his own way, was a historical figure. Whether I should be ashamed of saying so I'm not certain, but I should have liked to meet Joe DiMaggio. And if I had done so, I would certainly have told a number of people about it — because I think it would interest them, of course, but also to establish that I was living at what the world reckons ethereal heights. "If you had told me in 1938 [when he was ten years old] that I would be Secretary of State and friends with Joe DiMaggio," Henry Kissinger has said, "I would have thought that the second was less likely than the first." Is Henry Kissinger being a snob here? I don't believe so, even though DiMaggio's celebrity, if not his seriousness, outranks Kissinger's, which is far from slight. Instead Kissinger nicely illustrates Andy Warhol's remark that the best thing about being famous was that one got the chance to meet so many other famous people.

Although very great wealth brings its own celebrity — we all know who Ted Turner, Rupert Murdoch, and Michael Milken are — the normally wealthy are usually ready to offer obeisance to the celebrated by paying high prices to attend one or another kind of celebrity dinner. At the University of Chicago I once attended a dinner in honor of Walter Cronkite, a high platitudinarian and a man with a face only a nation can love, at which I noted the spectacle of a gossip columnist named Irv Kupcinet and a television news reader named Walter Jacobson shake hands warmly while each looked over the other's shoulder in the hope of discovering more important people than they in the room.

Such has been the mania in America over celebrity that, as Tyler Cowen writes in *What Price Fame?*, "it is estimated that 20 percent of all television commercials include a famous person." An economist with an interest in popular culture, Cowen describes ours as "an economy of fame." (Soon, doubtless, there will be an academic specialty called Celebrity Studies.) By this Cowen means that fame, which he uses synonymously with celebrity, is central not only in the sale of products but in the promotion of culture. The repercussions from this often cause the division between celebrity and quality to be all but unbreachable; certainly it has made the line separating the high, middle, and low in culture more blurry than it has ever been before.

I was once at a party, in the Rainbow Room at Rockefeller Center, at which were present a number of powerful political personages. Among them were George Shultz, then secretary of state; Jeane Kirkpatrick, then ambassador to the United Nations; Ed Koch, then mayor of New York City; Daniel Patrick Moynihan, then senator from New York; and Henry Kissinger. Lots of security men in the room, many walkie-talkies. I was seated at a table with a number of artists and critics. At the table with me was a dear friend, now dead, who was, though he would not be pleased to have it said about him, a power snob. Looking around the room, he leaned in and whispered to me, "I see that we have been put at the children's table."

The snob, recognizing where the action is, goes weak in the knees at the prospect of meeting or actually spending time with celebrities. The celebrity, he recognizes if his social radar is in good repair, is the new American aristocrat. But, as in a reverse limbo dance, the bar of celebrity rises higher and higher, allowing more and more people to pass under it.

"Reputation may be the major American art form," wrote Harold Brodkey (for reputation here read: celebrity). Brodkey himself had achieved considerable celebrity, at least in the small literary world of Manhattan, based on a long unpublished novel, said to have been a masterwork in the making. Once the novel was published and proved, alas, far from a masterpiece, Brodkey, who had something akin to genius in garnering celebrity, shifted into confessional mode, and recounted, in the pages of *The New Yorker,* his own forthcoming death resulting from AIDS. Poor man, right up to the end he kept his celebrity, which then expired with him.

"Can a nation remain healthy, can all nations draw together," Winston Churchill asked in an essay of 1930, "in a world whose brightest stars are film stars?" But of course things have gone much lower than film stars. Along with designers, chefs and models nowadays ring the celebrity register. Fame has long been separating itself from real achievement, but for the celebrity snob achievement hasn't much to do with anything. The celebrity's most serious achievement is in keeping his or her name before the public; and perhaps the greatest achievement of all, as the public understands it, is a talent for celebrity itself.

I have not till now called for sympathy for the snob, but life over the past fifty years cannot have been easy for him. His social radar would have been almost constantly atwitter as one hierarchy after another in American life has broken down and been replaced by new ones, ever more blurry and more ephemeral. The chief problem of how to gain and maintain a place from which to look down on all but a handful of his countrymen has shifted on him almost continuously. Piolets, at the ready for the great social climb, the snob has the challenge of discovering a peak that keeps changing and disappearing. American social life must have come to seem to him so many illusory tips and no iceberg whatsoever.

21

....

Anglo-, Franco-, and Other Odd philias

I HAD A FRIEND, now deceased, named Peter Jacobsohn, who attracted many people in a way that for a long
while I couldn't comprehend. Peter was born in Germany,
was Jewish, came to this country as an adult not long after
World War Two. He was small, bald, cared about clothes, and
had a nice sense of whimsy. He had a cosmopolitan accent,
part British, a touch Teutonic, free of all American idiom. His
father, Siegfried Jacobsohn, was a distinguished drama critic
and editor of *Die Weltbuhne,* an important intellectual magazine in Weimar Germany. But Peter's early life — with the advent of the Nazis, his and his mother's forced exile to England, his subsequent internment by the English in Australia
during the war — had robbed him of all ambition and left him
with only two goals: survival and the enjoyment of everyday
life in America on a modest scale.

Married, with a son born when he was in his fifties, Peter
achieved both these goals, but at the high cost of anxiety
about whether he had a real understanding of his adopted
country and was doing, if not the right, at least the approved
thing. Although he would live in America for more than half a
century, he never, one sensed, really got the hang of it. He was

a man who asked for lots of advice, had many consultants, of
whom for a long period I was one. (He called me, amusingly,
"Colonel.") History had rendered Peter a permanent guest,
not a host; a supplicant for, not a dispenser of, favors; a re-
ceiver much more than a giver.

What was interesting, and what for a while I couldn't
fathom, was why so many people, of a great range of ages and
types, were always pleased to help Peter. Part of the explanation is that he was a gentle, charming man with no edge to him
whatsoever, a genuinely sweet character. Yet I finally concluded that something else, something deeper, was going on.
All these people wanted Peter to like them — not that he
could do anything for them, or that they longed for a deep
friendship with him — because if they were liked by Peter,
they seemed to have passed an unspoken test. If Peter liked
you, it felt as if Europe approved of you. Peter's friendship
had a way of deprovincializing us, or those among us who
prefer to think of ourselves as more than *mere* Americans.

Most Americans of any educational pretension, as I have
remarked earlier, have long felt a cultural inferiority toward
Europeans. In the nineteenth century, no one felt this more
strongly than the best-educated Americans. Bostonians of the
Brahmin caste regularly ventured to Europe, many of them settling in Florence, Rome, London, and Paris, and having a
wider European than American circle of friends. The lure was
a denser, richer culture. Henry James, in his little book
on Nathaniel Hawthorne, puts best what this class sensed
was missing from an America that was then less than a hundred years old. Here is what one might nowadays call James's
wish list:

> One might enumerate the items of high civilization, as it exists
> in other countries, which are absent from the texture of
> American life, until it should become a wonder to know what
> was left. No State, in the European sense of the word, and in-
> deed barely a specific national name. No sovereign, no court,
> no personal loyalty, no aristocracy, no church, no clergy,
> no army, no diplomatic service, no country gentlemen, no
> palaces, no castles, no manors, nor old country houses, nor

parsonages, nor thatched cottages nor ivied ruins; no cathedrals, nor abbeys, nor little Norman churches; no great Universities nor public schools — no Oxford, nor Eton, nor Harrow; no literature, no novels, no museums, no pictures, no political society, no sporting class — no Epson nor Ascot!

The absence of all these and still other things caused James to emigrate — to England but really to Europe, where he became, as T. S. Eliot once called him, "a European but of no known country." James would later write to Mrs. William James, his sister-in-law, that he "could come back to America . . . to die — but never, never to live." While Eliot never spelled them out, his motives in departing America for England may not have been all that different from those of Henry James: the promise of a richer culture. George Santayana, one of Eliot's philosophy teachers at Harvard, was said to lecture not looking at his class but gazing out the window. When someone asked him what he was looking for out that window, Santayana is said to have replied, "Europe."

It's not uncommon for younger nations to yearn for the richer culture of older ones — as the Romans for a long while did for that of the Greeks — nor for the older nations to look down on the younger. In his novel *Money,* Martin Amis has his chief character, walking the streets of New York, think: "Speaking as an Englishman, one of the pluses of New York is that it makes you feel surprisingly well-educated and upper-class. I mean, you're bound to feel a bit brainy and blue-blooded, a bit of an exquisite, when you walk through 42nd Street or Union Square, or even Sixth Avenue — at noon, the office men, with lunchbox faces and truant eyes." A more amusing, if wildly more oblique, treatment of this subject comes up in Evelyn Waugh's *A Handful of Dust,* where the wife of the novel's protagonist is attempting to fix him up with another woman so that she may carry on her own love affair without distraction:

". . . We must get him interested in a girl."
"If only we could . . . Who is there?"

"There's always Sybil."
"Darling, he's known her all his life."
"Or Souki de Foucauld-Esterhazy."
"He isn't his best with Americans."

Sometimes the upper classes of one older nation will snobbishly imitate their counterparts in another. The Russians' aping of the French in the eighteenth and nineteenth centuries is but one example; any Russian caught speaking French in a Tolstoy novel is automatically a figure, if not always of ridicule, at least to be distrusted. For a spell the French looked to England for its best models of *hauteur*. The English upper classes are, historically, perhaps alone in not looking for models elsewhere. In their journal the Goncourt brothers note that "the wing of the chicken at a *table d'hôte* always goes to the Englishman. He is the only person the waiter serves. Why is this? Because the Englishman does not look upon the waiter as a man, and any servant who feels he is being regarded as a human being despises the person considering him in that light." As if in confirmation of this, Elizabeth Gaskell has an aristocratic woman in her novel *Wives and Daughters* say: "I never think whether a land agent is handsome or not. They do not belong to the class of people whose appearance I notice."

The English are more practiced in snobbery than any other people. The English also thought, Copernicus-like, that the earth revolved around them: "Continent Cut Off by Fog," read a famous headline in an English newspaper, when of course things ought to have been put the other way round. The English had a stricter class system, and one that lasted for a longer period than any other. "You couldn't go for a walk anywhere in Scarborough," writes the English novelist Pat Barker in *The Ghost Road*, "without seeing the English class system laid out for you in its full intricate horror." The cruel little distinctions that go along with this system are learned early — or had damn well better be learned if one is to stay socially afloat. Lord Berners, in *First Childhood*, the initial volume of his autobiography, notes that from earliest school days "it became necessary to exercise a nice judgment between the people to whom deference was due, those who were to be treated on terms of equality and those who might be looked on as inferior and who could be snubbed and bullied."

The French, though sometimes subtler, can be even crueler in these matters, as Proust, preeminently, has shown. The great French vice is no doubt too great an emphasis on taste, and judging others on their want of it. Perhaps this was owing to the repeatedly poor showing of the French in war, but after World War One Misia Sert noted that, among the French, "the clever insult replaced the gallant compliment." The French are of course death on anyone who uses their language badly. The English find in the use of their language measures of status and vulgarity and signs of the user's social-class origins, all of which they are prepared to use against him. (In America today it is said that the use of standard — which is to say, correct — English is a sure indicator of social class, and increasingly of being in the upper middle class and above.) But whatever the manifold disagreements between them, the English and the French — with many distinguished exceptions — have long been able to agree on one thing: the naiveté, the vulgarity, the sheer awfulness of Americans.

Coming at things the other way round, the American picture of the perfect snob is usually someone either English or with strong Anglo-American affectations. In American movies of my youth, the snob was often played by Clifton Webb or George Sanders, with Adolphe Menjou playing the snob in a more continental version. They were pedants and cads all, highly cultivated, effete, unfeeling, ostentatious, alike in their hauteur and disdain.

While the Anglophilic snob was mocked in popular culture, among the putatively cultivated Anglophilia was always taken seriously. In academic life, men such as Professor Barrett Wendell, of the English Department at Harvard, gave Anglophilia a bad name by suggesting that only students of English descent were suited to study English literature. Quieter, less heavily italicized ways of adopting an Anglophilic outlook than those suggested by the Clifton Webb, George

Sanders, and Barrett Wendell models were available. Italo-
philes would come later. They had early representatives in
Bernard Berenson and George Santayana; though both men
loved Italy, they never attempted to model themselves on
the Italian upper classes. The Italian spirit seems all but opposed to snobbery, except perhaps on the fashion front.
Germanophilia, attractive for sexually adventurous Englishmen during the Weimar period, seemed no longer a serious
possibility after Hitler, although the poets W. H. Auden and
Randall Jarrell were both Germanophilic in their cultural
interests.

American Anglo- and Francophiles tended to be men and
women who had grander conceptions of themselves than did
many of their countrymen. They thought of themselves as
somehow belonging to a larger world where tradition (England) or culture (France) played a larger role than it did in
the United States. Americans who married Europeans took
this yearning to belong to a wider world to a much higher
level, and often took on the status of half-naturalized Europeans even while remaining in this country. In my experience,
most such people turn out to be just a touch contemptuous of
their countrymen.

The influence of Anglophilia is seen in many American
institutions — eastern boarding schools and universities chief
among them — that have been based directly on English
models, both in their organization and in their architecture.
Some American customs — fox hunting in full regalia in Virginia is an outlandish example — quite out-English the English. Large American cities have chapters of the institution
known as Alliance Française, in which the French language is
taught and French culture, in rather a force-fed way, infused;
in New York one can still send one's children to a *lycée* where
they will acquire something like the education originally set
up by Frenchmen abroad so that their children could train for
the *baccalauréat*. England and France don't have or feel the
need for comparable American institutions; it is difficult to
imagine just what they would be like. And when the English
or the French come to America to live, they do so not because

they feel our culture is superior, though of late some among them may feel America more open and lively than their own countries; more likely they come for the economic opportunities offered in the United States.

When Americans have gone to live in Europe, they have tended to do so in the hope of a richer, deeper, more cultured life. Whether they found it or not remains an unanswered question. American expatriates in the last century, including the most elegant among them — Gerald and Sara Murphy, hosts to the not really all that lost generation, come first to mind here — finally remained tourists, if close to permanent ones. American writers, with the possible exception of Gertrude Stein, left the impression that their European years constituted a kind of camping out. Bernard Berenson, who from his villa in Tuscany enjoyed perhaps the grandest twentieth-century expatriation of all, can scarcely be said to have integrated himself fully into European life, becoming if not so much a tourist then something close to a tourist stop.

Henry James said that "it's a complex fate, being an American, and one of the responsibilities it entails is fighting against a superstitious valuation of Europe." By this James meant that, owing to its allure for Americans of sensibility, one is always in danger of rating the quality of Europe too highly. The temptation to do so has always been there and remains in place, even though one knows that Europe has neither the political power nor the cultural resources it once possessed.

My own taste has run more strongly to Anglo- than to Francophilia. I cannot visit either Oxford or Cambridge without a wisp of regret for never having gone to school there, even though many Americans, Bill Clinton among them, seem to have done so without either place ever having laid a cultural glove on them. The pronunciation of certain words — *teerod* and *sheerod* for *tirade* and *charade,* the mere use of *whilst* — fills me with a combination of envy and admiration. Certain English clothes — well-made shoes, sweaters, suits — can turn on my yearning switch. (Think Yiddish, the old motto had it, dress British.) Randolph Churchill, when asked if Harold Macmillan, then a candidate for prime minister, had the common touch, replied: "Common touch? To hell with the common touch! He's got the *un*common touch. We want men of distinction and education." England can still turn out people filled with impressive learning, elevated common sense, and delicate wit. Being well educated and openly distinguished has always seemed easier in England than in the United States, where either quality could be held against one, especially in public life.

It's the aristocratic air — social or intellectual, usually both — that Anglophiles often admire. For a good spell in America, having an English secretary was a mark of high status in corporate quarters. In American universities, an English-born academic with a good accent ought to have been able to earn an extra $20,000 or so more than an American academic of roughly the same scholarly attainments. Pathetic snobbery, all of this, of course. (When confronted by a genuinely upper-class English accent, Anglophile that I am, the old Communist in me comes out, and I think how, on balance, Oliver Cromwell was on to a good thing but really should have finished the job.)

Tocqueville gets it dead right yet again when he notes: "Aristocracies often commit very tyrannical and inhuman actions, but they rarely entertain groveling thoughts; and they show a kind of haughty contempt of little pleasures, even while they indulge in them." Until only recently, when English politicians, entertainers, and cultural figures began descending to imitate their Americans counterparts, the English were thought, at least by we Anglophiles, to have both a larger and more detached view of life.

In intellectual journalism, novel writing, theater, movies, scholarship, comedy, deployment of language generally — in most of the things that I cared most about, the English for so many years did it better. I rarely acted on my Anglophilia: didn't put on an English accent, wear heavy tweeds in summer, let my teeth go, favor gristly meat and overcooked vegetables. I long ago eschewed using such Anglicisms as "early on" and "in the event," though I wasn't above slipping an occasional Anglicism into my speech, saying that this "put paid to that," or that something or other "would see me out." I bought the odd item of English clothing, most notably thick corduroy trousers purchased in a shop on High Street in Oxford that come close to standing up on their own without aid of a hanger and that really will see me out. I occasionally published an essay or a review in one or another English magazine — *Encounter,* the *Times Literary Supplement,* the *London Review of Books* — which caused me to feel a pride not altogether dissimilar to that of being accepted as a member of a superior club. But my snobbishness on this count was almost entirely of an interior kind; that is, I could use it only to pump myself up into the belief I was traveling among the intellectual swells, not — to complete the full snobbish act — to make others feel a little worse because of this.

American Francophilia is a different kettle of snails. Unlike the English, whose accomplishments in acquiring and running their empire were immensely impressive, whose sense of fair play and decency were genuine, the French are not easily admired. They have no record of bravery, unless it be that of individual French men and women — Joan of Arc, Alfred Dreyfus, Albert Camus in the Resistance — winning out against stupid and vile French governments. Not for nothing have the French had the bitterest writers, from La Rochefoucauld to Flaubert to Celine, for the French have given ample examples of humanity at its most selfish upon which these writers could formulate their dark thoughts into works of literary art.

American Francophilia therefore takes a different turn than does American Anglophilia. For one thing, Francophilia isn't aristocratic in nature or impulse, for one can't really hope to imitate what is left of the French aristocracy — the de Noailles, the de Carbonnels, the de Greffulhes, the de Courcels, et alia — whose society is so exclusive, whose culture is so rarefied, whose style of living is so high as to be finally inimitable. Instead American Francophile imitations take the form of an amalgam of French peasant and upper-bourgeois life — cassoulet and the $100 bottle of wine. Francophile snobbery revolves around French food, wine, and the French language, at none of which can we gringos hope to compete.

American Francophiles can't really win. *A Moveable Feast,* Ernest Hemingway's memoir of Paris, had almost no Frenchmen in it, though its author was eager above all to show how very native he had gone; Hemingway's days were spent chiefly among fellow Americans and Englishmen. The French weren't hospitable to Hemingway, or any other Americans. The American novelists Irwin Shaw, James Jones, Diane Johnson, and others have lived their later lives in France, but all under the protection of that greatest of cultural buffers, fairly serious wealth.

In *French Lessons,* Alice Kaplan reports how American teachers of French in universities in the United States who work in departments with native speakers live in terror of making even the smallest mistake in pronunciation or grammar. This does not, of course, stop the American Francophilic speaker of French from looking down on the less accomplished American speaker. "French brings out the worst in all of us," Max Beerbohm wrote, but then the mispronunciation of words, foreign or English, always excites the snob when he is in possession of the correct pronunciation.

To live in the French way, the American Francophile thinks, is to live with sensible good taste, where sensuality is given its due, and a certain dry precision of manner is much admired. The Francophile's fantasy would be composed of friends among the wellborn, the artistically talented, and the amusing, dining on fine fresh light food, where the chic combines with the abstract, and high expenditure with a dramatically dark outlook. Only Americans with the Francophile virus could have fallen for the philosophical emptiness that passed under the rubric of existentialism.

Dazzled by what seems to him the ease of the French in the world, the casual elegance they bring to everyday living, the American Francophile fails to understand that beneath the overlay of French culture is the solid, sordid fact that every Frenchman is fundamentally in business for him- or herself, with every luxury allowed but that of altruism, if Molière, Stendhal, Balzac, Proust, and other of the more trenchant writers on the French social scene are to be believed.

The stock American Francophile, with his baguette and beret, his Alliance Française French, his Brillat-Savarin quotations accompanying dinner, is a figure from the past, though he may occasionally still be found on backwater American college campuses. The newer edition of the American Francophile is more likely to turn up today speaking no French, toting a $4,000 Louis Vuitton bag, and happy to fork over $500 or more for a three-star lunch. *Vive la France! Vive le schmuck!*

Henry James's superstitious valuation of Europe continues well into our day, making an especial appeal to American snobs, still ordering their clothes from London, linen from Vienna, furniture from Milan, toiletries from Paris. Along with a snobbery of European consumption, there is the American snobbery of European travel. One sees this highlighted in Paul Fussell's book *Abroad,* which, though ostensibly about the travel of the English between the world wars, badly tips its author's heavy-handedly Anglophilic, clearly snobbish mitt. An American himself, Fussell posits that "travel" is over, long ago replaced by tourism, for which read: vulgar American tourists are everywhere mucking things up for elevated chaps of high sensibility such as — you've guessed it — Professor Fussell. Once the going was good, to adapt a title of one of Evelyn Waugh's travel books, but now, in Fussell's view, the good is gone and all that remains of the going is package tours, pollution, the Americanization of the once exotic, leaving only, in Claude Lévi-Strauss's word, monoculture.

But hasn't it almost always seemed so? Henry James, in the 1880s, speaks of wishing to get to the Uffizi well in advance of the crowds composed, in his witty phrase, of "my detested fellow pilgrims." Jacques Barzun, in a different context, has remarked that art, once the handmaiden of religion, has now become "the pimp of tourism." This, too, has long been true. Part of the snobbish pleasure of travel is in having someone down upon whom to look: that busload of thick-legged Germans; those gaggles of Japanese, cameras slung round their necks; best of all for deploring are one's easily detested fellow Americans.

Yet it can be more than exasperating, it can be genuinely crazy-making to hear these same dear detested fellow Americans attacked by others. Some years ago, planning a trip to Israel, I was called near the last moment by one of the managers of an artists-and-scholars hostel in Jerusalem where I was planning to stay, informing me that my reservation had been canceled and was being put ahead by three weeks. I complained of the difficulty this caused me to an Israeli I knew who was then teaching at the same university I do. He replied that the hostel dealt with "so many vulgar Americans" that there probably wasn't much to be done about it. Vulgar Americans, I repeated silently to myself, and made a mental note to run this man over if ever he should step in front of my car.

I have also been "privileged," as the literary theorists say, by some Europeans who have complained to me about the lack of refinement and culture of Americans — all those McDonald's, that wretched television, ugly shopping malls — unlivable, hideous, ghastly! As a man of obviously deep culture, or so they pay me the halfhearted compliment of assuming, I must share their contempt for the grotesque American scene. When this happens, I find myself wanting to defend American culture to the last animal-fat-saturated fast-food french fry, and thus the jingo in me wins out, however briefly, over the snob.

22

....

Setting the Snob's Table

W HEN DID my dentist begin using the word *pasta?* When did anyone? I have checked this with friends who grew up in Italian families, and in their memory the word of choice was inevitably *spaghetti,* sometimes *macaroni.* I'm not sure I can nail down the exact date when *pasta* came into currency, but around that time, my guess is, one can discover the beginning of food snobbery in America.

Sometime in the 1970s, among the enlightened classes food replaced movies as the subject of passionate interest on social occasions. Instead of people chattering away ardently about what Pauline Kael, in *The New Yorker,* thought about the most recent Robert Altman or Arthur Penn movie, they were buzzing about the latest Ethiopian, Madagascan, or Corsican restaurant. At their homes, one would be served what can only be called the results of ambitious cooking. Limits removed from pretensions as easily as the tops of salvers from warm dishes, meals would run to six or seven courses. At one such dinner I attended, bits of ginger were provided between the fourth and fifth of seven courses to refresh "a tired palate." Not an easy thing to live with, a tired palate, surely I don't have to tell you.

As readers of this book by now cannot mistake, no subject, apart possibly from podiatry, is impermeable to snobbery, but

for a long while food in America seems to have been kept relatively free of it. Food was fresh or not, plentiful or not. There
were good and bad cooks. Upper-class Americans, or at least
some among them, ate extremely well. In her description
of the food served at her parents' table in the middle-late
nineteenth century, Edith Wharton, engaging in a fine bit of
gastronomic nostalgia, remarks of the cooks of the era, "Ah,
what artists they were!" Simple yet sure were their methods,
she says, working with plain good foods: "Who will again
taste anything in the whole range of gastronomy to equal their
corned beef, their boiled turkeys with stewed celery and oyster sauce, their fried chickens, broiled redheads, corn fritters,
stewed tomatoes, rice griddle cakes, strawberry short-cake
and vanilla ices." She goes on to describe the fare for a large
dinner party, which is more of the same but richer, at the close
of which she writes: "Ah, the *gourmet* of that long-lost day,
when cream was cream and butter butter and coffee coffee,
and meat fresh every day, and game hung just for the proper
number of hours, might lean back in his chair and murmur,
'Fate cannot harm me' over his cup of Moka and his glass of
authentic Chartreuse." No snobbery here, I would say, just
damn good vittles hugely enjoyed.

Complaints about the low quality of food in America were
entered by such official snobs as Lucius Beebe, who wrote
about travel and food for the old *Holiday* magazine and who
was once described by Wolcott Gibbs as "menacingly well-
groomed." (A woman, hearing that Beebe was to go in for ex-
ploratory surgery, is said to have remarked: "I do hope the
surgeon has the decency to open Lucius at room tempera-
ture.") Excitement about food, especially in the France of his
youth, was exhibited in delicious prose by A. J. Liebling in his
book *Between Meals.* Some American novelists who had
put in time in Europe — Mary McCarthy comes to mind —
rattled on in the most patently snobbish way about the hor-
rors of the American supermarket, making American white
bread seem nothing less than poison to the soul.

But food in America was no big, certainly no very complicated, deal. Plain fare was pretty much the order of the day,

with ethnic dishes, if one happened to be of an ethnic group, served at home. Beef — steaks, roasts, hamburgers — held primacy in American cookery. The ideal, nonregional meal at an American restaurant might consist of a shrimp cocktail, a salad (iceberg lettuce with Thousand Island dressing), steak and a baked potato and a vegetable as a main course, pie, cake, or ice cream for dessert. One might have a strong appetite for oysters or lobster, or the perfect hot dog, or Italian sausage, but for the most part the American diet was steady and solid, if a little dull in its want of variety. Then Americans began to develop complicated attitudes toward food, and cooking became a serious matter, so that a few months ago, an acquaintance whom I was to meet for lunch suggested a place that, he assured me, has "a fairly reliable risotto."

Several things greatly widened the American menu over the past thirty or so years, among them increased foreign travel, the happy acceptance and rising interest in ethnic food, the growth of supermarkets, the spread of vegetarianism, the national preoccupation with healthful eating, the endless worry about nutrition and diet. Suddenly a groaning sideboard of gastronomic possibilities was on offer. I recall, in 1951, at the age of fourteen, having tasted my first piece of pizza, at a restaurant on Broadway Avenue in Chicago called Gabriel's, and thinking I had gone to heaven. But pizza, to avail myself of one of those goofy mixed metaphors of the kind known as a punafor, was only the entering wedge. Over the next twenty or so years everyone not only began saying "pasta" but could tick off ten different kinds, with breath enough left over to say "pesto," "Marsala," and "infused white-truffle oil." Turns out — who would have thought it? — there were more varieties of balsamic vinegar than American states, possibly more virgin olive oils than actual virgins.

As with Italian food, so, soon enough, with the help of Julia Child and others, Americans of the enlightened classes became gastronomically literate about French cooking. The chop-suey-and-egg-foo-yung level of knowledge about Chinese food rose greatly, and Cantonese gave way to Mandarin and Szechuan. If one lived in a gastronomically sophisticated city — New York, San Francisco, Toronto — Eritrean, Malaysian, Vietnamese, and other once unknown cuisines become de-exoticized. As just about everyone in America was an expert on the movies, now, quicker than you could say quiche Lorraine, almost as many people began to think themselves food experts, if not in the preparation of food then in its consumption. Which sounds fine: as in language, so in food; the more variation and distinctions to be made the better.

Except that such proliferation, such an extension of possibilities, brought novelty, trendiness, exclusivity, finally snobbery in its wake. I once went to dinner in Washington, D.C., with a man who asked the waiter what kind of water — the astonishing phrases "designer water" and "still water" had not yet come into being — he had available. The waiter named six different brands, and my companion, obviously disappointed at not finding his favorite among them, shook his head, saying, "Never mind." On another occasion in the same city, in a French restaurant called Jean-Louis at the Watergate, I asked a waiter for salt for a female friend, only to be told, in a slightly suspect French accent, "I am sorry, sir, Jean-Louis does not permit salt at the table." With such behavior, on the part of patrons and restaurant owners alike, we know we have arrived in the dense and humid jungles of snobbery.

Restaurants have long been the scene of social exhibitionism and anxiety. In *Sister Carrie,* a novel of 1900, Theodore Dreiser sets a scene at the famous Sherry's restaurant in New York, where "there began that exhibition of showy, wasteful and unwholesome gastronomy as practiced by wealthy Americans which is the wonder and astonishment of true culture and dignity the world over." But even the sophisticated could be made edgy by posh restaurants, and anxiety in this realm has not been felt by Americans alone. "In restaurants," writes Martin Amis, "my father [the novelist Kingsley Amis] always wore an air of vigilance, as if in expectation of being patronized, stiffed, neglected, or regaled by pretension." In the contemporary age, not an entirely paranoid point of view.

Snobbery sets in when much more seems at stake than the taste of the food on the table. It has arrived when guests will later talk about a host's having served iceberg lettuce as the gastronomic equivalent of having made a serious grammatical slip or even an alimentary miscue. It's there when, at table, one is put to the torture of listening to a discussion of the relative merits of various types of fennel, capers, and arugula, and someone brings out a truffle shaver he recently purchased from Dean & Deluca for only $18.95. It was there with the actor Richard E. Grant, in the middle 1980s in a New York restaurant, seated among "new money [and] old flesh" and served "child-sized portions of pasta [that] clock in at thirty dollars." It's there when, as is recounted in an Ann Beattie short story, at a dinner party for twenty, sashimi is cut at table from a live fish.

In gastronomy, snobbery rubs up against decadence, charlatanism, and high if often unconscious comedy. Decadence, usually passing under the more elevated name of epicureanism, has always been around. One reads of those Roman meals in which a number of birds are stuffed inside larger birds, in the manner of Chinese boxes, to be prepared for emperors, usually after a nice starter of nightingale tongues. Today's decadence usually has more to do with the size of the bills people are willing to pay for not very good food — and in the restaurant of Alain Ducasse in New York one is offered a selection of expensive pens with which to sign for them. For a time, during the sad siege of the food regime called nouvelle cuisine, people paid more for receiving less food, as minuscule portions prettily displayed made for some of the most expensive dining on two continents. Nouvelle was replaced some years later by vertical, or Viagra food presentation, in which food was piled high on the plate. The past twenty-five years have seen lots of those places, as the restaurant-anxious Kingsley Amis puts it in his novel *The Biographer's Moustache,* "whose pleasure is small and whose cost is great."

One knows one is in the presence of decadence, with a reverse snobbish twist, when people begin ordering in restaurants food that would almost certainly disappoint them if it were served to them at home. At the Tavern Club in Chicago a popular lunch is corned beef hash served with a fried egg on top, an old working-class dish, as the word *hash* implies. Some restaurants began tarting up old favorites, pot pies but with lobster instead of chicken for the filling. More recently, a few New York restaurants are serving what is called comfort food, which includes macaroni and cheese, rice pudding, and, in one instance, Swanson's TV dinners (at $6 a throw).

William Grimes, the restaurant critic of the *New York Times,* calls this "slob food" and regards it as a fall from the heights of adult eating. He considers it a regression from all the efforts to educate American palates fearlessly to chomp on such delicacies as sea urchin and andouillette sausage (chitterlings got up in French costume). "Learning to eat is a kind of education," Grimes writes. "It rewards the adventurous." He sees this desire for the mediocre food of childhood as a setback, but it may be that this new decadence — it's the high prices that make for the decadence — comes about through fatigue with food endlessly gussied up, overseasoned, fiddled with, mounted and presented as if in an art gallery. Some people have had enough of Mr. Grimes's notions of educated and adventurous eating, and with all the snobbery implicit in both; they just want to chow down, man.

Good food is one of the world's great blessings, but, as with sex, one of the quickest ways to take the edge of it is to talk about it too much. The novelist Mary Renault nails the point when, after having been visited by a gastrolator who was to be her publisher, she wrote: "He is one of those Food and Wine kings. Food is nice but to make a career of it is a bit much. He sniffs a lot. It was a tacky evening, I can tell you."

One knew that food had entered the domain of snobbery when it became all right to announce that one's son or daughter was studying to be, or already was, a chef. This, as noted earlier, is one of the few downward-mobility jobs that is deemed — more than acceptable — positively meritorious. (True, chefs at upmarket restaurants were also earning six-figure salaries, so the mobility hasn't been entirely downward.) During the past thirty or so years, the young began to dominate the restaurant business. Now waiters and waitresses not only frequently announce themselves by their first names, but, when reeling off the list of (often) goofily ambitious "specials" on offer that evening, make plain that they had tasted them all; and then, after one has ordered, exclaim, if one were lucky, that one had "ordered very intelligently." ("What, may I ask," I can hear my mother saying, on being told by a waiter forty years younger than she that she had ordered well, "is it his business how I ordered?")

One might say that one was paying for the sizzle and not the steak, a metaphor greatly weakened by the paucity of steak on most upscale menus. (Upscale is of course a thin euphemism for expensive, or, as the English used to say, pricey.) For along with the snobbery of adventurous and expensive eating has gone the snobbery of healthful eating, which brings our old friend the virtucrat to the dinner table, and with his politically correct palate he's not, as will scarcely surprise you, the most expansive of guests.

If one nowadays gives a dinner party, it is understood that serving steak is a serious error, veal an unforgivable sin. A politically correct diner concerns him- or herself with what are currently called food miles; that is, the number of miles it has taken to get the food to market and thence to the table, and if the fuel output is too great, the food is disqualified. The organic-food movement has grown to the extent that, in England, one can now buy organic gin, by which, presumably, one can get three organic sheets to the doubtless somewhat polluted wind. "Sweet," runs the caption of a *New Yorker* cartoon showing one enlightened-class couple driving off after a visit to another such couple, "but a little more organic than thou."

Healthful eating took two forms, both tinged with snobbery: vegetarianism was one, fear of death before age 106 the other. Sometimes toward the end of the 1970s, vegetarianism began to spread among university students, and one would hear such statistics as that a fourth of all students at one or another time tried a form of vegetarianism while at college. Vegetarianism itself turned out to have all sorts of subdivisions, variants, schools: from the pure vegan, who along with not eating meat won't eat any fish or dairy products, to the selective vegetarians, some of whom won't eat anything that has eyes — potatoes of course excepted — and at least one of whom (reported to me very recently) won't eat any *cute* animals: she'll eat chicken (uncute) but not duck (cute).

The Vows section featuring unusual marriages in the Sunday *New York Times,* always good for a social laugh or two, recently discussed the coupling of two middle-aged people whose vegetarianism is at the center of their marriage. Along with the obvious things, he won't eat tomatoes, eggplant, anything with artificial flavors or with wheat or dairy products in it. He impressed her by teaching her to make soy milk kefir (a yogurt-like drink); when he visited her, he brought his juicer along, knowing her pleasure in carrot juice in the morning. May they have a happy marriage, these two people, during the long course of which I hope never to be invited to their home for dinner.

In Ann Beattie's story "The Women of This World," a hostess reflects: "What hadn't seemed fussy and precious before now did, a little: people and their wine preferences. Still, she indulged the vegetarians in their restrictions, knew better than to prepare veal for anyone, unless she was sure it wouldn't result in a tirade. Her friend Andy liked still water, her student Nance preferred Perrier. Her mind was full of people's preferences and quirks, their mystical beliefs and food taboos, their ways of asserting their independence and dependency at table. The little tests: would there happen to be sea salt? Was there a way to adjust the pepper grinder to grind a little more coarsely? A call for chutney? That one had really put her over the top. There was Stonewall Kitchen's Roasted Onion and Garlic Jam already on the table." Fatigue sets in at the contemplation of all these little demands that, though constituting a claim for individuality of taste, are at bottom and in their essentials deeply, almost aggressively snobbish.

Not all vegetarians are snobs or virtucrats or even left wing in their politics (I know a vegetarian who publishes articles *against* gun control). Some are genuinely repulsed at the prospect of eating animals, which is honorable; others claim simply to feel much better for not eating meat at all, which is believable. But there is something about dining with a vegetarian that is a touch off-putting, and what puts one off has to do with snobbery, even if there is not the least snobbish intention on the vegetarian's part. It's the feeling that somehow he or she is living at a more advanced stage of culture, is more highly evolved than a mere carnivore such as oneself. "Vegetarianism is harmless enough," Robert Hutchison, a former president of the Royal College of Physicians, has said, "though it's apt to fill a man [and woman] with wind and self-righteousness."

The other healthful food eaters, in which category I too often find myself, are those who are a bit — how to say it? — shy of death, sometimes also known as the Ugly Customer, or the Ruffian on the Stairs, and would like to postpone meeting the fellow for as long as possible, preferably forever. We are careful about cholesterol, calories, sodium; we dine with the single criterion that anything that tastes especially good surely cannot be good for us. We are a pain in the neck and in tenderer lower parts, to ourselves, our hosts, our waiters in restaurants. Our snobbery consists of our thinking ourselves, however much we grumble about so many good things being off limits to us, a lot smarter than people who eat what they like and in the quantities they like.

A social-class phenomenon this healthful eating turns out to be, for the adults who do eat what they like and in the quantities they want are almost always of — hmm, harummph — the lower orders. We see them in McDonald's or Taco Bell, or in small, usually Greek-owned luncheonettes, scarfing up one or another sort of flavorful yet one expects deadly dish: hamburgers or bacon and fried eggs or hot dogs — those cartridges, as Mencken called them, composed "of all the sweeping from the abattoir floor" — and vast quantities of french fries, washed down with tankards of beer or cola. Happy wretches, they remind one of no people so much as the Epsilons in Aldous Huxley's *Brave New World:* gross, misshapen, deliberately underbred to do society's drone work, and deprived of all insight into the reasons for their own being. They shall die early, we think, the cause of death being lower-class ignorance, poor creatures. Distinctly not People Like Us.

Nor do you find the American Epsilons drinking much wine, unless it be out of gallon-sized bottles. Throughout the 1960s not many Americans drank lots of wine. Americans knew about chianti, whose empty bottles were so useful for the insertion of candles for that bohemian touch in a college room; champagne — a bit of the bubbly — was there for New Year's Eve; and Jews on holidays drank the thick, sweetish Mogen David wine.

America was a booze- and beer-drinking nation. Odd that this should have been so, for we have also been a middle-class nation, and the middle class is nothing if not moderate, and wine is, as Robert Parker, the editor of the *Wine Advocate,* rightly says, "the moderate drink," leaving one neither bloated nor befoozled, unless one drinks it in large quantities. The increase in the American consumption of wine is owing in part to the Europeanizing of American culture and in part to the growth of good homegrown wines. Another part, alas, is owing to snobbery.

By the 1980s, wine among the middle class no longer seemed very foreign. But the historical Europeanness of wine drinking made it a pushover for the snobs — and an even greater pushover for European vintners and restaurateurs directing the traffic in American snobbery. Americans, the feeling was, did not grow up drinking wine; it was not part of their culture, as it was for Europeans, so they could never claim anything like real authority in this line. This was a serious disadvantage in a field, that of oenology, that required gurus, or people with real authority, to be guiding one's choices.

Knowing wines is no dilettantish activity. I long ago made the decision not to know them, at least not in any serious way. I have a friend named Max Ponder, a former All-State high school football player and Big Ten wrestler and among the least pretentious people I've ever met, who really knows wines. He offered to teach me, but, sensing the complication entailed — all those *appellations,* those obscure grapes, the various shoulder-shapes of bottles — I decided I'd sooner spend the time failing to learn another foreign language, and dropped out.

That wine drinking is rich material even for the oenologically ignorant snobographer is self-evident. In the realm of consumption generally, snobbery sets in as soon as one has essentially the same object offered at many different prices. Snobbery becomes richer still in wine, where one must trust one's sense of taste or the delicacy of one's palate, which can vary immensely from person to person. Snob territory, in other words, par excellence.

Because of wine drinking's origins in European culture, Americans who know a few things about wine tend to take snobbish pride in their knowledge. (Though not, of course, so much so as the French; in *Cousin Pons,* Balzac says of one of his characters, "Being German, she relished the different kinds of vinegar which in Germany are commonly called Rhenish wines.") Wine talk has for long been comic in its reliance on metaphors to describe tastes and smells: "a promiscuous little wine but ultimately responsible, with a bouquet that partakes of the combined taste of peaches and olives wrapped in cedar." What the use of such insane language means is that physical taste is an area of great uncertainty, providing fertile ground upon which the false authority, or simple con man, likes to trod.

Apparently very few of even the best wines cost more than $10 per bottle to produce. But that doesn't deter people in the business from selling some of it for hundreds of dollars a bottle. Pierre-Antoine Rovani, who works with Robert Parker, was recently quoted in the *Atlantic Monthly* as saying that one can sell even bad wine for an enormous price "if the bottle says 'Grand Cru,' or 'Premier Grand Cru,' or 'Pomerol,' or, you know, if there's a word on there that some rich guy recognizes." Such stuff can be sold, he added, "in small quantities in a place like New York, where there are *lots* of idiots." Later in the same article, Rovani says: "I know collectors with forty thousand bottles who if you poured them a glass of Gallo Hearty Burgundy wouldn't know the difference. I know collectors who, believe me, if you mixed Kool-Aid into cheap Chilean merlot, they'd taste it and say, 'Well, yeah....' "

To be sure, there are men and women who really know and love good wine. But not all of them are wine collectors. Rovani goes on to report that the people — most of them men — who buy recent vintages for $600 to $1,000 a bottle are collecting trophies, the way they might buy an ostentatious boat or a hot sports car or acquire a young wife. Owing to such characters, and many others at a slightly lower level of idiocy, wines have increased greatly in price in recent decades. I have a friend, far from being a rich man but a collector since his twenties, whose wine not long ago became too expensive for him to drink. He wound up donating it to his city's symphony orchestra and deducting it from his taxes at current prices, which allowed him to take his family on two extended European vacations. (The symphony auctioned off the wine.) Who, one wonders, bought it? People, one assumes, who have no difficulty drinking a bottle of wine that costs anywhere from $100 to $500 a bottle.

I've drunk enough wine to know that some wines are a lot better than others. I've never been at a table where people — young investment bankers, commodities market men after a killing in pork bellies, lawyers having settled a large case in their favor, manic-depressives on an upward swing — guzzled wine for which they were paying $300 or $400 a bottle. Such people must feel themselves flying so high as to imagine themselves on another planet. As they pull the cork on that third bottle, I suppose it wouldn't do to break the mood by telling them that their pleasure is, at its piggish heart, merely another trivially snobbish one. *Salut!*

23

·············

The Art of With-It-ry

Spin, stir, crackle, sizzle, and buzz,
How quickly the Land of Oz turns to Was.

— Anonymous

IN JUNE OF 1911, Sara (not yet Murphy) Wiborg wrote to
her future husband, Gerald Murphy, apropos of Gerald's
brother, Fred, who did not make Skull & Bones, that most exclusive of Yale's secret societies: "There is *nothing* in this
world so ghastly as to feel 'out of it.' " Sara twice underlined
"nothing." About herself she needn't have worried, for during
their fling as the most charming of all American expatriates,
no one was less out of it, no one more splendidly with it, than
the Murphys, beautiful, rich, artistic, friends with everyone
who really mattered, always not merely up to the moment but
usually a good furlong or two ahead of it.

The fear of being out of it, referred to by Sara Wiborg Murphy as "ghastly," is felt by many as a genuine terror. Behind
the terror is a fear of growing old, or seeming to be used up, or
on the way out. This used not in itself to be a crime, though in
the United States, a country where youthfulness has always
been vaunted, it has come to seem a sad, if not deplorable,
condition. To be out of it is evidence of one's becoming a
back number, a fogy, superfluous, superannuated, beside the
point, distinctly not in the game, no longer on the attack, a

player, a part of the life of one's time — in the view of many, snobs prominent among them, to be out of it is a form of slow but real death.

Yet what precisely is the It in the phrases "out of it" and "with-it"? Not easily pinned down, for the thing is changing all the time, this It. To reel off some synonyms, *It* is the action, what's happening, the buzz, the stir, the sizzle, all the things in which the cognoscenti are, at this very moment, most keenly interested. These people, too, change faster than the pitchers in a major league bullpen. One year they have the names Slim Keith, Jerome Zipkin, Babe Paley, Ahmet and Mica Ertegun; a few years later they are called Sonny Mehta, Julian Schnabel, Cindy Sherman, Tom Ford, and Barry Diller; and a few years further on, fresh names, like fresh plates in a Chinese restaurant, shall be brought on. *Vanity Fair* not long ago ran lists of regular well-known patrons of New York's Four Seasons restaurant in 1979 and 1999, and so many of the once powerful names of '79 are now off the screen, dropped from the charts, gone with the wind of with-it-ry. But the particular names don't really matter; what matters is that there are always such names and that one must know them, go to the places they go, where one might with luck encounter them. With great good luck, one might perhaps become one of them, and find oneself with-it at last and well out front on the envy curve, doing a little touchdown dance — free at last! — in the snob-free zone.

The It is also the going thing, the hot thing, above all the Now thing as represented by the right restaurants, magazines, movies, designers, dance groups, singers, writers, photographers, psychotherapists, painters, and billionaires around whom people urgently interested in being up to the moment swarm. They are the people whose photographs or names one sees over and over in *Vanity Fair, Talk, W, Rolling Stone, Vogue, Details,* the *New York Observer,* and other periodicals that set out to be the chroniclers of the lives of the with-it. After the opening of a show of her photographs — which sold for $30,000 a shot — Cindy Sherman gave a party at Mr. Chow's restaurant in Los Angeles; in attendance were

Robin Williams, Jacqueline Bisset, David Hockney, LL Cool J, Chloë Sevigny, Cheryl Tiegs, Eli Broad, Mike Leigh, Elle Macpherson, Steve Martin. As a guest list for the with-it, this is fairly good — for the moment. As for the next moment, who can say?

Some people seem to be as naturally with-it as others are as naturally out of it. Some feel themselves quite happily, even fortunately, out of it; others acquire the spiritual equivalent of a hernia trying to get or stay with it. Snobs in this realm are of two kinds: those who struggle hard to be with-it and those who are altogether too pleased to find themselves already there.

With-it-ry represents, of course, the higher — perhaps the highest — conformity. To stay ahead of the pack, as the with-it snob desires above all to do, is to find oneself in formation with a smaller pack, sometimes known as the herd of independent minds. "To have a horror of the bourgeois," notes Jules Renard in his journal, "is bourgeois." To worry about falling out of it probably means that one has already done so; to desire to be with-it probably means that one really isn't, with the distinct likelihood that one never will be.

The expenses — the outlay of cash — of being with-it are never low. One cannot hope to achieve with-it-ry in contemporary America on an income of less than six figures, probably the middle to high six figures. Consider real estate. Can one claim to be anywhere near with-it and live in, say, Minneapolis, Salt Lake City, or Tulsa? With-it American cities today include Chicago, Los Angeles, San Francisco, Portland (Oregon), Seattle, New Orleans, Key West, Santa Fe, Princeton, Jackson Hole, maybe Austin, and above all and primarily New York; abroad, with-it cities include London, Rome, Florence, Tangier, and Paris. This list of OK places recalls Robert Mitchum's response when asked how he found jail, after he had done six months in a Los Angeles County prison for being in possession of marijuana: "It was like Palm Springs," he said, "but without the riffraff."

New York and Paris over the past thirty or so years have vied with each other for being the with-it capital of the world, with London enjoying a brief run in the late 1960s, during what might be called the Age of the Beatles, but tradition, not with-it-ry, has always been London's strength. "Vogues, fashions, crazes," these, Balzac affirmed, found their proper atmosphere in Paris, where "great achievements are so harshly received and trivial ones welcomed with such disdainful indulgence" and where "ideas tread on one another's heels like travelers filing into a hostelry." But New York, in this realm, has long been coming up fast on the outside.

Within the with-it cities one then has to find the right neighborhoods in which to live, those SoHos, NoHos, TriBeCas, none of which comes cheap. Moving on to wardrobe, one has to hit this just right, too: wear that $200 Prada T-shirt, the right jeans, jacket, shoes, eyeglass frames. Probably best also not to walk around with too droopy — that is to say, too old — a face, for which, in cosmetic surgery, remedies, also not cheap, are at hand.

Without going much further, one can readily see that a high expenditure of time and energy is required to stay with-it. Entailed is a race, more like a chase, to keep up with the young. Richard E. Grant, in his journal, refers to "middle-aged trendism" in which "desperadoes attempt to be-bop themselves into frillier fashions, tighter pants and nightshade red or black hairdyes, the haunted look of 'last call at the singles bar' furrowing up a pack of brows. Please, God, when my turn swifts up, do NOT let me fit a rug to my balding cranium or wrench some designer jeans around my sagging 'cheeks.' Remember this wisdom."

A losing race, then, that of keeping up with the young, for even the young, getting older, eventually have to drop out of it. They're a transient class, the young, permanent only in the sense that they are always different but always the same, and rather like the avant-garde in this respect. "Everything changes," said Paul Valéry, "but the avant-garde."

The avant-garde, more precisely the myth of the avant-garde, provides the blueprint for with-it-ry. With-it-ry always assumes there is further yet to go in the development of new forms, styles, behavior, and the with-it snob must be in on them — present, with luck, at the creation, or if not then, soon thereafter. "That was *so* twenty minutes ago," a British comedienne used to say, but by now she is herself doubtless more than half an hour ago—or, in another with-it phrase, "so over."

The with-it act as if always advancing, perched at the edge, where boundaries morph and everyone is reaching for the white-hot center, taking the next nihilistic plunge. Being with-it, for those wishing to play the game, can be exhilarating, exciting, sexy. But the new — or not so new — twist is the disappearance of the philistine, which gave the old avant-gardian his happiest reason for being. "The philistinism of our day," Lionel Trilling wrote as long ago as 1961, "is likely to manifest itself in ready acceptance rather than in stubborn resistance."

To live the with-it life requires immense knowingness. Nothing can kill you quicker in the with-it world than owning up to improper beliefs. People who live on the with-it standard believe that life is about change, constant change, and that the best change is in the direction of deeper, ever more radical discovery, through (once) psychotherapy, (then) drugs, (then) sexual liberation, (then) consumption, (then) wait for it, whatever it's going to be, don't worry, it will arrive soon enough.

Lives lived on the with-it standard have a volatile quality and always have had, for the with-it, a historical phenomenon, have always been with us. In his journal, Mihail Sebastian, in the early 1940s, writes about the family of Antoine Bibescu (Bibescu was earlier a friend of Proust's), with their "declared liking for something that one day suddenly disappears without trace and makes way for some new craze." Captivating and charming though they could be, there is finally an insubstantial quality to the Bibescus, and anyone else in their condition; certainly, one senses, one would be foolish to count on such people in a crisis.

I had a friend who made a career out of his with-it-ness. He wrote books about popular-culture figures — Lenny Bruce, Elvis Presley, John Lennon — in a hopped-up style, freighted with much psychoanalytic interpretation. He lived in New

York, and, because sometimes a few years would go by between our seeing each other, sighting him afresh was always
an adventure. For one thing, I couldn't be sure what he might
be wearing, how he was cutting his hair, what new hip phrases
dominated his vocabulary. Did he, in good with-it snob fashion, look down on me, still wearing the same kind of clothes,
using the same language, breaking no barriers, hopelessly yet
contentedly out of it? I never sensed that he did, though I
could of course be wrong. He died in his late sixties. Had he
lived, he would doubtless have had to end his days in a gray
ponytail and write books about grunge, gangsta rap, and the
rest of it. Got out, maybe, just in time.

A more spectacular with-it career than my friend's was that
of Kenneth Tynan, a more talented but in the end perhaps not
much happier man. Tynan had been easily the best drama
critic of the past fifty years, one of the main forces behind
England's National Theatre, and the chief force behind the
musical revue *Oh! Calcutta!* He began life as a fan and ended
it as a snob, and was, at least in his forthright snobbery, uncomplicated. ("Last year," he wrote to friends, "met Cary
Grant. Top that.") Michelangelo Antonioni claimed he got
the idea for his movie *Blowup,* about swinging London in the
1960s, from a party he went to at the apartment of Ken Tynan
and his first wife. Impossible to have one's with-it-ness more
highly endorsed than that.

The first man to use the F-word on the BBC, Tynan was simultaneously left wing and in love with privilege, slashingly
critical about selling out and mad about success. Successful
right out of the starting gate, he allowed that his education at
Oxford "gave me a superiority complex." Socially dauntless,
he seems to have had no difficulty approaching the celebrated
on a basis of equality from an early age; in a characteristic gesture, he asked Katharine Hepburn, whom he had just met, to
be his soon-to-arrive daughter's godmother. She said — what
the hell! — yes.

With-it-ry was of the air Tynan breathed, and he ended, an
emphysemic, both literally and figuratively out of oxygen. Sex
was the division of with-it-ry that came to interest him most,

and he tried to change sex from the pleasant indoor sport it can be to a full-fledged ideology that would lead to understanding the mysteries of life. Sex, revolutionary politics, an adoration of success, all this mixed together, made for a with-it cocktail that Tynan drank regularly and that no one could survive for long. He died at the age of fifty-three, having spent his last days lashed to an oxygen tank reading his subscription to the *Fetishist Times* in a wheelchair out on a patio in the California sun.

Kenneth Tynan was of course English and his main theater of operations was England, though he wrote for *The New Yorker* and his snobbery did not include anti-Americanism. Far from it, he loved America for its cultural excitement and the glamour he found in New York and Hollywood. He was also the first of many English men and women who would be key figures in the American saga of with-it snobbery. Martin Amis, another pro-American Englishman, in a brilliant essay about the poet Philip Larkin, who was his father's dearest friend, wrote that "Larkin is separated from us, historically, by changes in the self. For his generation, you were what you were, and that was that." Amis goes on to say that his father, Kingsley Amis, was this way, too, but that he and members of his own generation are not. He doesn't elaborate on the point, saying only that "there are too many forces at work on us." Nor does he say what these forces are, but I infer that he means nowadays people live in greater fear of seeming old and out of it, and thus are willing to do a great deal to be, or at least to appear, with-it. This partly explains their regular and often drastic changes in appearance, ideas, or whatever else it takes to look still with-it.

In the realm of with-it snobbery, those who can call the shots, telling the larger society, with the proper air of authority, what precisely is with-it and where the with-it resides, come to seem culturally important figures. In this line, no one has shown more acumen than Tina Brown, also English, a journalist with something close to a genius for spotting and promoting the with-it. This gift for unearthing the with-it for Americans may have something to do with the sad collapse of the British Empire, leaving the English with only memories of the great days, a burdensome weight of personal irony carried by their intellectuals and artists, and very little worth competing for, really, but trying to establish one's own superiority through establishing one's with-it-ness. English with-it-ness, owing to lingering American Anglophilia, is still highly exportable, at least to our particular colony.

Tina Brown's specialty as an editor has always been that of producing magazines that postulated a world of glamour. Her genius resides in her having had all but to invent this glamour, since it doesn't, if one looks closely, appear quite to be there. She supplies the sizzle; one must look elsewhere for the steak. In her first American editorship, that of *Vanity Fair,* she set out a fantasy world composed of what was left of European royalty, clothing designers, big-money writers, and Hollywood actors and directors, and assigned journalists to write chiefly enthusiastic articles about these people while filling up the rest of the magazine with lovely scandal, psychobabblous explanations of the character of politicians, and stories of old American families still clinging to power. The mix made for a snobbish bouillabaisse found delicious by many. Small photographs appeared in *Vanity Fair*'s pages of bright young things — and a few rusty old ones — at play at various parties in Hollywood, the Hamptons, and elsewhere. *Vanity Fair* under Tina Brown was said not to have made much money — to have in fact lost a lot of money — but it became, as they say in the trade, "the hot book."

When Miss Brown shifted her base of operations to *The New Yorker,* she kept the fantasy alive, adding a strong element of *épater le bourgeois,* by printing the occasional cover meant to outrage, stories and articles and cartoons that were unshy about both choice of subject and the use of what was once thought rough language, lots of material about Hollywood and homosexuality and anything else that might cause a stir. If something more exciting came up near deadline, she was said always to be ready to rip up the magazine and rework everything required to get it in, no matter what the expense. Subscribers may often have been disappointed after reading what she printed, but felt nonetheless that they ought — *had* — to read it. She seemed to equate journalism with being talked about, and under her editorship the magazine was, if not more loved, surely more talked about than at any other time in its seventy-five-year history. In "Under Which Lyre," his 1946 Harvard Phi Beta Kappa poem, W. H. Auden offered as the best advice for keeping one's perspective, "Read *The New Yorker*, trust in God; / And take short views." Tina Brown put paid to the first part of that advice.

Miss Brown's editorship of *The New Yorker* was also significant for being central to the shift from the old, vaguely Anglophile, upper-middle-class-aspiring, Ivy League–centered snobbery, for which *The New Yorker* was in many ways the house organ, to the new with-it snobbery that we live with today. Buzz was the name of Tina Brown's game, and, as a veritable one-woman beehive, buzz she created, week after week. Many older readers of the magazine spoke of despising what she had done to their revered *New Yorker*, home of E. B. White and James Thurber. She, my guess is, viewed this old-guard readership as so many out-of-it snobs, and liked to rub their noses in the less than brave new world they had had the misfortune to live on into. If they missed the old *New Yorker*, she gave them an issue on women — whose guest editor, Roseanne Barr, was known for being foul-mouthed — and the photograph of a work of sculpture in which the artist fashioned a number of figures of himself, forming a sodomistic daisy chain. Whoever thought that our social Mme. Defarge would be a smallish woman with an English accent.

(Tina Brown could not repeat this odd success at her next venture, *Talk*. Being paid for by the Miramax film studio, the magazine was chiefly about Hollywood, designers, and kid singers. Making glamorous the current crop of actors, directors, and producers was a brutal assignment; not even the talented Miss Brown could make Tom Cruise, John Travolta, and Hugh Grant, despite their worldwide fame, seem even mildly interesting.)

The New Yorker became the weekly bulletin board of the with-it. Kurt Andersen, who when editor of *New York Magazine* claimed he was out to discover the Zeitgeist of the week, was hired by Tina Brown to write about changes in the culture, or more specifically about the world of the with-it. Andersen would later write *Turn of the Century,* the novel in which he put much of his — how to say it? — Zeitgeistical knowledge into one literary package. Such knowledge made it possible for him to produce the following scene in which an ultra-with-it television executive describes a new television channel, the Reality Network, as

> a New Age cable channel, although New Age is a no-no. Demi, Deepak, Marianne Williamson, Mars and Venus. Mayans and the Sphinx, gyroscopes, high colonics, homeopathics, chiropractic, yoga, Enya, John Tesh, Dr. Weil, Kenny G., vitamin E, herbs, Travolta, Cruise, lifestyle, feng shui, ginseng, ginkgo, tofu, emu, psychics, ESP, E.T. et cetera, et cetera. Aromatherapy. VH1 meets Lifetime meets the PBS fundraising specials meets those good-looking morning-show doctors meets QVC meets the Food Network. You know? And in the late-night daypart, tantric sex.

Andersen is a walking barometer–Geiger counter–seismograph of social weather, pop treasure, and cultural tremors, able to imitate insiderishness at a high level, as when he has another character in his novel do business in Seattle and writes about the new culture of three different cities:

> But at the moment, each of the three places — New York and L.A. and the Northwest digitalopolis — hungers for an ingredient only the other two can provide. It's the Fred and Ginger symbiosis (class for sex) extended into a Metternichian three-way alliance. Give us publicity, and you can underwrite our IPO; you give us gravitas, we'll give you the sheen; you supply the video, we'll provide the stream; you give us the candy, we'll give you the eyes; you let us meet the movie stars, we'll invest in your studio; you advertise us, we'll advertise you; you pro-

mote our shows, we'll take you seriously; you take *us* seriously, we'll give you a 600-megahertz set-top box. Deal; deal; deal. And we all go on *Charlie Rose.*

Genuine with-it-ry calls for precisely this kind of knowingness, part of which has to do with knowing about snobbery up to the moment. Of the main character in his novel, Kurt Andersen, who would seem to be writing of himself here, writes: "He cannot abide dumb snobbery, easy snobbery, snobbery ten or twenty years behind the curve." Yet the question intrudes: when you know all that Kurt Andersen knows, how much that is serious do you have to forgo knowing? And when you know all these things, do you really possess anything more than high-level trivia, and of a kind that is likely to change every year? Already all that talk of IPOs feels a touch archaic and will soon require a footnote explanation.

Feeling with-it can of course bring its own pleasures. Among others, it allows a person to think that he or she is in touch with the life of his or her times. No small delight, this. As a younger writer, I used always to feel the need to keep abreast of the culture, wanting to know what songs were on the Top 40, the names of all the U.S. senators, all the sports results and statistics; I watched the television talk shows, glimpsed scores of magazines, not least the women's fashion magazines, and read studiously the ten or twelve main intellectual journals and the *New York Times.* All this was done in the name of keeping up with the life of my time, of trying to stay with-it.

I sensed myself slipping badly in the late 1960s, when the curtain dividing the young from the not-so-young fell, never again to be lifted, leaving America with two cultures: a perpetually changing youth culture — with its own music, interest in drugs, special clothes — and an adult culture that, even though demographically in the majority, seemed perpetually in retreat. Although only thirty, owing not a little to personal temperament, I found myself on the adult side of the divide. The slope I was on was not at all slippery, but gentle, affording a genial slow slide into out-of-it-ness. That this may be the natural state of men and women is suggested by the still relatively youthful F. Scott Fitzgerald, than whom in his own time no one was more with-it (or more of an upward-looking snob), and who, in the following passage from *The Crack-Up*, seems to be expressing a desire to be released from the endless pressure of staying with-it:

> Trying to cling to something, I liked doctors and girl children up to the age of about thirteen and well-brought-up boy children from about eight years old on. I could have peace and happiness with these few categories of people. I forgot to add that I liked old men — men over seventy, sometimes men over sixty, if their faces looked seasoned. I liked Katharine Hepburn's face on the screen . . . and Miriam Hopkins's face, and old friends if I only saw them once a year and could remember their ghosts.

With-it snobbery relies wholly on style for its standard of the acceptable and on aesthetics for its sense of right and wrong. Newness, for the with-it snob, is worthiness. The new and the true are one — that is all they know and all they feel they need to know. With-it snobbery also relies on continuous youthfulness to sustain itself. Perspective of the kind that normally comes with growing older, or even growing up, is death on with-it-ry. Perspective makes plain that style, while always appealing, is much less important than honor or integrity, and that integrity requires coherence of personality, which precludes constant change of one's personality to keep up with the spirit of the moment. The deepest style, perspective teaches, derives from living one's life as if it were a work of art, a work that from time to time requires touching up, sometimes even serious revisions, but is essentially a unitary story always seeking — alas, not always finding — its moral. In this scheme of things, with-it-ry is entirely beside the point — of interest, finally, only to a certain kind of snob.

Coda

*To excuse one's own failings as being only human na-
ture is, provided one has meant well, every writer's
first duty to himself.*

— G. C. Lichtenberg

24

A Grave but Localized Disease

I SHOULD BE SURPRISED if there is anyone outside a Trappist monastery who has gone through this book who hasn't at one point — and perhaps at several — met up with his or her own snobberies, some congruent with my own, some perhaps the reverse of mine. What ties all snobberies together is the need we all seem to have to elevate ourselves above those among whom we live — to feel an edge, however slight, over the next person. Even caring a great deal for someone does not lessen the need most of us feel to think ourselves oh just a touch better: smarter or wittier or more commonsensical or better looking or larger-hearted or subtler, better adjusted, more logical — pick any three, and add a few items of your own invention not listed here. Why can we not simply allow that another person is our superior, without qualification or stipulation, and walk away, pleased with what we have, content to be what we are, happy not to be limping. But most of us cannot.

"Snobbery," wrote Santayana, "haunts those who are not reconciled with themselves; evolution is the hope of the immature. You cannot be everything. Why not be what you are?" Yet how difficult to be reconciled to oneself, to be oneself and nothing more. This is especially difficult if doing so means conceding one is not extraordinary, unusual, powerful, great, and shall in fact disappear tomorrow without leaving a scratch on the earth — a being, like the vast vast majority, whose life did not finally, as the Victorians used to say, signify. Is there something in our nature that prevents us from cultivating this kind of difficult but useful objectivity about our true standing in the world?

"There are two truths which most men will never believe," wrote the nineteenth-century poet Giacomo Leopardi. "One, that they know nothing, and the other, that they are nothing." Add to this that there is something about being an American that makes it particularly hard to accept that some people are born with much greater luck than others — the luck of being born to the right parents, of having the right physique, the right brain power — while others struggle against nature to make themselves something they were perhaps never intended to be. Yet struggle most of us do.

The problem of snobbery in its contemporary manifestations lies not in some small number of pure snobs in the world, but in the multitudinous little snobberies that infect us all. Not least myself, as I have plainly demonstrated here. I am someone who glories in distinctions large and small. Invoking to myself Henry James's advice to be a person on whom nothing is lost, I prefer to know everything about anyone I encounter: his or her ethnicity, social class, education, family background, opinions, passions, general point of view. So deeply ingrained is this in me that I cannot separate these things from the notion of taking a person for him- or herself alone. There is, in my view, no him- or herself alone. A person, I realize, is more than a list of his sociological data — his ethnicity, social class, education, and the rest — but he is that, too. And I find it difficult to ignore what the poet Zbigniew Herbert calls "the oppressive levity of appearance."

Leopardi, who was a hunchback, and often mocked for being so, remarked that people couldn't seem to resist using another person's flaws against him. "A man," he wrote, "who has a physical or moral defect is always being given its name: *il sordo, lo zoppo, il gobbo, il matto* [the deaf man, the lame man, the hunchback, the madman]. . . . The reason is that this gives the speaker a sense of superiority: his self-love is flattered." He adds that others' doing so gives them "an inner joy and a malignant satisfaction." In Naples, Leopardi was called by his fellow artists and intellectuals, all men whom time has proved much inferior to him, *o ranavutollo,* which means "little toad."

The snob operates similarly, except that he generally prefers to go for social over physical deformities. Being born in the lower middle class can be such a deformity, so in our day can be being a Christian fundamentalist, or having the wrong art on one's walls, or living in a neighborhood that requires explanation, or having gone to Central Michigan University.

Aldous Huxley once compared the multitude of modern snobberies to fleas on a dog, not allowing the poor things — the dog and society — to rest easy. Perhaps the best that can be said for snobbery is that, in consonance with Huxley's metaphor, it keeps society astir, and thus always in action. Snobbery also makes life in at least one respect easier for snobs, freeing people who employ it from the need to pass individual judgments and instead at one stroke to write off entire groups, types, social classes. And despising humanity in general, allowing snobbery to blend into misanthropy, adds a piquancy to everyday snobbery. Virginia Woolf was on her way to achieving such a blend. "I begin to loathe my kind," she wrote in her diary for January 3, 1915, "principally from looking at their faces in the tube. Really, raw red beef and silver herrings give one more pleasure to look at."

When one believed more strongly in a class system than it is perhaps sensible to do today, one could think of the status struggles of the bourgeoisie against the aristocracy, of *parvenus'* ceaseless banging on the gates of the upper classes, of the *nouveaux riches* doing their (always inadequate) best imitation of the established rich. Less and less of this now applies. One of the things that makes current-day snobbery different, and in some ways more perplexing, is that it doesn't seem to be carried on in anything like the traditional context of social class. In snobbery, as in so much else in contemporary America, everyone is in business for him- or herself.

Under the current dispensation, where the old notions of hierarchy have broken down — in most places for better, in a few others for worse — the nature of snobbery, at least in certain key areas, has radically altered. Democratic snobbery would seem to be a contradictory notion, but as we have seen in the case of the virtucrat in politics or in political correctness as it has entered into daily life, snobbery in our day can revolve around the question of who is the least snobbish person of all and hence, yes, just a bit better than everyone else.

When I think of my own snobberies, they are directed partly toward my own class, with its rather sad insistence on its special sensitivity toward art and cultivated living, which I often find comical and worth looking down on. The members of this class, which I have throughout this book called the so-called educated or enlightened classes, believe they live their lives guided by ideas and ceaselessly enriched by culture, but of course neither is generally true. They are themselves chiefly (unconscious) snobs and conformists who congratulate themselves on what they think the superiority of their taste, the sensitivity of their opinions, the uniqueness of their point of view. A fair amount of my own snobbery has to do with my desire to separate myself from them, though why I should need to do so is itself perhaps worth questioning.

How different this sort of snobbery — mine and that of the so-called enlightened classes — from the bad old days of (capital-S) Society, when there was something called a Society page in the newspaper of every American city, and in the larger cities a book called the *Social Register* in which the names of those allowed to play the Society game were actually inscribed. (Socially, an old joke had it, she doesn't register.) Society and all its subsidiary institutions — debutante balls, cotillions, charity events — have now all but disappeared, and gone with them is the once dominant Wasp culture, with its interlocking directorates made up of select prep schools and Ivy League colleges, the Episcopal Church, exclusionary city and country clubs, legal and investment firms. (All the institutions of Wasp culture continue to exist, of course, but in a vastly attenuated form.) But this is merely the first of the hierarchies that have broken down.

In the arts, the lines separating highbrow from popular culture were once boldly drawn, with many critics devoting much intellectual energy to sorting out the highbrow (James Joyce, Stravinsky, Picasso) from the middlebrow (Arthur Miller, Rodgers and Hammerstein, Andrew Wyeth) and worrying a good deal about the infusion of commerce into art. These distinctions, too, are furiously under attack, if not by now completely routed. An insistence on the purity and elevated status of the highbrow in art used to be considered one of the hallmarks of the snob in culture. But to subsist today on highbrow culture means adopting a cultural diet made up almost exclusively of the culture of the past. Highbrow culture in our day exists only in pockets, is itself almost never free from the intrusions of commerce, and — excepting perhaps only the large audiences that turn out to see supershows at art museums (with what combination of mixed motives who can say?) — has an aging, if not already quite elderly, audience. (If you ever wish to feel young, take yourself to a chamber music concert.)

"Nobrow culture," according to John Seabrook, is the order of the day. In *Nobrow: The Culture of Marketing, the Marketing of Culture,* Seabrook sets out to demonstrate how "during the second half of the twentieth century," and unto our day, what he calls "the townhouse of culture" had collapsed. The agent of change here has been marketing. Once marketing had become the chief element in American life, Seabrook argues, consumption patterns began to replace social class as an organizing principle of contemporary society, a kind of with-it avant-gardism became commercially mainstream, and the old distinctions everywhere began to break down, so that today, for example, one learns that the most fiercely independent, militantly, deliberately out-of-the-mainstream rock musicians supply the music for television commercials.

"The very culture had changed," Seabrook writes. The

highbrow-lowbrow distinction has been all but done in. Commercial success, no longer presenting a reason on the artist's part for feeling dubiety, became the most satisfying success. All hierarchies were out, excepting "the hierarchy of hotness" — all that mattered was what's hot and what's not, as the lifestyle magazines put it. Turning things on their head, anti-status became status. It isn't any longer a question, as in the famous Yeats poem, of the center not holding; the center — poof! — has disappeared.

In this maelstrom of change, the snob has been sent out to a choppy sea in a frail craft, without a sail and without a compass. Not to worry, though, for snobs have a wondrous capacity for reading the wind and usually find their way to shore. In some ways a social scene controlled by market considerations is easier for the snob to crash and manipulate to his own ends than one controlled by birth or achievement. The breakdown of the old systems, social and cultural, may have made snobbery simultaneously more amorphous and more pervasive than ever before.

Early in 2001, an Englishwoman named Betty Kenward died, at the age of ninety-four. Mrs. Kenward was a society columnist, and, in the words of the *New York Times*'s headline writer, she was a "Snobbish Chronicler." Mrs. Kenward wrote about the upper classes for the English magazine *Harpers & Queen.* She purveyed no gossip but instead offered lists of people who attended important social events. She employed her own punctuation system, using commas after the names of commoners, semicolons after those of members of the royal family and other well-connected people. Those who worked in business and advertising and publishing, though they might have been in attendance at the events she covered, were never mentioned in her column. Lord Snowdon, or Antony Armstrong-Jones, as he was known before he married Princess Margaret, always remained a photographer to Mrs. Kenward, and so his name was never mentioned, except as "HRH Princess Margaret and her husband."

An amazing performance really, and all the more amazing

in that Mrs. Kenward kept it up until 1991, when she retired. The daughter of divorced parents of no great social standing, divorced from a man whose family was in the brewery business, she called gossip columnists "gutter rats" and considered journalists vulgar. "A snob and proud of it," the obituarist for the *New York Times* called her. But I wonder if that is accurate. I wonder if Mrs. Kenward wasn't instead a fantast who wanted to believe in a world — composed of upper-class elegance and honorable nobility — that no longer existed, that may never have existed, but that she wanted terribly to believe in.

Might it be that snobs, too, are finally fantasts? They see themselves living a life of ease, of elegance, of with-it-ry, of endless sunny days in which they are surrounded by the best and most exciting people, charming, beautiful, confident, all of whom take the snob at his or her own high self-appraisal. An exhilarating fantasy, or so it might seem if the reality behind it didn't inevitably entail so much energy in the sad acts of sucking up to, and putting down of, others. Yet even if the snob attains the fantasy, it isn't enough for him or her to have arrived; other people must be made to understand that they haven't. And there's the rub, the quite raw rub.

Every act of snobbery is at bottom an act of weakness. Often it is weakness striking out, showing its cruel side. Sometimes it shows this by condescension, sometimes by pretension, sometimes by unconscious vulgarity. In *Pygmalion*, Professor Henry Higgins tells Eliza Doolittle that the great secret about manners is not whether they are arbitrarily good or bad, but whether one behaves the same toward everyone. This is what the snob finds it all but impossible to do. He or she cannot seem to understand that only natural distinction and genuine good-heartedness are what truly matter. Snobs cannot see through the artificialities of social rank nor through the world's silly habit of offering prestige to many people who are utterly unworthy of it.

John O'Hara, in whose novels the cruel side of snobbery is so often chronicled, said that the true gentleman — and,

of course, lady — is "sure enough of himself to find it un-
necessary to be a snob." Yet how many people have been
able to divest themselves fully of snobbish feelings? (It is not
clear that O'Hara ever came close.) Avarice, lust, fear, and
snobbishness — are these, as Hilaire Belloc once suggested,
the four powers that govern human beings? Some days it
certainly seems so.

The old barrier of ancestry — our family came over on the
Mayflower, that sort of nonsense — has long been knocked
down, but with very little effect on snobbery. Instead of being
a beneficiary of privilege, one can nowadays make quite
as great a snobbish claim for him- or herself as a victim.
The United States is an immensely more tolerant country
today than it was even twenty-five years ago: an African
American is secretary of state, a Jewish candidate has run for
the vice presidency, Spanish-surnamed Americans have for
years served in cabinet posts. Ethnicity is everywhere recognized as a source of pride and, rightly, no longer of shame.

Yet people nowadays attempt to outdo one another not
in the distinction of their forebears but in the purity of their
suffering — my holocaust is greater than your slavery —
establishing snobberies of virtue by way of victimhood. High
culture has for so long been under attack that people now
stake out snobbish positions for themselves in their allegiance
to the grossest popular culture. Snobbery, it seems, will find
a way: it will seek out things to attach itself to, even if
things have to be stood on their heads, or have almost to be
invented.

An intelligent person of a certain age ought to be able to
fight free of all forms of snobbery, if only to keep his or her
mind clear for larger thoughts. Now past sixty, I do not require any new jobs, honors, or friendships among the famous;
I do not wish to wear the ribbon of the *Légion d'honneur* or
any American equivalent thereof. Once asked by an inter-
viewer whom I would like to be if I weren't Joseph Epstein,
my answer was Joseph Epstein, only a little smarter and a lot
better looking. The grave awaits, and any notion of social

climbing I might once have had is now, I believe, properly dead. So all remnants of snobbery ought to be. Yet if I no longer look up to anybody but the distinguished dead, why do I still find it necessary to look down on some people?

Why do I need to feel myself above the overdressed lawyer with the $200 haircut entering the Standard Club? Why, encountering someone at a party who tells me that Woody Allen's *Annie Hall* changed her life, do I think to myself, "Poor baby"? When shown by an acquaintance a wretched new painting for which he has paid $6,000, why do I think, "One of a man's first obligations is not to be duped, and you, friend, haven't met it"? Why, when I learn of a colleague who is teaching Jack Kerouac, do I think about inciting his students to begin a malpractice suit against him? Why, when I read a young director of commercials say, in a newspaper interview, that the three words that describe him best are "creative, compassionate, and considerate," do I feel the need to add that he seems to have left out "smug"? Why, when passing a woman I know who has been married to a shrink and a professor of journalism, do I say to myself, "I hope her third husband isn't also a charlatan"?

Why do I need to continue to make such harsh, essentially snobbish judgments? They could be construed as expressions of jealousy, petulance resulting from aging, or — happy thought! — deep intolerance. Possibly they are all these things, but more likely they serve to reinforce me in my own point of view and what I take to be its clear superiority over those I feel nicely above. Pure snobbery, you might say, though I would be happier with a judgment against myself of impure snobbery. If I didn't make these little judgments — and, out in the world, I make them all the time — I'd feel almost as if I didn't exist, so much are they a part of my consciousness, my very being.

You will have to take my word for it when I claim that I never act on what is my downward-looking snobbery, and that in everyday actions I am not a snobbish person. It is only in my thoughts that my snobbishness lives so active a life. Yet why can't I leave it alone, let it go, continue to make my little distinctions, social observations, but do so without feeling just a touch of corrupting snobbery when going about it?

W. H. Auden, who thought himself a Christian, claims one warm June evening in 1933 to have been sitting with three colleagues — fellow teachers at a boys' school, two women and a man — and for the first time in his life he "knew exactly — because thanks to the power, I was doing it — what it means to love one's neighbor as oneself." No alcohol was involved, and no sexual interest among any of the four people. Auden recounts at that moment he "recalled with shame the many occasions on which I had been spiteful, snobbish, selfish, but the immediate joy was greater than the shame, for I knew that, so long as I was possessed by this spirit, it would be literally impossible for me deliberately to injure another human being." The heightened feeling, he says, continued for roughly two hours, and lasted, in diminishing force, for two more days. "The memory of the experience has not prevented me from making use of others, grossly and often, but it has made it much more difficult for me to deceive myself about what I am up to when I do."

What Auden apparently had undergone is the experience, or vision, of *agape,* or Christian love feast, in which one feels a purity of love for all human beings, without invidious distinction of any kind, the powerfully certain feeling that one's fellows are worthy of the same respect, sympathy, and consideration as one pays oneself. Wholehearted love with the power of pure objectivity behind it, how glorious it must have been to undergo — and, as Auden was too honest not to add, all but impossible to maintain.

"Live and let live" remains the most sensible of mottos, and so much less demanding than the Golden Rule. Time for me to adopt it as my own. What I should prefer is to go through the rest of my life snobbery-free, looking neither up nor down but calmly off in the distance. I should like to spend the rest of my days without anger or bad feeling and with a fine social indifference, cultivating the kind of objectivity that Schopenhauer thought constituted genius.

"Snobbery," Marcel Proust contended, "is a grave disease, but it is localized and so does not utterly corrupt the soul." It would be good to think Proust is right about this, yet if snobbery is localized, why, despite strong efforts, can't it be eliminated? Why does it still thrive? In an age of great social mobility, with a wider tolerance than any hitherto known in this country, when perhaps less and less can be used against a person to make him or her feel in any way socially inferior, in such an age why doesn't snobbery simply disappear, or at least begin to show some signs of beginning to do so?

Snobbery will die on the day when none of us needs reassurance of his or her worth, when society is so well balanced as to eliminate every variety of injustice, when fairness rules, and kindness and generosity, courage and honor are all rightly revered. But until that precise day arrives — please, don't mark your calendar just yet — snobbery appears here to stay.

A Bibliographical Note

Index

A Bibliographical Note

"WHAT DO YOU have to do to be able to write a book about snobbery?" someone to whom I mentioned I was writing such a book not long ago asked. "You only have to look around you," I replied. "That, and a little selective reading."

This book, as it turns out, is based not so much on selective as on a lifetime's desultory reading and the attempt, from a fairly early age, to keep my eyes open to the world into which I was born. These two highly unscientific activities constitute such research as has gone into this book.

Novels having always been central to my education, it is not surprising that I have found far and away the best writers on snobbery to be the novelists: Jane Austen, Balzac, Proust, Henry James, Thackeray, Dickens, Dreiser, F. Scott Fitzgerald, Evelyn Waugh, Anthony Powell, and others. Some among them (Dreiser and Dickens) have felt the sting of snobbery firsthand, and were able to write about it with heart's blood. Others (James and Powell) have brought a lordly detachment to the subject, and were able to work it from a distance for all its cruel comic potential.

Not all that many books in the category of nonfiction have been written about snobbery, but a vast number touch on the subject, and quite a few do more than touch on it — the *Historical Memoirs* of the Duc de Saint-Simon is a stellar example — providing accounts of institutions that were at the heart of a world of snobbery now largely and unlamentedly departed. In the list that follows, I am certain to have left out a number of books from which I have profited, even though their authors are not mentioned in my own book, for which I apologize. But here, to the best of my memory, is a list of the books that have contributed to the writing of *Snobbery, The American Version*.

Adams, Henry, *Democracy* and *The Education of Henry Adams*
Agins, Teri, *The End of Fashion*
Alsop, Joseph, *I've Seen the Best of It*
Amis, Kingsley, *The Biographer's Moustache*
Amis, Martin, *Money* and *Experience*
Amory, Cleveland, *Who Killed Society?*
Andersen, Kurt, *Turn of the Century*
Ansen, Alan, *The Table Talk of W. H. Auden*
Austen, Jane, *Pride and Prejudice, Sense and Sensibility, Persuasion*, etc.
Baltzell, E. Digby, *The Protestant Establishment*
Balzac, Honoré de, *Lost Illusions, Cousin Bette, Old Man Goriot, Cousin Pons*, etc.
Beattie, Ann, *Park City: New and Selected Stories*
Benson, E. F., *Alcibiades*
Berners, Gerald, *First Childhood*
Bourdieu, Pierre, *Distinction: A Social Critique of the Judgment of Taste*
Braudy, Leo, *The Frenzy of Renown*
Brookhiser, Richard, *The Way of the Wasp*
Brooks, David, *Bobos in Paradise*
Cannadine, David, *The Rise and Fall of Class in Britain*
Castiglione, Baldassare, *The Book of the Courtier*
Chesterfield, Philip Dormer Stanhope, *The Letters of Lord Chesterfield*
Cowen, Tyler, *What Price Fame?*
Cramer, Richard Ben, *Joe DiMaggio: The Hero's Life*
Diesbach, Ghislain de, *The Secrets of Gotha*
Dickens, Charles, *Martin Chuzzlewit, David Copperfield*, etc.
Dreiser, Theodore, *Sister Carrie, Jenny Gerhardt, An American Tragedy*, etc.
Dunne, Dominick, *The Way We Lived Then*

Fitzgerald, F. Scott, *Tender Is the Night, The Great Gatsby,* etc.

Frank, Robert H., *Luxury Fever*

Fraser, Kennedy, *The Fashionable Mind* and *Scenes from the Fashionable World*

Fussell, Paul, *Abroad*

Gold, Arthur, and Robert Fizdale, *Misia*

Goldstein, Rebecca, *The Mind-Body Problem*

Griffin, Jasper (ed.), *The Art of Snobbery*

Haskell, Francis, *Taste and the Antique*

James, Henry, *The Princess Casamassima, The Portrait of a Lady, Hawthorne,* etc.

Kaplan, Alice, *French Lessons*

Lemann, Nicholas, *The Big Test*

Liebling, A. J., *Between Meals*

MacShane, Frank, *The Life of John O'Hara*

McDowell, Colin (ed.), *Fashion*

Mugglestone, Lynda, *Talking Proper*

Nisbet, Robert, *Tradition*

O'Hara, John, *Appointment in Samarra, Ten North Frederick, Collected Stories*

Packard, Vance, *The Status Seekers*

Perry, Thomas Sergeant, *The Evolution of the Snob*

Post, Emily, *Etiquette in Society, in Business, in Politics, and at Home*

Powell, Anthony, *Dance to the Music of Time*

Proust, Marcel, *Remembrance of Things Past*

Reitlinger, Gerald, *The Economics of Taste*

Richardson, John, *The Sorcerer's Apprentice*

Rollyson, Carl, and Lisa Paddock, *Susan Sontag: The Making of an Icon*

Rorem, Ned, *Lies*

Saint-Simon, Duc de, *Historical Memoirs, 1691–1715*

Santayana, George, *Soliloquies in England*

Seabrook, John, *Nobrow: The Culture of Marketing, the Marketing of Culture*

Sebastian, Mihail, *Journal, 1935–1944*

Shklar, Judith, *Ordinary Vices*

Singer, Irving, *George Santayana: Literary Philosopher*

Thackeray, William Makepeace, *The Book of Snobs, Vanity Fair*

Tocqueville, Alexis de, *Democracy in America*

Trollope, Frances, *Domestic Manners of the Americans*

Turner, James, *The Liberal Education of Charles Eliot Norton*
Vaill, Amanda, *Everybody Was So Young*
Veblen, Thorstein, *The Theory of the Leisure Class*
Warhol, Andy, *The Andy Warhol Diaries*
Waugh, Evelyn, *A Handful of Dust, The Diaries of Evelyn
    Waugh, The Letters of Evelyn Waugh,* etc.
Wecter, Dixon, *The Saga of Society*
Weiss, Michael J., *The Clustered World*
Wharton, Edith, *A Backward Glance, The House of Mirth,
    The Age of Innocence,* etc.
Ziegler, Philip, *Diana Cooper*

Index